REAL ESTATE
DEVELOPMENT
STRATEGY
FOR INVESTORS

REAL ESTATE DEVELOPMENT STRATEGY FOR INVESTORS

RON FORLEE

WILEY

First published in 2022 by John Wiley & Sons Australia, Ltd

42 McDougall St, Milton Qld 4064
Office also in Melbourne

Typeset in Liberation Serif 11pt/14pt

ISBN: 978-1-119-88732-4

NATIONAL LIBRARY OF AUSTRALIA

A catalogue record for this book is available from the National Library of Australia

Cover design by Wiley

Cover Image: © RomanBabakin/Getty Images

Disclaimer
The material in this publication is of the nature of general comment only, and does not represent professional advice. It is not intended to provide specific guidance for particular circumstances and it should not be relied on as the basis for any decision to take action or not take action on any matter which it covers. Readers should obtain professional advice where appropriate, before making any such decision. To the maximum extent permitted by law, the author and publisher disclaim all responsibility and liability to any person, arising directly or indirectly from any person taking or not taking action based on the information in this publication.

Printed in Singapore
M121446_220422

CONTENTS

ABOUT THE AUTHOR

Ron is an architect, property developer and author. He is also the CEO of Phaeton Pty Ltd, a blockchain technology enterprise creating innovative blockchain solutions in real estate development and investment.

Over the past 42 years, Ron has been involved in a range of real estate developments, from housing estates and hotels to shopping centres, which he has managed and financed. As an architect, he has master-planned large-scale communities and infrastructure projects and designed commercial buildings such as shopping centres, office blocks and tourism developments in Australia, South Africa and China.

Ron has hands-on experience in real estate and infrastructure development through undertaking personal real estate developments. As an expert in real estate development, infrastructure, master planning and architecture, Ron has written and published several books on real estate development and building construction. He has also delivered papers at seminars about his primary interest.

In addition to his books, Ron provides online educational courses on real estate development through his website www.ronforlee.com. These courses are based on his experience over four decades as an architect and real estate developer. In providing these programs he aims to educate people to undertake developments properly. Developers make money by taking a significant risk, but this should not be their sole motivating factor. Developers are decision-makers in creating environments for future generations. Their responsibility is therefore to create ecologically sustainable environments that all can enjoy.

ACKNOWLEDGEMENTS

This book would not have been possible without the support and encouragement of certain people. They have contributed to my life in many ways. I express my gratitude to:

My late mother, Mabel, who supported and encouraged me to live my dreams and taught me the importance of assisting less fortunate people.

My late wife, Cindy, who loved and supported me throughout our 38 years of marriage and showed me the importance of being happy and positive.

My children, Taryn, Jared and Charisse, who have loved and supported me in every possible way.

Ron Forlee B.Arch
info@ronforlee.com
January 2022

PREFACE

In 2004 I published my first book, *An Intelligent Guide to Australian Property Development*, followed by *Australian Residential Property Development* in 2010. In 2014, due to overwhelming interest, I wrote *Australian Residential Property Development for Investors*. This book is a sequel to that 2014 volume.

A significant aspect of real estate development is that it is creative in its built form. Deciding how to tackle a new development requires lateral thinking. There is no static or structured approach for a new project. Understanding alternative strategies places a range of options at your disposal.

This book covers various strategies, including forming syndicates and joint ventures, developing with minimal cash, creative financing, securing low-cost development sites and creating a real estate portfolio with passive income. It concludes with a review of modern technological developments such as cost-effective construction techniques and blockchain technology. My case studies demonstrate how using these strategies over my long career has resulted in favourable project outcomes.

If you want to advance your career in the exciting world of real estate development, this book is a 'must read'. Most readers will have acquired some development experience or at least have read my previous book, *Australian Residential Property Development for Investors*. This will make it a lot easier to understand and appreciate the ideas in this book and will arm you with a greater understanding of various development strategies.

A confident grasp of the strategies examined will give you an edge over your competitors, help you secure the respect of your peers and development team, and prepare you to communicate on an equal footing with seasoned real estate developers.

Real Estate Development Strategy for Investors is comprehensive, providing important details on each topic. It does not follow a specific sequence, and you may choose to turn to a topic of particular interest as you need to. However, I recommend that you read all the chapters so you are acquainted with the broad range of options and strategies you can draw on during your career as a real estate developer.

INTRODUCTION

Creativity is essential to successful real estate investments and developments. Real estate development is not static, and there is no standard structure beyond the basic principles. A project does not come to life from following a set formula. It starts with being creative and applying various development strategies. Seasoned developers who have worked on multiple projects approach a new development equipped with multiple creative options. It is creativity that distinguishes one real estate developer from another.

As you transition through a real estate development career, you should study the various real estate development strategies to resolve any problems in a project, such as financing or structuring a new concept for the market. First, though, you will need to fully understand the fundamentals and principles of real estate development, whether residential or commercial. In this book, we cover the following real estate development strategies.

Real estate development syndicates

A real estate development syndicate pools money from a group of investors in order to fund a development project. The money contributed can be used as the equity for a construction loan provided by a senior lender. A development syndicate is created to develop a variety of asset classes, from residential apartments to commercial property. The structure will vary depending on the type and scale of the development. To safeguard the public's interest, all syndicates are regulated by the Australian Securities and Investments Commission (ASIC).

The benefits for the developer and syndicate members are that as a group they can participate in a more substantial property development than they could develop on their own. Additional syndication benefits include obtaining a more significant quantum of financing, investing in a larger property under professional management, diversifying by investing in several properties rather than just one, and investing in property in different geographic locations.

Joint venture developments

A real estate development joint venture (JV) is an arrangement between two or more parties to work together and share resources to develop a property. The parties in a JV maintain their own business identity while working together to complete the project. JVs allow property developers with extensive development experience to work with real estate capital providers, investment funds or landowners. Each party's role and responsibilities within a JV can be assigned as needed to progress a project to its successful conclusion. Profits are then shared as agreed upfront between the JV parties.

The following example demonstrates the benefits of a joint venture. A landowner owns a potential development site with mixed-use zoning for an apartment and retail centre. The landowner is approached by a professional developer. The landowner is not interested in selling the land but is willing to participate in a JV with the developer. Under the JV, the landowner provides the land as equity for the project, and the developer finances the construction and manages the project. When completed, the project can be sold to third parties, or the JV partners can hold it as an investment for a medium to longer term.

Developing with minimal cash

A common problem among developers is a lack of cash and cash flow. Developers are visionaries and entrepreneurs. They are not cashed up and are always looking for alternative ways to finance their projects. Many people believe it is impossible to become a real estate developer without substantial capital. However, there are strategies that enable you to get started in this industry with only a small amount of seed money.

Most financial institutions require at least 25 to 30 per cent deposit or equity before advancing any development funding for a project. The developer's goal is to develop without cash or any cash deposit. So how do cash-poor developers overcome this problem? Fortunately, there are solutions, but they require creative and lateral thinking. The solutions depend on several factors, such as the developer's experience and an adequate understanding of development finance and the various lenders' policies.

Securing development land at a lower cost

In the real estate development industry, there is a saying: 'You make your development profit when you buy the land.' What exactly does this mean? It means land is where the value grows. If you buy or secure land at lower than market price, you create an instant increase in equity. Conversely, you will always be behind the eight ball if you buy or secure land at above the market value. Adding a building to the land does not increase its value to the same degree. Building construction cost is relatively consistent, whereas land prices can fluctuate according to supply and demand.

Development land promoted by real estate agents on various marketing platforms is sold at current market price. If the market is buoyant, there is no room for negotiation. The key is to source 'off-market' development land. It is not always easy to find. Techniques for securing off-market land include finding government land, securing development rights, rezoning or assembling blocks of land to create a higher value.

Alternative forms of development finance

Traditionally, banks have been the primary source of development funding. In recent years, the credit crunch has seen the banks tighten their lending and apply stringent criteria for lending to developers. There are alternatives available to developers, though. Understanding these alternative options will raise you to another level in terms of your knowledge of how to finance your development.

With advances in modern technology, we have seen the rise of *crowdfunding* and other alternatives such as *social impact bonds*. At the same time, some developers have created their funding source through *development funds*. More seasoned and knowledgeable developers have pre-sold their entire project to a significant investor, making the development funding a lot easier.

Development economics and cost control

In a career spanning more than 40 years as an architect and developer, I have seen many projects shelved or delayed due to cost blowouts. In analysing the reasons for this problem, I found that the development team, from the developer to their consultants, did not comprehend the value of *development economics*. Understanding the simple elements that cause cost blowouts and how to prevent them will help you bring in your project within the budget.

Development economics is only one of several facets that make up the package of a successful development. Its role is to guide developers to ensure that all cost factors are considered when a decision is made at each stage of the development process. The exercise enables you as developer to build the intuition to recognise elements that create unnecessary costs and to avoid them through the process. With this intuition, you can guide and lead your team to keep your project within budget and ensure that it remains viable. It can also assist you in making significant decisions, including whether to proceed with a project, or to set it in the right direction so it becomes bankable. (I discuss this area more fully in my previous book *Australian Residential Property Development for Investors*.)

Creating a passive income real estate portfolio

One of the main reasons for building a real estate portfolio is to increase your wealth so you can achieve financial independence by creating a passive income in your retirement. Many real estate investors who follow this strategy have become extremely wealthy through capital growth over time, but a property portfolio is not a short-term investment. In the short term you may receive only minor or no profit from the rent after expenses like mortgage, insurance, rates and maintenance are taken into account.

There is a faster way to increase this capital growth, however, and that is through real estate development. The secret is to develop quality properties and retain as much of your project product (assets) as you can to add to your long-term property portfolio. Holding these assets as investments allows you to acquire your property at the developer's wholesale cost, holding it for further capital growth and deferring the tax on the development profit until sold.

Smart technology and blockchain strategies

The world is changing at a pace it is hard to keep up with. We are living longer, but our daily lives have become overloaded. The speed of progress means things quickly become obsolete. No industry is immune to the pace of change, and any business that is not looking to keep up with the changes in modern technology will be left behind by its competitors.

The real estate industry is exposed to these changes and has embraced new technology in research, marketing and sales through digital communication. Real estate developments are also starting to adopt new construction methods that are faster and more cost-efficient.

One innovation that will impact the real estate industry is the creation of *blockchain technology*. It has already disrupted the financial sector, with cryptocurrencies affecting payments, remittances and foreign exchange. It is not surprising therefore that this technology is now being adopted in other businesses such as real estate. Real estate transactions have traditionally been conducted offline, involving face-to-face meetings between interested parties. With blockchain, smart contracts allow assets like real estate to be tokenised and traded like cryptocurrencies such as bitcoin and ether.

When blockchain technology is applied to real estate development, it has many social benefits due to its transparent, cost-efficient and secure platform. It provides a better system through which governments and businesses can minimise problems of human interference while maximising access to professional services. Moreover, it is a transparent system that can disrupt the norm to reduce fraud, speed up approvals and provide a more efficient way of completing a project.

The development and investment strategies I outline in this book draw on my experience as a developer and an architect. They are also supported by case studies taken from developments in which I was involved. Of course, other developers adopt different methodologies. Indeed, such strategies are limited only by our imagination and creativity.

CHAPTER 1
REAL ESTATE DEVELOPMENT SYNDICATES

Given the scale and dollar value of most real estate developments and investments today, the popularity of syndication continues to grow, as it has over the past three decades. Financing is one of the primary factors affecting its popularity. Typically, the interest and cost of debt financing place a burden on a project's cash flow. This burden is eased through attracting investors to pool their resources to finance a project and achieve a financial goal that could not be accomplished by an individual investor acting alone.

Real estate syndicates are also known as unlisted property trusts (UPTs), listed property trusts (LPTs) or real estate investment trusts (REITs). They offer investors the opportunity to participate in the ownership of higher-quality properties that would ordinarily be beyond their reach. In this chapter we focus mainly on the private real estate syndicate or UPT, explaining its structure, benefits and risks, and how to manage it.

A syndicate can develop or invest in various asset classes, from residential apartments to commercial real estate. The structure may vary depending on the syndicate's strategy. Most syndicates are regulated by government authorities to safeguard the public's interest. In Australia the governing body is the Australian Securities and Investments Commission (ASIC).

The benefit for the developer and syndicate members (investors) is that, as a group, they can participate in a more extensive real estate development. Additional syndication benefits include obtaining a more significant quantum of financing, investing in a larger property, using professional management, diversifying and investing in several properties, and investing in different geographic locations.

What is a development syndicate?

A real estate syndicate is organised by a developer or investment manager. The manager will source suitable real estate and form a real estate investment company (usually a limited liability company) to acquire it. The manager will then coordinate a group of investors. These investors will contribute money to the company for the property purchase (less any bank loans), settlement costs, operating capital and reserves. In return for their contributions, investors will receive membership or ownership interest in the company and a return on their investment. The manager will conduct due diligence on the real estate before acquiring it and will manage the project on behalf of the investors during the development or ownership of the property until it is sold.

Real estate types

The types of real estate developed by a syndicate vary significantly, from small residential projects to industrial complexes to office towers to retail, hotels and other tourism-related ventures. Each real estate syndicate will have different objectives. For example, a development syndicate could develop and sell a group of residential buildings, with the profits shared among its members. An investment syndicate, by contrast, invests in commercial rental real estate with quality tenants, long-term leases, stable returns and excellent capital growth potential.

Syndicate structures

A syndicate can be based on several legal structures such as partnerships, limited liability companies or incorporated joint ventures or unit trusts. Schemes complying with the Managed Investments Act must be offered through a trust structure. The syndicate usually has a specified term of around five to 10 years. It will then be sold and the net proceeds returned to the investors.

Legal requirements

Most larger syndicates offered to the public will require the promoter or manager to prepare and lodge a prospectus or information memorandum with ASIC. The prospectus sets out detailed information about the syndicate and the risks and expected returns relating to the investment. Smaller and private syndicates can also create a prospectus but do not have to lodge it with ASIC unless they exceed the regulator's limit on the number of investors.

Types of members

The syndicate may be promoted to the public through licensed securities dealers, property managers, financial planners and accountants. In comparison, private syndicates are formed when a small group of individuals, perhaps friends, band together to develop and sell or own a small residential project or office building.

Types of real estate syndicates

There are several types of real estate syndications. Typically, they fall into two specific categories: (a) private syndicates with particular offerings; and (b) public syndicates listed on the stock exchange. In a private syndicate, the sponsor or manager identifies a specific asset to be acquired and raises the capital necessary to either invest or develop the particular asset. In this case, the investors are acutely aware of the specific asset being managed. The second most common type of syndication is a REIT. This publicly traded company pools investors' capital to invest or develop various real estate assets.

Private syndicates vs REITs

The most fundamental difference between a syndicate and a REIT is their relative size and scope. REITs are by definition more extensive than private syndicates. They have more investors, and they manage portfolios aimed at longer-term holdings. Private syndicates tend to be less formal than REITS, with fewer specific legal guidelines or restrictions. They are usually limited to a small number of development projects. And they tend to focus on holding assets with revenue streams on a shorter time scale than REITs. Table 1.1 outlines the differences between the two structures.

Table 1.1: the difference between a REIT and a private syndicate

	REIT	Private syndicate
Number of assets	It holds a property portfolio across multiple markets and focuses on specific asset classes, such as shopping centres, offices or healthcare centres.	It invests or develops a single property for a single market specific to that property using a particular strategy.
Ownership	Ownership is through shares in a company. Investors do not own the underlying assets but share in the company that owns those assets.	Investor ownership is directly through a company or unit trust investing or developing a specific property.
Access to invest	Most REITs are listed on major stock exchanges and are easy to find.	Private syndications can be more challenging to find, and the investment process can involve a bit more time and effort.
Minimum investment	There is no minimum amount under a REIT. Typically, investors buy as many shares as suits their budget.	Syndications have higher minimum investments, as there may be a limited number of investors for a specific development or investment.
Liquidity	Buying shares in REITs means investors are free to buy or sell shares at any time, making REITs a liquid investment.	Private syndicates are not liquid, as the investment includes holding the asset for a specific period until the investment is realised.
Tax benefits	A REIT investment is made through a company, not directly in property. So the tax benefits are through that company. Dividends are therefore taxed as income.	Investment is direct in a property that benefits from various tax deductions, including depreciation (writing off the value of an asset over time).

Types of REITS

These include:

- **retail REITs.** Retail REIT investments include shopping centres and freestanding retail outlets. The REIT represents the single most significant investment by type in most Western countries. However, there are longer-term concerns for the retail REIT space as shopping is increasingly moving away from the mall model towards online sales.

- **residential REITs.** These REITs own and operate rental apartment buildings and retirement villages. They are not as active in Australia as in the United States, for example, as Australia still has relatively high home ownership rates.

- **healthcare REITs.** Healthcare REITs invest in hospitals, medical centres and aged care facilities. The success of this real estate class is directly tied to the healthcare system. Rentals in this sector are more reliable than other REITs as the medical profession is more reliable.

- **office REITs.** Office REITs invest in office buildings. They receive rental income from tenants who have usually signed long-term leases. Most office REITs invest in prime office space within or near the central business district.

- **other REITs.** These include industrial buildings, industrial parks, logistics centres, hotels and serviced apartments and entertainment.

Variations of real estate syndicates

Real estate syndicates vary in scale and structure. There are private and public syndicates, unlisted and listed property trusts. Some unlisted real estate funds will be 'open-ended' funds, which means the fund can continue to issue units and acquire new properties as time goes on. These unlisted property funds will have no set term and will continue to grow. Generally, the fund's underlying properties are valued every year, so they do not display the same level of volatility as listed property funds, also known as REITs. There are typically three types of syndicates.

Wholesale real estate syndicate

Under this structure, the promoter or developer may have already secured the land, set up the syndicate structure and prepared the project's information memorandum, and can then sell individual shares or units. It is important to note that the financial services industry is highly regulated. Offering shares in a public project requires ASIC compliance documentation and a licence. A wholesale real estate syndicate restricts the offer to wholesale or sophisticated investors. The investors' minimum investment is usually higher than for a retail real estate syndicate.

Retail real estate syndicate

A retail real estate syndicate enables retail investors (mums and dads) to invest in a syndicated project. The minimum investment for a retail real estate syndicate investor tends to be much lower than for a wholesale real estate syndicate. Typically, the minimum investment starts at $10 000. A retail real estate syndicate requires the issuance of a Product Disclosure Statement. In addition, it requires that a responsible entity or manager with an AFSL (Australian financial services licence) run the syndicate.

Private real estate syndicate

Under a private syndicate, business associates, friends, family or other parties known to each other agree to form a syndicate between them. They typically establish a budget then actualise a project. They set up the legal and accounting structure first then look for a site to develop or invest in a property that suits their strategy.

Crowdfunding

Another form of real estate syndication gaining market interest is crowdfunding. Real estate crowdfunding can be described as peer-to-peer lending or financing for real estate projects. The process of raising funding is conducted through an online crowdfunding platform. The borrower or developer joins a platform to secure funds to start a real estate project. Investors join a platform to invest capital in exchange for returns on their investment.

SUMMARY

There are various real estate syndication models. The choice you make will depend on whether you are a promoter looking for investors to buy an existing income-producing property or a developer looking to raise equity capital for your project. When selecting the type of syndication model, I recommend you speak to your accountant. It is vital to ensure that the syndicated project complies with the strict rules imposed by ASIC and the Australian Taxation Office.

Advantages and disadvantages of real estate syndicates

While real estate syndicates have grown in popularity over the past few decades, sponsors and developers need to understand the advantages and disadvantages of syndicated real estate investments or developments.

Advantages of syndicates

Let's first look at the advantages.

Access

The price tag attached to most larger development projects is generally well beyond most individual investors' means. Forming a syndicate allows investors to access such properties' returns in proportion to the amount they can afford.

Higher-income return

Real estate syndications offer the opportunity to earn a higher income return on capital funds not available with many other forms of investments. With typical real estate developments, funds required are equity (30 per cent), which is leveraged against a lender's debt (70 per cent). With residential developments, home units are sold with at least a 20 per cent profit, equating to a 66 per cent (20/30) return on equity. In commercial buildings, tenants are obliged to contribute towards many of the outgoings on the property, such as rates, insurance and maintenance expenses. Therefore, rental income is higher than most residential investments where landlords pay these outgoings.

Assurance

In general, a syndicate develops or owns a specific property or a limited number of properties for a set period. There may also be restrictions on the syndicate's sale of any existing properties. The investment attributes are much more specific than a listed property trust, where a portfolio can change significantly from year to year.

Management expertise

Managing a more substantial development takes considerable knowledge and time. Like a listed property trust, a syndicate run by a professional manager has an advantage. It frees investors from the day-to-day management of the property (such as managing the development team or negotiating and signing leases). Investors also benefit from the manager's expertise in real estate matters (including financial, taxation and legal issues).

Security of capital

Depending on each syndicate's structure, your name or the name of an approved trustee will appear on the Certificate of Title. Your interest will be according to the proportion of your capital invested against other investors in the property. Therefore, you will have the security of tenure with freehold title, as you would ordinarily hold with any other real estate investment. In addition, the syndicate will borrow 60 per cent to 70 per cent of the total development cost from a lender who agrees that it will not have recourse to you or other investors but only against the property. That means that in a worst-case scenario your other assets are never exposed.

Tax advantages

One of the advantages of investing in a completed development property is that the government provides tax advantages through an investment allowance on building the property and depreciation on all fittings and fixtures within the building premises.

Disadvantages of syndicates

Now the advantages have been outlined, it is important to understand the disadvantages. As with all real estate ventures, there will be cons or risks on new investments or developments.

Liquidity

An investment in a syndicate is an investment in real estate, not tradeable shares. Accordingly, it suffers from the limitations of real estate investment. The principal one is that it is not liquid. For example, investors in an LPT or REIT can sell their shares on the market provided by the Australian Stock Exchange (ASX). However, there is a limited secondary market for unlisted trusts and private syndicates. Syndicate members cannot exit the syndicate before the end of its term unless there is a buyer for their units. This illiquidity means that syndicates should be viewed only as a long-term investment, unless it is a residential syndicate where home units are sold on completion.

Lack of management skills

Many syndicate managers are well schooled in investment and development, property analysis and acquisition. However, not all possess the necessary management skills. As opposed to a simple transaction, syndication is a long-term commitment. The amount of continuing communication between managers and investors, such as through quarterly and annual reports, can be overwhelming. Very few developers are trained for this type of group communication and management.

Valuation

As REITs are traded virtually daily on the ASX, holders of REIT units can continuously monitor their investment value. However, the lack of a secondary market in other forms of syndicated property makes it challenging to monitor its value.

Clarity of sponsor compensation

One of the primary reasons sponsors or developers create syndications is the potential for good returns. No law dictates the fee-splitting arrangement between sponsors and investors in a private offering. There are many different possible arrangements.

Too many investors

Managers of a syndicate have found themselves unprepared to handle investors' care and maintenance. Managers can deal with this problem in two ways. First, they can limit investor numbers in each group. With these smaller groups each investor must make a more substantial minimum investment. In comparison, sophisticated investors who can contribute more money can better absorb the risks associated with real estate investment. Second, the limited liability company's structure almost demands fewer investors. Each investor may have a say in management. Too many investors make the decision process complicated.

Too much risk for too little reward

Often there is more risk in real estate development than anticipated. This problem is especially significant for a syndicate's manager, who may take on the risks of ownership for all the group members. The mistake most often mentioned is that managers assumed significant personal liability in return for the expected profits. Whatever the cause, managers should examine their expected benefits carefully when starting a syndicate. The best option may be to collect a development fee for specific projects and leave the syndication to someone else.

SUMMARY

This section has listed the broad advantages and disadvantages of syndicated property. Sponsors or developers need to undertake a similar exercise before launching their project. The devil is in the detail, so draw up two columns on a piece of paper and list your project's specific advantages and disadvantages. You may find items you have not considered. It will assist you in deciding whether the project is worth syndicating or not.

Creating a syndicate

Before you decide to create a development syndicate, consider the following factors. In addition, you may need to engage experts in real estate investment, legal, accounting and finance.

Type of real estate

Consider whether you want to develop residential or commercial property, as the development strategies are different for each. Generally, most residential developments are sold to individual homebuyers, whereas commercial properties are developed then leased.

Management

Assess whether you have sufficient skill and knowledge in the type of development you intend to syndicate. If not, you can engage a professional manager to supervise the syndicate's affairs.

Return and yield

Consider what returns you expect to receive on the development's completion and the anticipated yield if the development is leased.

Taxation

Evaluate the tax implication of whether the project is sold on completion or held as a longer-term investment. Again, it is wise to consult an accountant to help you understand the tax implications and the best strategy to minimise tax expenditure.

Government policy

Ensure that you fully understand the government's rules and regulations through ASIC and that your syndicate complies with the current legislation. A good real estate lawyer will assist in this regard.

Exit strategy

With most residential developments, the exit is defined by the sale of home units. With commercial buildings, however, the developer will consider when to sell to extract the best value for syndicate members.

Reinvestment

After the exit, some syndicate members want to reinvest, so consider how the syndicate agreement will accommodate reinvestment. Having happy syndicate members saves time looking for additional investors for the next project.

The process for a wholesale syndicate

The following list outlines the typical process in creating a syndicate registered under the Managed Investments Act.

1. **Find a suitable investment or site.** The sponsor or developer who acts as the manager researches the market and finds an appropriate development site that will suit a syndicate.

2. **Secure the site**. The manager obtains an option over the property or exchanges a contract of sale conditional on the manager's obtaining finance through the syndicate.

3. **Concept and prefeasibility.** The manager and development team prepare a concept plan and prefeasibility study of the project to be developed.

4. **Offer to investors.** The manager then offers interest in the syndicate to interested investors or, if promoted to the public, prepares a prospectus registered with ASIC.

5. **Financing.** Investors then subscribe for an interest in the syndicate, using their own funds plus money borrowed from a lender organised by the manager. The loan is secured by a mortgage over the property. In addition, there is a fixed and floating charge over syndicate assets under a company or trust structure.

6. **Property acquisition.** The syndicate then acquires the property for and on behalf of each syndicate member. The syndicate will then proceed with the investment or development.

7. **Sale of the asset.** If the development is sold on completion, the profit after tax is distributed to the syndicate members. However, the completed product may be held as an investment. In that case, the manager will regularly distribute to the syndicate members any net income and provide audited financial and tax statements.

8. **Long-term investment.** The syndicate manager may decide to hold the property as a long-term investment. In that case, the manager will arrange for regular maintenance and repairs and ensure the property is fully tenanted.

9. **End of syndicate's term.** At the end of the syndicate's term, the manager will arrange for the property to be sold, the syndicated loan repaid and all syndicate expenses paid out. The balance of the proceeds is then distributed pro rata to the syndicate members.

The process for a private syndicate

Setting up a private real estate syndicate can be challenging because of the amount of knowledge about finance, the law and the tax system needed. Following is a step-by-step guide.

1. **Find your partners.** This is probably the most challenging step, as money is a dynamic and personal matter for most people, so investing with others is not going to be for everyone.

2. **Agree on your objectives.** The main thing is to agree on and establish a broad strategy, refined in the following two stages.

3. **Analyse a finance strategy.** This is based on how much each partner is willing to invest, the type of investment or development, and how much a bank will lend towards the project.

4. **Decide on an investment structure.** You can use various structures, such as a partnership, tenants in common, a private company, a unit trust or a discretionary trust.

5. **Agree on a real estate strategy.** Once the group's finance strategy and investment structure are decided on, the syndicate can choose and agree on a real estate strategy.

6. **Put a legal agreement in place.** Once these items have been decided on, a legal document is established. Each syndicate member will then be required to sign off on it so there can be no misunderstanding in the future.

7. **Execute your strategy.** When all legal documents have been signed off, the manager will start looking for an investment or development opportunity aligned with the syndicate's purpose.

SUMMARY

Setting up a syndicate, whether under the Managed Investments Act or privately, is easier said than done for a manager. It can be time-consuming with all the relevant parties involved and the documentation needed before a project can be actioned. The manager therefore needs to be patient and must fully comprehend what is required at each step. This will assist parties at each stage to complete their task and start the next step.

Syndicate structures

Although there are several ways to structure a real estate development syndicate, figure 1.1 shows a typical syndicate with equity investors and a separate management entity.

Syndicate entity

A special purpose vehicle (SPV) is set up as the holding entity, as shown in figure 1.1. The borrower on any bank loan sells interests to investors in the SPV. Suppose you use a limited liability company as the SPV. In that case, it will be managed by a 'manager' and 'members' as the investors.

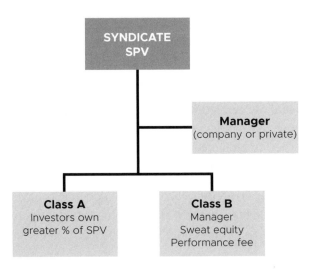

Figure 1.1: structure of a typical development structure

The SPV will need an agreement between the manager and investors to govern how the SPV will operate. The company agreement defines the management and investor rights and duties, and how cash will be distributed to each participant.

Manager

The manager could be a management company controlled by the developer. If an individual is named the manager, the SPV could be harmed if something happens to that person. It will have no manager until a new one is found. Therefore, whether a partnership or company, the manager should have several possible alternatives for continuity. The manager does not have voting rights in the company but can be granted shares for certain pro-bono services. However, the manager will earn specific fees for their active role in managing the SPV, including project procurement, due diligence, development and asset management.

Members

The SPV in a syndicate will typically have multiple classes of members. These can be broken into two categories; namely, Class A (for cash-paying investors) and Class B (the management or 'sweat-equity' class). In addition, if certain Class A members have different returns, Class A can be broken into separate sub-classes (A-1, A-2 and so on).

CLASS A SHAREHOLDING

Investors who purchase Class A interests in the SPV are Class A members. Class A members contribute 100 per cent of the capital contributions necessary to capitalise the SPV in exchange for a portion of its own interests.

Class A is offered a preferred return (meaning they get paid their returns before Class B members). Preferred returns can be cumulative, accruing even if no cash is available to pay it until future events. Preferred returns are typically calculated on an annualised basis but determined quarterly.

CLASS B SHAREHOLDING

Class B is the service class. This class typically includes the manager and others who provide services to the company, as determined by the manager. Class B members keep the company's remaining ownership interests in exchange for a nominal amount, typically $100 or $1000 plus their 'noncapital contributions' to the SPV. Class B can also establish a cost basis for their investment by paying for their interests. They may be taxed at capital gains level rather than paying ordinary income tax when they receive distributions.

Class B members receive their portion of the distributable cash during operations only after Class A members have received their annualised preferred returns. In addition, Class B members receive distributions only after Class A's capital contributions are refunded on a capital transaction and any arrears have been paid. Consequently, Class B members' returns are subordinate to Class A members'.

Bare trust syndication structure

A *bare trust* syndication structure may be used when a project is initiated by a group of friends or a group with a common interest in jointly developing a property (see figure 1.2). This applies mainly to residential developments, such as co-housing or housing developments initiated by a developer who has ready buyers and investors. This structure can also apply to commercial property if the project involves strata units such as offices, showrooms or small factory warehouses.

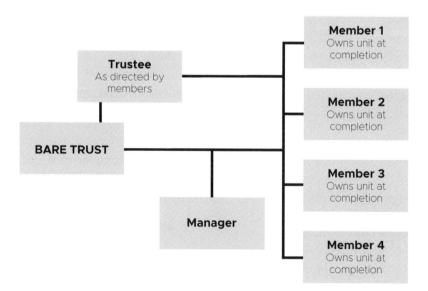

Figure 1.2: structure of a typical syndicate using a bare trust

Bare trusts

A bare trust is used where the trustee holds the property on behalf of the beneficiary. In this case, the trustee has no discretion and no active duties other than to transfer the property to the beneficiary when requested by the beneficiary. For example, in the case of a syndicated real estate development, the bare trust will purchase the land. Then, with the manager's help, it will develop the strata units, whether residential or commercial.

The trustee

The trustee is purely a nominee of the beneficiaries. Legally, a bare trust is a trust under which the trustee (or trustees) holds a property without any specific interest in the trust, other than having the legal title as trustee. The trustee does not have a duty or other duties to perform, except to convey it upon demand to the beneficiaries or as directed by them — for example, on sale to a third party.

Members

The syndicate members are the beneficiaries who will direct the bare trust. These members will place the initial funds into the bare trust to purchase the land. Then the bare trust will borrow funds to construct the buildings. On completion, each member will pay for their strata unit and take a transfer after paying out their portion of the bare trust's construction debt.

The manager

Under a bare trust arrangement, the manager is an independent development manager, appointed by the syndicate members and contracted to provide development services for a fee. Selecting an independent manager for a bare trust structure avoids conflict between syndicate members. For example, some members could be more dominant than others, leading to disagreements.

Other syndication structures

Trusts come in different forms and are substantially more flexible than other structures as they offer more asset protection. In addition to the bare trust structure, others are as follows.

Discretionary trusts

These structures are often referred to as family trusts with beneficiaries. The beneficiaries' entitlements are not fixed under these trusts, which means beneficiaries can receive different entitlements. Discretionary trusts allow all income plus capital gains to be distributed to beneficiaries by the trustee according to the trust deed. At the same time, creditors cannot gain access to the asset held by the trust. Therefore, there is the opportunity to distribute income in a tax-effective way, and the trust is entitled to the 50 per cent capital gains tax (CGT) exemption.

Unit trusts

Each entitlement in a unit trust is fixed. This means that if you own 20 units of the 100 income units issued by the trust, you are entitled to 20 per cent of the income produced by the asset. Under a unit trust structure, the beneficiaries have predetermined entitlements and can also claim negative gearing. The trust is also entitled to the 50 per cent CGT exclusion. In some states, property ownership can be transferred without a stamp duty charge only if it was the initial intent when setting up the trust and was declared to the authorities.

Hybrid trusts

This type of trust is a blend of discretionary and unit trust. Entitlements can be either fixed or flexible. This trust usually takes the form of a trust deed and a trustee. The written agreement sets the guidelines for holding and managing the asset on behalf of the group of people in the trust. Discretionary and hybrid trusts have an 'appointer' and have the authority to recruit and discharge the trustee. The asset is registered and held in the trustee's name. The trustee can be a person or a company, known as a corporate trustee. The benefits of a hybrid trust include its flexibility in allocating income and gains to the beneficiaries. There is also the opportunity to gain from the negative gearing benefits in the initial phase of the investment life cycle. At any time the trust can be switched to a discretionary trust.

SUMMARY

The selection of the type of syndication structure will depend on your investment and development strategy. It should suit the real estate project you are undertaking and the variety of investors who will make up the syndicate members. It would help if you spoke to a lawyer about the project's legal implications. Furthermore, do seek advice from an accountant on tax-related matters that will affect the syndicate project and its members.

Role of a syndicate manager

Winning the confidence of investors to participate in a new development syndicate is vitally important. Investors need to be convinced that the manager has the credibility and experience to deliver the outcomes promised. It must be remembered that a manager in a syndicate is appointed by syndicate members. If they do not have the required skill set, they can be dismissed and replaced by a competent manager even if they were the initial founder or sponsor of the syndicate.

The manager's role is to analyse the viability of a development before a final commitment is made to proceed with construction. All development factors should be studied in detail, including planning issues, land and building costs, investment value, funding options, rental value, market value, demographics and environmental factors. It provides potential syndicate investors with a realistic assessment of a project's feasibility in terms of both planning outcome and commercial aspects such as timing and financial projections. Following is a summary of the duties to be performed and the skill set required of the manager.

Roles and responsibilities

The manager must take the lead and captain a development team to ensure that the syndicate will be financially successful and should therefore perform the following duties.

Strategic planning

- Evaluate market sectors in terms of emerging opportunities.

- Monitor market and competitor trends.

- Define and review project goals and constraints.

- Establish strategies for further review.

Preliminary feasibilities

- Define and evaluate the best options for property to be developed.

- Work with credible consultants to create concept designs and do preliminary costing.

- Conduct a preliminary financial analysis on preferred end-use options.

- Implement risk minimisation strategies to secure optimum economic and financial returns.

- Liaise with real estate agents, consultants, and marketing and leasing agents.

Concept design and planning

- Develop a design brief together with external consultants.

- Arrange a site audit and due diligence.

- Establish a development budget and cost plan estimates.

- Control and manage the design phase.

Funding

- Work closely with lenders or finance brokers, and review the best financing options for syndicated development.

- Negotiate the terms and conditions of the senior debt with lenders.

Approvals

- Liaise with approval authorities and relevant parties.

- Negotiate and secure approvals in a timely and cost-effective manner.

Development

- Liaise with management and consultants to ensure that appropriate financial, commercial and legal risks are documented.

- Manage the evaluation process and negotiate formal documentation such as development leases.

- Ensure compliance with relevant ASIC regulations.

- Negotiate amendments to legal documentation.

- Monitor progress and manage cash flows and taxation issues as they arise.

- Appoint and manage marketing agents.

- Together with appointed consultants, prepare tender documentation.

- Manage the tender process within probity guidelines.

Construction

- Instruct and manage external project management consultants.

- Review, prepare and negotiate the contract with the selected tenderer.

- Review the preparation of the building contract documents.

- Supervise the management of the building contract and report progress regularly.

- Manage the completion of each construction stage and approve the construction certificates.

- Monitor and oversee the practical completion and final certificates in consultation with management and the appropriate certifier.

Management reporting

- Ensure accurate and timely information is available for monthly reports to syndicate members covering all aspects of the project.

Skills and experience

Investors in a syndicate will look for the following skills and experience from the manager:

- a demonstrated track record in real estate development with expertise in project delivery

- a tertiary qualification in a real estate discipline, preferably in business management, real estate or financial investment

- a minimum five years' experience in real estate development

- experience in a range of asset classes, from residential to commercial, with projects exceeding $10 million.

Behavioural competencies

The following behavioural traits and skills will be helpful when dealing with investors and the development team involved in syndicated developments:

- able to work autonomously and independently but communicate and consult with all stakeholders

- able to build strong and positive relationships with investors, external stakeholders, consultants and advisers

- excellent negotiation and influencing skills

- demonstrated leadership skills with vision, commitment, engagement and results

- excellent verbal and written communication skills to communicate at a high level

- ability to manage and prioritise several essential tasks within defined deadlines

- a lateral thinker who can resolve complex problems

- a strategic thinker and planner with the ability to deliver results

- a high level of professionalism, honesty and integrity.

SUMMARY

As indicated, the role and responsibilities of a syndicate manager are not simple. They require significant experience and knowledge, and the personality and skills to deal with people at all levels. If you decide to establish a real estate syndicate, it is worth doing a self-assessment to evaluate if you have the skill set to manage a syndicate. Be honest with yourself. If there are areas where you lack certain skills or traits, look for a coach or mentor who can assist you or find a suitable candidate, such as a professional development manager, to fulfil this role. Remember, the success of a syndicate depends heavily on the manager.

Fees and expenses

The fees and expenses of operating a typical real estate syndicate are administered by the manager on behalf of the syndicate members. The manager may collect these fees and expenses monthly, quarterly or annually. The costs and fees can vary depending on the asset type and whether the syndicate is a development only or development and investment. A breakdown of the fees in each phase of a typical syndicated project follows.

Development stage

The manager will spend a great deal of their time and energy researching and evaluating potential developments. They will also supervise and manage the project from inception to completion. Therefore, they should be rewarded with a fee payment for their effort. The fee should be factored into development as an outgoing. This fee can be used to cover your overhead cost, or it can be left in the development as part of the required equity. Examples of these fees are now explained.

Project procurement fee

This fee is paid to the manager for their initiative in finding a viable project. It includes using their time to research the market, networking with various people within the real estate industry, creating the vision and structuring a deal with the landowner. This service fee is usually based on a percentage of the land cost or a fixed figure. Fees can vary from 2 to 3 per cent of the land cost.

Development management fee

The manager's role is to represent the syndicate members and direct the development to ensure its viability so it can be financed and the projected returns achieved. The manager also analyses the development's potential, sets up a strategic policy framework and ensures the appointed project manager is doing their job. Depending on the development's scale and complexity, development management fees range from 2 to 5 per cent of the total development cost, excluding land.

Syndication fee

This fee is for services rendered in creating the investment syndicate, negotiating with potential investors, arranging a new partnership or company, negotiating debt finance, and setting up the management and accounting systems. For example, the manager could take a small fee and a more substantial shareholding. The fee can be either a flat fee or a percentage of the equity raised, in the range of 2.5 to 5 per cent of the monies invested by the syndicate members.

Performance fee

A performance fee is a payment made to the manager for generating positive returns. It is separate from other fees, such as the development management fee, which is charged without regard to returns. A performance fee can be calculated in several ways. Most common is a percentage of the surplus profit after paying investors a targeted return on their investment. For example, if a targeted return of a two-year development is 10 per cent per annum on investor funds, and if the project shows a 50 per cent return on equity, the first 20 per cent (2 × 10 per cent) is distributed to the investors. The 30 per cent balance is split between the investors and the manager.

Operation stage

Should the development be held as a medium- to long-term investment after completion of the project, then the following costs and fees may apply.

Asset management fee

The manager may charge a fee of 1 to 2 per cent of gross collected revenue for managing the property on behalf of the syndicate members. It is separate from the property management fee, which is generally contracted to a third party. The property manager takes care of the tenants and leases, while the manager manages the property and reports to the syndicate members.

Performance fee

Like the performance fee under the development stage, the performance fee under operations may be based on offering equity investors a preferred return calculated against the amount of their initial investment. Any remaining distributable cash is split between the manager and syndicate members. For example, suppose an expected return is 10 per cent and the investors' preferred return is 6 per cent. In that case, the 4 per cent balance is split between the members and the manager.

Refinance fee

A syndicate manager may charge a fee for refinancing the current mortgage of the syndicated property. For example, if the manager sees an opportunity to secure a better mortgage from another lender that will benefit the syndicate, a refinance fee of 1 to 2 per cent of the refinance loan amount may be applicable.

Loan guarantor fee

Where the lender requires a guarantor for a loan to the syndicated property, and if the manager provides the necessary guarantee, the manager may charge a fee of 1 to 3 per cent of the loan amount or just a flat fee.

Expense reimbursement

In addition to the fees and distributions charge, the manager can get reimbursed for payments it makes to third parties during the syndicate's operational period. This may include valuations, legal advice, accounting, auditing and any third-party related cost.

Other fees and costs

Other fees and costs include the following.

Property management fees

Property management services will generally be contracted to a third-party professional company, especially if the syndicated property falls under the commercial category. Property management fees vary between residential and commercial properties. It is best to research these fees before appointing a property manager. On average, commercial property management fees range between 7.7 and 9.9 per cent (including GST) of the monthly rent. Management fees may also be based on two other pricing structures: flat fee and hybrid.

Leasing fees

For securing a lease, an independent leasing agent's fees are based on a percentage of the transaction they secure on behalf of a building owner. They work on a success basis, and there is no fee payable if the property is not leased. The following is a guide:

- lease for three years or less — 12 per cent + GST

- lease above three years — 12 per cent + 0.5 per cent for each year or part thereof + GST

- lease or option renewals — 50 per cent of the fee mentioned above + GST.

Again, research the leasing fees, as they can vary between residential and commercial properties and from state to state.

Sales commission

When exiting a syndicated investment, a real estate agent will be appointed to market and sell the property. Upon the successful conclusion and settlement of the sale, the real estate agent will charge a fee of between 2 and 3 per cent of the final selling price.

Directors' fees

Depending on the structure and size of the syndicate, a board of directors may be appointed to give direction and vote on the syndicated property or make significant decisions. Some of these directors may be independent of the syndicate. For their time attending board meetings, the directors may be reimbursed as agreed by the board.

SUMMARY

These fees are based on industry standards and apply to most real estate syndications. Fees are not fixed, and the manager can vary them according to the scale and complexity of the syndicated project. However, as pointed out, there are variations to acceptable standards. These fees and costs should be researched and justified, because some syndicate investor members will do their homework and query any differences.

Taxation implications

The tax areas within real estate syndication can vary depending on the syndication structure and the type of entity holding the property. Whether to structure the project under a company, unit trust or discretionary trust is a critical decision that a manager of a syndicate must make. A tax specialist should be appointed to provide the best tax advice.

Most developers use companies as a development vehicle. In contrast, investors use trusts to hold an investment property for long-term growth. Unlike companies, trusts may be eligible for the 50 per cent CGT discount on the eventual sale. Therefore, if a syndicate develops and holds the completed property within a single entity vehicle, this can create problems with the Australian Taxation Office (ATO). A potential solution is to set up a joint venture (JV) at the start, in which a JV company and trust structure develop the property, share costs proportionately and split the assets (not the cash) on completion. It means that the trust acquires the property at cost, which boosts its rental yield compared with acquiring it at market value. In addition, upon the sale of the property by the trust (subject to meeting certain conditions), the capital gain will be subject to tax at 22.5 instead of 45 per cent.

While the structure plays an integral part in a syndicate relating to CGT, other taxes should be considered during the development and operating stages. Listed next are the tax items to consider.

Development stage tax

During the development process stage of a project, the following taxes should be considered.

Stamp duty

Every state and territory within Australia has its stamp duty when buying a property, whether land or an existing building. The applicable local stamp duty rate should be checked and included in a syndicate's budget.

Goods and services tax

When a typical strata development, such as residential units or factory units, is sold to third parties, the GST component of the development cost can be claimed. However, when the units are sold, they must include a GST component. In contrast, if the development is to be held as an investment, then the GST component on the development cost cannot be claimed during the development stage unless the future rent includes GST. It is mainly applicable to commercial property.

Income tax

When the syndicate is structured under a company, a 30 per cent company tax will apply if the building(s) is sold to a third party on completion. But, of course, there is no income tax if the building is held as an investment.

Operating stage taxes

The following taxes should be considered when construction has been completed, and the building is occupied.

Goods and services tax

If a residential property is held as a rental income investment and the holding entity is GST registered, then GST is not applicable on rent, as GST is not charged. In contrast, GST applies to commercial properties that are leased.

Tax deductions

In addition to everyday operating expenses such as interest payments, rates and taxes, building insurance and advertising, further tax deduction applies to rental properties. These are big-ticket items including any capital works and depreciation. Different items have different rates of depreciation based on the item's practical life. The ATO offers a comprehensive guide on what it considers appropriate. These depreciation benefits can be easily calculated by engaging a qualified quantity surveyor to prepare a depreciation schedule.

Income tax

Should there be a surplus income from the rent after taking all tax deductions into account, this surplus is subject to income tax paid yearly. If the holding entity is a limited liability company, a 30 per cent income tax will apply. If it is a trust, however, the income tax will depend on the structure of the trust.

Capital gains tax

On the sale of the property, capital gains tax will come into play. If a property is held for at least 12 months, any gain is discounted by 50 per cent for a trust or 33.3 per cent for a company. Capital losses can be offset against capital gains, and net capital losses in a tax year may be carried forward indefinitely.

SUMMARY

Australian taxation laws are among the most complex globally. Moreover, changes are frequent, especially when a new government is elected. It is therefore difficult for a syndicate manager to keep on top of these recent changes when they occur. Consequently, it is advisable to find a competent real estate accountant with real estate syndication experience. Their advice can be invaluable when setting up the structure of the real estate syndicate.

The appointed accountant should meet with your syndicate members to explain its structure and tax on the syndicate. At such a meeting, it must be remembered that the accountant may not give individual tax advice to each member. Members should approach their own accountant when it comes to personal tax.

Finding syndicate members

Before you look for potential syndicate investors, it is vital to evaluate your profile and ask yourself, if you were an investor, would you invest in your syndicate? The project may be great, but do you have the credibility and track record of successful developments? Intelligent investors know that a good project must have a reliable manager backed by an experienced development team.

Essentials

Before presenting to potential investors, you will need to do the following.

Establish credibility as a manager

If you do not have the credibility and track record in syndication and the type of asset class to be developed, consider appointing a seasoned development manager with the required expertise as part of your development management team. As most syndicates are 'one-off' projects, you may use the development manager's skills on your first project, learn from it then undertake the next one on your own.

Prepare an information memorandum

A serious investor will only consider an investment proposal with a well-presented and detailed information memorandum (IM) or prospectus. This IM should cover all the relevant project information including market research, site information, prefeasibility study, concept plans and so on. In addition, an outline of the syndication and how potential investors can participate should be presented.

Prepare a brochure or flyer

Most investors do not have the time to review a full IM. Therefore a brochure or flyer of no more than two pages should be produced from the IM. The brochure or flyer should contain an executive summary of the syndication project, together with the critical points of the investment. These short marketing documents can be emailed or printed for the initial meeting with investors. If they show an interest, then the full IM can be presented.

Be prepared for questions

It is always best to prepare for questions that investors will ask and to give honest answers. Following are two of the most common questions that investors ask.

IS THERE A GUARANTEE THAT I'LL GET MY MONEY BACK?

The short answer is no, as there are risks in every investment. However, advise them that the property secures their investment. Remember that the lender will have the first charge over the property should something go wrong for whatever reason.

WHEN WILL I GET MY MONEY BACK?

The answer will depend on your exit strategy. It could take two years for smaller residential projects where the units are sold. With a develop-and-hold strategy, the exit could take five years based on a two-year development period and a three-year holding period.

Sources of syndicate investors

There are several forums in which your syndicated project could be presented to attract investors.

Family and friends

This is usually the first contact. Nobody wants to compromise a friendship or cause a family rift. You need to consider how they would react if things went wrong down the track. You should have very few family members or friends as syndicate members, or none at all if you have other potential investors.

Local investment clubs

Look out for local real estate investment clubs, as people who attend these clubs are already interested in real estate investments. It may be helpful to have a presentation evening with club members to present to a broader audience.

Associations

You can present to other groups, such as the local Chamber of Commerce or Rotary Club. Also, presentations can be made to high-profile organisations that attract professionals who often need tax shelters. These are business network groups, and people who attend those functions look for business opportunities and will want to connect.

Professional advisers

Approach accountants, lawyers and financial planners, as they generally have clients looking for investment opportunities or need a tax shelter. Professional advisers cannot recommend their clients to invest in your syndicate. Still, they can suggest they contact you should they be interested.

Angel investor networks

There are several online angel investor group networks. Typically, you will submit your investment proposal through their website, and should an angel investor be interested they will contact you.

Crowdfunding platforms

There are several property-based crowdfunding platforms on the internet. Look for the ones that are marketing real estate opportunities. It is essential to check the criteria and credentials of the platform you choose. Assuming your project passes the platform's credit checks, it will be marketed to investors on its platform.

SUMMARY

It is not easy to find new syndicate members, especially those who are like-minded and on the same financial level as other members. Syndicate members come from all walks of life, with different personalities and varying personal finances, and not all know how syndication works. Therefore, the manager should be prepared to assist those unfamiliar with a syndicate and guide them through the process. Also, not all those you talk to will become members of your syndicate, so be prepared for rejection and work on more significant numbers as only a small percentage will take up membership.

Rules and regulations

Real estate developers have probably been putting syndications together since the concept of private land ownership was first devised. In Australia, real estate syndicates are regulated by ASIC, as it usually involves the sale of 'securities' in the form of an 'investment contract'. Generally, a securities offering must be registered and approved by the regulatory agencies. Still, there are areas where this may be exempt.

In most syndicate structures, the key driver is tax. However, understanding the *Corporations Act 2001* (Cth) requirements is essential, because these can impact the structure. For example, the Corporations Act can require the manager of a real estate syndicate to hold an Australian financial services licence (AFSL).

As pointed out earlier, there are two commonly used structures to establish and operate a real estate syndicate: companies and trusts (usually unit trusts). In addition, several other structures may be used, such as unincorporated joint ventures. This section focuses on the more common company and trust structures and when an AFSL will be required to operate a real estate syndicate.

Companies

In general, a company does not require an AFSL to issue its shares. However, it may be considered a financial product when a company promotes an investment business such as real estate, shares or other investments. It means that where a real estate development company raises funds for its development, it will require an AFSL to issue its shares. There are qualifications and exceptions to this rule that should be verified by your lawyer and through ASIC.

Trusts

A unit trust can be used to conduct real estate syndicates. Investors acquire units in the trust, which a trustee manages if the trust is a registered managed investment scheme (MIS). As a result, each investor has a beneficial interest in assets of the trust in proportion to the number of units they own. A unit trust is generally considered an MIS under the Corporations Act, and there are two categories of MIS— namely, registered and unregistered. Note that an MIS will require an ASIC registration in specified cases, which should be verified by your accountant or lawyer.

Registered MIS

A registered MIS is complex as the registration process involves approval from ASIC. A specific AFSL, and significant financial conditions can apply. The complexity and cost of such schemes often outweigh the benefits for small real estate syndicates.

Unregistered MIS

An unregistered MIS is generally less complex as it does not require registration. However, an unregistered MIS will require an AFSL if the number of investors exceeds ASIC's limit. Also, the identity of the sponsors of the MIS is required.

When is a prospectus required?

Generally, a prospectus is required to issue securities to a retail investor. Therefore, if your syndicate includes mainly retail investors, you may be required to provide those investors with a prospectus or a Product Disclosure Statement (PDS) to allow them to participate. On the other hand, if your syndicate includes only sophisticated investors, not retail investors, then there is no need to provide a prospectus or PDS. However, you may still have to provide investors with an information memorandum (IM) for investors to make an informed decision on whether or not to invest in the syndicate.

SUMMARY

This area of the law is complicated, and failure to comply with the various regulations can have profound legal implications, both civil and criminal. Furthermore, the foregoing is only an outline of the rules, and it does not cover all situations or specific structures. I strongly recommend, therefore, that you seek legal and tax advice (from your lawyer and accountant) before starting a real estate development syndicate.

Managing a syndicate

Whether for investment or development, the success of a real estate syndicate depends on how effectively the manager deals with the syndicate members and the property project. If you intend to set up a new syndicate, you have certain obligations as a founder. The following are summarised recommendations on working with and managing relations with investors.

Manage relations

Managing relations with investor members is one of your key responsibilities as a founder manager. It takes considerable personal time that does not directly impact business operations. However, the time spent is helpful as it lays the foundation for open communication and trust. If the project is extensive, with several team members, the founder or manager should still take this role.

Build mutual understanding

A mutual understanding between the manager and investor members is essential for long-term collaboration. It ensures that investors understand the project strategy and the pathway to achieving its goals. To ensure that investors fully grasp the project, it is worth inviting individual investors to join you in your office periodically to participate in an open discussion.

Establish a set of rules and policies

One way to ensure there is no misunderstanding between the manager and investors is to establish a written set of rules and procedures. It should outline the roles and responsibilities of the manager and investors and the protocol when dealing with important matters. Some investors may believe they know more than the manager and can be vociferous. Having policies in writing will provide a formal guide.

Draw up a mutual program with milestones

To avoid misunderstandings and at the same time benefit from your investors' input, I recommend that a program with critical milestones be drawn up. This program should be regularly updated when and if changes are made. Members' meetings are ideal for sharing and discussing the program and milestones to be prioritised, how they will be achieved and by whom.

Regular meeting update and agenda

To keep investors updated on a project's progress and involve them in strategic decisions, set up regular monthly or bi-monthly meetings with an agenda listing items for discussion. The meeting should be chaired by you or your representative and recorded in writing to distribute to members, especially for those who could not attend the meeting.

Do's and don'ts

When managing successful real estate syndications, a manager should keep in mind some key 'do's and don'ts'. Here is a list of things that a manager should and should not do.

Do your research

Whether it is detailed around the proposed project or the finance structure, you must research each area thoroughly. Member investors will be looking to you for answers in all project areas and financing. So, it is important not to embarrass yourself by not providing the correct answers when asked.

Do select the proper structure

Each syndicate member's financial situation will be different, so it is essential to choose a flexible structure for the individuals in the group to maximise their benefits. Speak to an experienced, commercially minded lawyer or accountant, and get the right advice on the structure suited to your syndicate.

Do have a clear exit strategy

As with all businesses, it pays to have a clear exit strategy as one never knows what may happen in the future. For example, the early assumptions made on the market may worsen, or some personal matters may arise. Therefore, it is always best to have contingencies in place if the exit takes longer than expected.

Don't accept just anybody in your syndicate

Disruptive members in a real estate syndicate can cause mayhem, especially those who think they know better. It is therefore wise to do background research on potential members before accepting them in your syndicate. Make sure you understand the motivations of all the people interested in joining your syndicate.

Don't start a syndicate without a legal agreement

Forming a legal agreement is critical when setting up a real estate syndicate. It ensures you think carefully about the different possibilities and eventualities during the project. It also provides answers on how to deal with those eventualities to ensure they don't occur during the syndicate's life.

Don't leave any questions unanswered

Syndicate members will come from different walks of life. Some are businesspeople or professionals; others may have a sales or trades background. Each will have a different outlook and level of knowledge on real estate and syndication. As the manager, you must provide answers and in turn ask them which area of the business they do not understand. Giving the correct answers and asking the right questions will create a more cohesive group of syndicate members.

SUMMARY

When starting a real estate syndicate you are effectively launching a new business. Whether the syndicate is created for real estate investment or development, you should treat the operation as a business. Depending on the project's scale, you may have to rent an office and employ staff for administration and record-keeping. In addition, there are taxes and operating expenses to be paid, and it is essential that the fees you charge for managing the syndicate cover these costs. Also, ensure that the fees charged are paid monthly and are in line with your cash flow.

CASE STUDY 1:
AN OFFICE DEVELOPMENT SYNDICATE

This case study is of a syndicate I created 30 years ago with people I knew through the construction industry. Even though it was over three decades ago, the principles applied in this project are equally applicable today. With our architectural business expanding, we needed additional office space. Instead of paying rent to a third party, we formed a syndicate and developed strata-titled offices.

Project:	88 Walters Drive
Type:	8 strata office units
Year:	1988
Total development cost:	$1650000
End value	$2075000

Description

At the peak of a building boom in 1988, a group made up of builders and architects decided to build their own strata office. We could see no merit in renting office premises, so we invited four other interested parties made up of investors. A syndicate of six members was then formed.

A new business park area site was found, which gave each office a street frontage. The final design included eight strata offices varying in size but with an average of 155 square metres. We decided that each member would own a strata unit at wholesale, while the two remaining units were to be sold at retail and any profits split equally between the six members.

The building boom had led to a shortage of bricklayers and they were also charging a premium for their labour. It was then decided to build the project with tilt-up panels, the first tilt-up office block in Western Australia.

Legal structure

After consulting a lawyer, we established a bare trust with the six syndicate members as beneficiaries. Before creating the trust, our lawyer had a meeting with the Australian Taxation Office and outlined the purpose of the bare trust. This was critical as the syndicate paid stamp duty only on the land purchased and not on the end value when completed, and strata titles transferred to each syndicate member.

Lessons learned

A development syndicate can work well if all members understand the ultimate investment goals. The rules should be clearly defined so there can be no misunderstanding between members.

There are significant benefits in developing real estate through a syndicate. For example, stamp duty is paid only on the land. In addition, members can increase their equity position faster by getting their unit at wholesale plus a share in the profits made from the sale of retail priced units.

CONCLUSION

Syndicates continue to play an integral role in residential and commercial real estate. With the increasing cost of land and construction, the high cost of raising finance and the risks of going it alone, a real estate syndicate is becoming a common approach to raising capital for real estate development.

For a developer, the profit on a project is much lower under a syndicate structure because it means sharing the returns with other syndicate members. However, the model carries significantly fewer financial risks. Furthermore, if the developer acts purely as development manager employed by the syndicate, there is the benefit of a management fee that pays monthly as the project rolls out. There is also the opportunity to share the project's profits through a performance-based fee. It provides a cash flow with less stress and a bonus at the end should the project turn out to be financially successful.

Not all developers are comfortable with a syndicate association, however. Some prefer to go it alone. They may lack the skills to manage a group of people having an equal say in a development they have conceived or found. Unless these developers have deep pockets, they will focus on smaller-scale developments.

CHAPTER 2

JOINT VENTURE DEVELOPMENTS

A joint venture (JV) is a business entity created by two or more parties characterised by shared ownership and sharing the returns and risks on a specific project. Joint ventures are usually short-term arrangements set up for particular projects. However, it is possible to use joint venture arrangements in a broader context. They are also used as flexible and clean structures to carry on a range of businesses.

The term *joint venture* has no statutory definition. It describes several different legal relationships, but is not a separate legal entity. The relationship between joint venture parties is governed by the agreement's terms and the general law.

A real estate development JV is an arrangement between two or more parties to work together and share resources to develop a property. The parties in a JV maintain their own business identity while working together to complete the project. JVs allow real estate developers with extensive development experience to work with real estate capital providers or investment funds.

The role and responsibilities of each party in a joint venture can be assigned in whatever manner they are needed to bring a project to its successful conclusion. Profits are then shared as agreed upfront between the JV parties.

The basic principle of a JV development can be demonstrated through the following example. Company A owns a potential development site suitable for an apartment block but is based in another city. Company B is an experienced developer in the city where the development site is located. Company A wants to develop the land, as the market is on an upward trend. Company A therefore forms a joint venture with company B. Company A provides the land and the capital; company B provides the development expertise.

Reasons for a joint venture

There are many forms of JVs and several reasons for using this arrangement. In a real estate development context, we can break these down into three main areas: land, finance and expertise. These three resources are usually the driving force for parties seeking to form a JV.

Development land

Securing well-located development land is the first step in a financially successful real estate development project. A development can be structured in several ways. In some cases, accessing and securing quality land can be completed only through a JV. Establishing a JV with the landowner can unlock an excellent opportunity for an experienced developer and for the landowner.

Development finance

Undertaking a new development requires significant upfront capital before any revenue is generated. If a developer does not have sufficient finance or equity, finding a JV partner who is financially secure will help. There are many JV opportunities with investors who have money. Some prefer to remain silent or passive in a project. In this case, the investor would take a share of the development profits rather than receive interest on the money invested.

Development expertise

Successful real estate development requires significant knowledge and expertise. It takes both time and effort to master real estate development.

The success of most projects depends on the developer's skills. Many landowners hold viable development sites that they cannot unlock or take forward. Forming a JV with a developer who has the requisite skills and ability opens up the land's potential.

Land, finance and expertise are the three main motivating factors for a joint venture, which may be driven by a combination of all three.

A joint venture versus a syndicate

Chapter 1 focuses on another form of partnership, a syndicate. There is a crucial difference between a syndicate and a JV. However, to determine if an enterprise is a JV or a syndicate is to decide whether it qualifies as an investment product or a contract. The critical question to ask is, 'Is there any profit derived from the efforts of a promoter or third party?' If there is, it is an investment contract through which a promoter sells shares or securities, and it is considered a syndication. If not, then it is a JV.

Under a syndicate

Under a public syndication, a manager or promoter sells shares. It must therefore register with the Australian Securities and Investments Commission (ASIC), which regulates securities law. Investors in a syndicate do not have an active role in the project's ongoing management and are passive investors.

In general, a syndicate is more expensive to form, as a Product Disclosure Statement is required to be registered with ASIC, on top of the ongoing costs of compliance, reporting and promotion.

Under a joint venture

In a JV two or more individuals or companies pool resources to accomplish a common goal. For example, both or all parties play an active management role in a real estate project and have unlimited liability. No single person can make decisions on behalf of the group. Decisions must be by majority or unanimous rule.

As a JV is a private commercial arrangement between two or more private parties, it costs less than the management of a syndicate.

Advantages and disadvantages of a joint venture

A JV has several benefits, but failing to structure it correctly can result in failure. Before entering a JV in a real estate development, consider the pros and cons of doing so.

Advantages of a JV

Unlike a partnership, a JV is a short-term arrangement. One of the main benefits is that each party operates under its own legal entity after completing the project. Each real estate JV is therefore structured differently. There are distinct advantages in a development JV, including:

- bringing together partners with complementary profiles

- ability to undertake larger projects

- spreading the risk

- two heads are better than one

- increased capability

- shared resources

- shared expenses

- access to additional capital

- access to further knowledge and expertise

- added credibility

- flexible arrangements between parties.

Disadvantages of a JV

While there are significant advantages to a JV development arrangement, there are disadvantages to consider as well. These include:

- the other party could add a degree of risk

- exit strategies can be complicated if partners have different goals

- lack of total control

- potential for disagreements

- conflict-resolution challenges

- the potential for obligations to be unfulfilled by the other partner

- project terms are not clearly defined

- lack of commitment by either party

- different management styles

- unclear or different objectives

- imbalance in levels of expertise

- different cultures and backgrounds.

The rewards of a JV can far outweigh the risks, but it is essential to do your homework thoroughly before signing an agreement. A JV development is effective only when each party is sincere and willing to move forward together. It might be better not to consider a JV project if one party questions the motives of the other. To prevent an inevitable failure, it might be better to exit a JV before any legal obligation arises. Better still, before formally entering into a JV agreement, do your due diligence on the other party and consider the following questions:

- Is there the potential of losing money?

- Will you be relinquishing any of your intellectual property?

- What is the critical return to entering the JV?

- Will your credibility be tarnished if the JV fails?

Examples of when JVs are formed

JVs are used when two or more parties recognise that something is missing in their organisation and seek to fill this gap. This lack might relate to many things, including finance, access to credit, experience or an asset such as land. For example, a developer finds a great development opportunity, and has the expertise to manage it, but needs a financial partner to make the opportunity happen. Following are some cases in which a JV is employed in real estate development.

Land contribution

A landowner owns a valuable piece of real estate but requires a developer with the ability to develop it. The landowner may not want to sell the land to the developer but would like to contribute to the venture. Or a developer finds a parcel of land that would suit a significant development but does not have the financial resources to buy the land. So the developer convinces the landowner to participate and share the profits.

Credibility

A small residential developer has found an opportunity to develop a much larger project such as a multi-storey apartment block or a new shopping centre. Although they have the required equity, they lack the expertise or credibility to convince lenders to finance their project. So they look for a seasoned commercial developer with the proper credentials and track record and form a JV.

Finance

An experienced developer has enough cash for a deposit on a potential development site but cannot secure a loan because of a shortfall on the required equity. The developer seeks a financial partner with either cash or access to credit to cover the critical shortfall. The developer might approach a building contractor with a significant balance sheet to provide the necessary funding for the project.

Government tender

In some Australian states, the government will invite developers to tender on government-owned land to stimulate the local economy. To increase their chances of winning the tender, the developer might form a JV with either a financial partner or a respected building contractor.

Public–private partnership

Another form of JV is a public–private partnership (PPP). A PPP is a JV collaboration between a government entity and a private-sector company such as a developer or building contractor. For example, a government entity may not have the capability to undertake a capital-intensive building project, so they partner with a private enterprise to undertake the project.

Types of JV entities

A JV is similar to a partnership, but they are not the same. Each party in a JV continues to do business under their own entity. The JV partners are just working together on a specific deal or project.

When the project has been completed, the JV partners split any profits based on an agreed percentage. Financial contributions are fundamental in these ventures. One party may provide all the necessary finance, or it could be an 80:20 split, a 50:50 division or another variation.

Often one partner brings most of the cash, while the other acts as the operating partner. A joint venture can use several legal structures depending on the agreed arrangement between the parties. A JV agreement will specify each party's contributions and responsibilities and how profits will be distributed. There are three common types of JVs.

Incorporated joint venture

A limited liability company (Pty Ltd) is probably the most common entity used in joint ventures. Setting up a business as a Pty Ltd is relatively easy and inexpensive. The terms of the JV agreement are spelled out in the shareholders' agreement. Each party in the JV will be a shareholder in the company, owning a certain percentage shareholding. Companies are attractive as they provide liability protection to the shareholders.

Unit trust

Under a unit trust, the joint venture partners are the unitholders, usually with a corporate trustee. It is a standard business structure for a venture between several unrelated interests. The JV parties are beneficiaries who have a fixed interest in the development managed by the trustees.

Unincorporated joint venture

The JV partners enter a contract to establish their legal rights and obligations concerning the joint venture. Depending on the terms of the agreement, the parties may constitute a partnership for general law purposes. In certain circumstances an alternative joint venture may be used instead of a partnership to carry on a business. In such a case, the parties would generally use a company to act as a manager carrying on the business on behalf of the JV partners.

JV development structures

While there are many different variants, these transactions generally fall into one of five general development structures.

Standard joint venture partnerships

Limited liability companies or limited partnership agreements remain the most popular ownership structure today. The generic terms of joint venture and partnership are used for this analysis. However, all legal arrangements should be investigated and analysed before agreeing to liability management and tax issues.

Advantages for the developer

- They earn a development profit based on equity contributed.

- It is easier to attract finance partners, many of whom prefer pro-rata structures with the developer putting in tangible equity.

- Shares in costs savings are pro rata per party.

- Each party has partnership rights.

- Tax treatment may be more favourable, as a CGT exemption may be available if the property is held for a sufficient period.

- Interim financing is more easily attainable, as the two partners' additional capital will allow for a better loan-to-value ratio for lenders.

Disadvantages for the developer

- Usually, the agreements will have buy or sell provisions that benefit the finance partner.

- The risk is pro rata and therefore not limited.

- Partnership documentation is complicated and usually more expensive and time-consuming.

- There is less flexibility on exit timing.

- The partners may be required to provide guarantees for interim financing.

Fee development

The safest strategy for a developer is a fee development transaction. Many developers prefer this type of transaction, especially in a high-risk environment. In a fee development transaction, the funding partner owns the property during the entire development period and the risk for the developer is limited. Usually the developer's risks are for cost overruns and are limited to a portion of the total development fee.

Advantages for the developer

- There is limited risk as the developer shares in the construction risk with a cap.

- No interim financing is needed as the funding partner provides funds.

- The developer can often negotiate to share in cost savings.

- Fee income is more certain.

- Entitlement and cost are generally reimbursed.

Disadvantages for the developer

- The profits are not shared or equity is not created.

- It is tough to negotiate as the funding partner recognises the developer has no capital at risk.

- The developer has less control of the project and any significant decisions.

Incentive development fee

A hybrid approach to a JV development is a development fee structure with the opportunity to earn profits through an incentive fee contract. Under this structure, the funding partner owns the property from the outset, and the developer receives a market development fee. The developer may earn additional incentive fees based on the project's financial performance.

Advantages for the developer

- A portion of the profit or equity created will be earned.

- Risk is limited (and can be capped).

- Cost savings are shared.

- There is some flexibility in operational decisions.

- No interim financing is necessary as the finance partner provides the funds.

- Entitlement and cost are generally reimbursed.

Disadvantages for the developer

- The most significant share of the equity created goes to the funding partner.

- There is generally some downside risk (exposure may be capped).

- There are significant 'partnership' provisions, but limited legal rights.

- Incentive profit is taxable as a fee.

Joint venture with landowners

This structure is used by a developer when the landowner retains ownership of the project. In most cases, the land value equals 10 to 20 per cent of the project's overall cost, and landowners would expect to have that percentage of the ownership with no additional risk. Generally, the landowner becomes a limited partner in the agreement.

Advantages for the developer

- The developer earns a pro-rata share of the profit.

- The developer controls and manages the project; the landowner is the silent shareholder.

- It is easier to finance as the land value is considered equity by lenders.

- It reduces the amount of equity required by the developer.

- There are tax advantages as a CGT exemption can generally be achieved upon sale.

Disadvantages for the developer

- Risk is not limited.

- The developer generally guarantees the construction or senior loan.

- The developer assumes risks for construction delays and cost overruns.

- The developer assumes all leasing and tenant risks if the development is held as an investment.

Agreement to purchase on completion

Most rewarding for the developer is an agreement to purchase the development on completion. It occurs when an investment institution such as a real estate fund agrees conditionally to purchase the project on completion. It is also referred to as a 'take-out'. Before starting the construction, the developer prearranges to sell the property to an institutional purchaser as a fully leased building with a guaranteed yield for a limited period. These types of opportunities apply mainly to commercial developments. In some instances, the institutional purchaser may finance the whole project and charge interest on any funds used by the developer.

Advantages for the developer

- The developer receives the entire development profit over the prearranged price.

- The developer retains significant flexibility over leasing and operational decisions.

- It makes development financing easier.

- Interim financing will generally carry better terms and pricing.

- The developer receives all cost savings.

Disadvantages for the developer

- The take-out terms and conditions can be numerous and onerous.

- The developer generally guarantees the interim loan.

- Pre-agreed pricing is generally at a higher capitalisation rate than the current market.

- The developer assumes all risks for construction delays and cost overruns.

- The developer assumes all entitlement and pursuit cost risk.

- The developer generally assumes all leasing and tenant improvement risks.

Selecting the right JV partner

The ideal JV partner has resources, skills or assets that complement what you lack for a project. The joint venture must work contractually, but there should also be a good fit between the parties' beliefs.

Screening potential JV partners is not easy, particularly if you are assessing a potential partner you do not know well or have never met before. Following are some of the many things you need to consider when selecting a JV partner:

- Do their skills complement rather than replicate yours?

- How well does the party perform?

- What is their attitude to collaboration?

- Do they share your level of commitment?

- Do they have similar work habits?

- Do you share the same business objectives?

- Are they honest and trustworthy?

- Do their brand values complement yours?

- What kind of reputation do they have?

- Do they share the same vision for the JV?

When assessing a potential new partner, you need to carry out some necessary checks:

- Are they financially secure?

- Are they self-sufficient?

- Do they have any credit issues?

- Do they already have partnerships with other businesses?

- What level of management team do they have?

- How well do they perform in production, marketing and personnel?

- What do their customers or suppliers say about their reputation?

Although a JV in a real estate development is a one-off project, it is still essential that the selected JV partner is the right fit for you and the project.

Unfortunately, I have seen many JV projects fail because their vision is not aligned or partners do not trust each other.

Structuring the shareholding in a JV

Structuring the shareholding in a JV is not simple. Some parties may believe they are bringing more to the table or they just want control. Both parties should consider and agree on what is fair and reasonable. If not, it may be helpful to let a third party, such as an accountant, undertake an assessment. Besides, shareholding is only one aspect of a JV. There are several options available on how the profits can be split. Before finalising the share structure, consider the following questions.

Who has control?

The major shareholder will always have the final say, although this may not be the case with operational matters. The major shareholder generally controls all major decisions, such as when selling the property. Who has the right to vote? Will there be restrictions on the transfer of shares? Should partners have the first right of refusal in a sale situation? These considerations and more need to be part of the JV creation process. On operational matters, the party appointed as manager makes all decisions in line with the goals set out for the JV and relating to achieving these goals.

How can profits be shared?

Most real estate development JV shareholding is based on the capital contributions made by the parties. If only one party is providing the capital, then the split could be 70:30 or 80:20, with a profit share based on the performance of the operating partner. The performance provisions dictate how any net income and profits are distributed. Generally, the capital partner should get a specified return on their investment before the balance or excess of profits is distributed. For example, after the capital partner is paid their return on capital, the excess profit can be split 50:50 or 70:30, with the latter portion going to the non-capital partner.

What are the tax and legal implications?

Each party will have different tax requirements, both business and personal, depending on how the JV decide to split the profits. An accountant is the best source of advice on this matter. Also, there are different liabilities to consider and other legal implications, depending on how the JV is set up and how profits are split. A lawyer should be appointed to provide the correct legal input.

Steps in setting up a joint venture

A JV opportunity occurs when any of the examples shown earlier comes to fruition. Before formalising a JV agreement, a developer should take the following steps in sequential order. Some steps may be skipped depending on the arrangement and type of JV.

1. Determine if a joint venture is a suitable arrangement

First, examine the two entities' operating structures to see if they are compatible. Consider the following issues before deciding:

- Do the structures complement each other?

- Are both parties committed to the success of the joint venture?

- Are the staff of each company receptive and supportive of the JV?

- Are both parties financially secure enough to support the JV?

- Do the parties trust each other to work well together?

- Are the values and ethics of each party similar?

- Are both parties trustworthy?

- Are there any personality conflicts that could derail the JV?

2. Undertake due diligence on the JV partner

Before setting up a JV, the potential business partner needs to be analysed thoroughly. It is essential to carry out thorough due diligence on the party concerned. Items that should be checked when conducting due diligence include:

- the company profile and credibility

- the integrity of the directors

- their financial status

- their complementary skills and resources

- if land is offered, its status and ownership.

3. Prepare a heads of agreement

If the earlier steps have been undertaken and found acceptable, prepare a heads of agreement (HoA). For a JV to be successful, the two companies must deal openly, sharing otherwise confidential information. The HoA is non-binding in-principle agreement before a formal JV agreement is structured and signed. The agreement allows both parties to agree to pass on more detailed information without disclosing or taking advantage of anything obtained from the other company. A sample HoA is available at the end of this book.

4. Review the scope of the JV

After the HoA has been signed, the parties sharing information will meet to further the joint venture's purpose. The parties should first determine the expected duration of the JV, shareholding, management and resources, then use that information to select the future course of action. The parties should then analyse the various forms of a joint venture and decide whether the structure should be a new limited liability company, a partnership or a simple contractual agreement.

5. Formalise a JV agreement

Once the parties have agreed to the terms and conditions plus any critical elements to the JV, a lawyer should be contracted to draft a formal

JV agreement. There may be further amendments after each party has scrutinised the draft agreement. Finally, when the parties are satisfied, the contract is signed and work can start on the JV development.

Key aspects of a JV agreement

Five main features will be considered in relation to a JV agreement involving real estate development.

Distribution of profits

An essential distinction to make when drafting a JV agreement is how the parties intend to distribute profits generated from the project. Profits may not always be equally distributed. For example, more active members or members who have invested more in the project may be compensated better than passive members or members who have invested less.

Contribution of capital

The JV agreement needs to specify the exact amount of capital injection expected from each member. Also, it must determine when this capital is due. For example, a funder may agree to contribute 25 per cent of the required capital, but only if these funds are made at the last stage of the development process.

Roles and responsibilities

Each party's roles and responsibilities should be clearly defined and detailed to avoid later misunderstanding, conflict or confusion.

Management and control

Besides the roles and responsibilities, the JV agreement is expected to specify the development project's management and control. If a company is formed, it must be decided who the directors are and the respective level of control on significant decisions.

Exit strategy

A JV agreement needs to provide details on how and when the JV will end. It is best for both entities to make the closure of the JV as economical as possible by avoiding any legal fees or costs. Also, the JV agreement must list all the events or trigger points that will allow one or both parties to initiate a premature dissolution of the JV.

The JV agreement

When structuring a joint venture agreement, consider the following items that should be included in the formal agreement.

Purpose of the JV

Most contracts start by naming the parties to the agreement and describing each party's business, then naming the new JV and including a brief statement of its intended purpose.

Relevant terms and definitions

If specific terms are essential to the joint venture, they should be clearly defined. This section falls under the heading of 'Definitions' to set it apart from the agreement portion of the contract. Some parties consider this section unnecessary. However, it is helpful to define the key phrases and terms.

Business objectives

This section should clearly define the JV's purpose to help the parties focus as the project progresses. The objective statement should be clearly described so the parties to the contract can identify when their specific goal has been met.

The JV structure

The JV parties need to define whether they will be creating a new business entity or acting as independent agents working together.

If a new company is to be formed, it should identify that new entity, its operating structure, directors and officers.

If a partnership is being formed, it should define how the partnership will share assets and liabilities.

Management

For the JV to succeed, the parties need to agree on operating it. A decision is to be made if a separate board of directors is created or made up of members of each party. Under this section, address the:

- structure of the management

- procedures for appointing or selecting the managers

- compensation or fees for the managers

- management's decision-making responsibilities or limitations

- frequency and purpose of meetings.

Financial aspects

Define what each party will contribute to the JV in cash or other resources. The sharing of profits also needs to be addressed. Following are some other considerations:

- What equity is each partner responsible for?

- When will profits be paid out?

- How are profits to be calculated?

- What share of profits will each party receive?

- How will tax obligations be shared and reported?

Roles and responsibilities of each party

Consider which company will contribute staff to the JV. The agreement must identify which staff members will perform specific tasks and responsibilities. Additional areas include:

- manager of the JV running day-to-day operations

- manager's level of decision-making

- administration and record-keeping

- staff who will support the manager.

Accounting

This section needs to specify who will be handling the day-to-day finances—who oversees the banking, payment of contractors and service providers. This should have been covered in the roles and responsibilities section. Also, it should be specified who has the authority to approve payments and to what level. Money distribution and disbursement is among the most critical areas to cover in a JV agreement.

Insurance

Most JV parties are not newly formed business entities. It should therefore be clear how the JV will be protected with insurance and which types of insurance must be maintained during the development. This section should specify the various insurances such as workers compensation, public liability and any other insurance to protect the construction and contractors working on the site.

Dispute resolution

It is crucial in any JV that the parties anticipate the possibility of disputes. The JV agreement needs to provide procedures the parties will follow to resolve any future disputes.

The first step should always be for the two parties to resolve any dispute in good faith. If the matter cannot be resolved between the parties, a mediator should be called in to meet with each party and help bring about a resolution. If the mediator cannot resolve the dispute, the matter should be taken to arbitration, which involves a sort of trial. The arbitration may be binding or non-binding. It can sometimes be costly, depending on the scope of the dispute.

It is essential to identify which state's laws govern any dispute and if the JV parties are from different states or countries. Dispute resolution can be costly. Therefore, it is essential to define upfront who will be responsible for the costs—whether they will be split equally or paid for by the party raising the dispute.

The term of the JV

As reiterated often, a JV is a temporary arrangement. The JV term is defined by a specified time or by clearly stating the business objectives—for example, when the goals have been reached and the JV will be concluded. Items relating to the term may include:

- a clear explanation of the completion of the joint venture project

- a confirmed date when the project is to end

- procedures and steps in winding up the JV

- the possibility of ending the JV if the project is failing

- periodic reviews to determine whether the JV objectives are being met and whether termination should be considered.

Confidentiality clause

If the parties executed a confidentiality agreement under the HoA, then the formal JV agreement should incorporate the clause or repeat similar terms.

Agree with signatures

The JV agreement must be signed by representatives of each party with the authority to enter the contract. In addition, both parties should keep a copy of the final agreement.

■■■

This list provides the general context of a typical JV agreement. As mentioned, each JV arrangement will be different, and a competent lawyer is required to finalise the agreement. Although a JV is a short-term contractual arrangement between two or more parties, it is vital to employ a skilled lawyer who has experience in JV agreements. You do not want to be a guinea pig for a novice lawyer, as they may not consider an area where a JV could go wrong.

While the agreement can cover the necessary clauses, some areas should be carefully considered. For example, what if a partner goes bankrupt during the JV period? Does the existing partner get the right of first refusal if one party wants to sell their share? And what is the unwinding process of the JV if anything goes wrong during the JV period without affecting each party's own business?

Public–private partnerships

Another form of joint venture is a public–private partnership, sometimes known as PPP or P3. A PPP is a JV collaboration between a government entity and a private-sector company such as a developer or building contractor. The latter parties provide the finance, build and operate projects. These projects can include public transportation networks, general hospitals, social housing, convention centres, schools and other community facilities.

How does a PPP work?

Sometimes a government lacks the financial capacity, resources or expertise to undertake a capital-intensive project on their land. A private enterprise may then be interested in developing the building in order to receive the operating income once the building is completed and rented out. Following are some critical elements of a typical PPP:

- **Term.** PPPs typically have extended contract periods of 25 to 30 years or longer.

- **Finance.** The financing of a PPP comes partly from the private sector but requires payments from the public sector and users over the project's lifetime.

- **Private partner's role.** The private entity's role is to design, complete, implement and fund the project.

- **Public partner's role.** The public partner focuses on defining and monitoring compliance with the project's objectives.

Advantages of PPPs

Partnerships between private companies and the government provide advantages to both parties:

- Private-sector technology and innovation can help provide better public services through improved operational efficiency.

- The public sector provides incentives for the private sector to deliver projects on time and within budget.

- They provide better development solutions than a wholly public or private initiative. Each party performs according to its expertise.

- They result in faster project completion and reduced delays by including time-to-completion to measure performance and profit.

- A public–private partnership's return on investment may be higher than only private or only government projects. This is because innovative design and financing are created when the two parties work together.

- Risks are fully appraised early to determine the project's viability. In addition, the private partner can serve as a check against unrealistic government promises or expectations.

- The project execution and operation risks are transferred from the government to the private party, which usually has more experience in cost containment.

- By increasing the value of the government's investment, a PPP allows government funds to be redirected to other critical socioeconomic areas.

- High standards are better achieved and maintained throughout the project's life cycle.

Disadvantages of PPPs

There are downsides too, however:

- If the project is not delivered on time, exceeds cost estimates or has technical defects, then the private partner typically bears the burden.

- The private partner faces availability risk if it cannot provide the service promised. In addition, a company may not meet safety or other relevant quality standards, for example, when running a prison, hospital or school.

- Every PPP involves risks for the private participant, who reasonably expects to be compensated for accepting those risks.

- Profits of the projects can vary depending on the associated risk, the type of competition, and the project's scope and complexity.

- If the partnership's expertise lies heavily on the private side, the government is inherently disadvantaged. For example, it might be unable to assess the proposed costs accurately.

Types of PPPs

There are several types of PPP contract models and no 'one-size-fits-all'. Each contract is based on the project's objective and sector and, more specifically, on the project's outcome. The public sector defines the essential standard services to be provided. In contrast, the private sector is responsible for meeting and improving vital standards. Following are some traditional models being adopted.

Build – Operate – Transfer (BOT)

The private sector is responsible for the asset's construction, operation and management when completed. Then, after an agreed process term when the developer recoups any capital investment and profit, the asset is transferred back to the public sector.

Build – Own – Operate – Transfer (BOOT)

A BOOT is similar to a BOT, except the project is in the private sector's name. The primary goal is to recoup construction costs (and more) during the operational phase. This structure is adopted when the government has a financing shortfall in equity, and the commercial risk remains with the private sector for the contract term. This model can be used for school and hospital contracts.

Build – Own – Operate (BOO)

A BOO is similar to a BOOT, except the facility is not transferred back to the public sector partner. A BOO transaction may qualify for tax-exempt status and is often used for water treatment or power plants.

Design – Build

According to the PPP contract's performance specification, the contract to design and build a facility is awarded to a private party. This partnership can save time and money, provide more reliable guarantees and allocate additional project risk to the private party.

Design – Construct – Maintain – Finance (DCMF)

In a DCMF the private entity creates the facility based on specifications from the government body and leases it back. This model is generally used for government offices or prison projects.

Concession contracts

In this contract, the private party is responsible for financing, constructing a new or modernising an existing facility, and operating the facility for a given period. The public sector takes over after the expiration of the contract.

■■■

There are many other types of PPP contracts. Some of these do not include development but cover just operation and management. For example, most PPP contracts focus on major infrastructure works such as railways, roads and utility plants. However, now and then a PPP is tendered with a building or development element.

CASE STUDY 1:
A TOWNHOUSE DEVELOPMENT

This is an example of a successful JV project between two willing parties, both of whom were experienced developers. A professional commercial developer approached me to take over a partially completed townhouse project.

The owner, whose core interest was in the commercial industrial sector developing industrial buildings, decided to try his hand in residential developments. After completing only five units, however, only one unit was sold, and that was to his own quantity surveyor. With no interest from other homebuyers, he approached me to redesign, build and market the project. After the council's approval on the redesign, my team and I completed and sold all the remaining units within a year.

Description

The initial development approval was for 24 double-storey townhouse units in an exclusive upmarket suburb on a one-hectare site.

As part of Phase 1, the initial developer took the risk of building a cluster of five townhouse units without any pre-sales except for one unit purchased by the developer's quantity surveyor. Although there was substantial marketing, the other four units did not draw any public interest and sat vacant for six months.

The developer then approached me to undertake a JV in which my role was to redesign, build and market the rest of the development. After our market research, we found that the potential buyers were independent retirees. They were looking to scale down from their large homes to more manageable, secure units without diminishing their current living standards.

In the redesign, we decreased the number of allowable units from 24 to 18 units, which meant 13 units were redesigned. Although there were fewer units, we increased the floor areas of the remaining units. The intention was to suit the targeted market who wanted larger rooms and fewer bedrooms to accommodate their sentimentally prized furniture.

After the first marketing launch, we pre-sold all 13 units and completed the construction within one year.

Legal structure

The JV agreement was quite simple, defining the role of each partner. My role was to redesign, build and market the project. The developer's role was to provide the land and finance for the construction. On completion, the developer would receive an agreed price for his land and charge interest on the construction. Any profit after that was paid to me.

Lessons learned

This JV worked because the landowner developer recognised the skills and experience he lacked and that he needed a residential developer.

A successful JV works when each party clearly understands their specific roles.

The financial structure was clearly defined upfront.

CASE STUDY 2:
A HOTEL DEVELOPMENT

This case study is an example of an unsuccessful joint venture. The JV was between two real estate developers, a residential developer and a hotel developer. My company, AYR International Pty Ltd, was appointed as the development manager, acting on behalf of the hotel developer. The residential developer owned an existing tavern surrounded by substantial vacant land to accommodate short-term accommodation. The site was in a booming mining town.

The landowner, who was experienced only in residential housing, approached the hotel developer seeking a serviced apartment development site to service the 'fly-in, fly-out' labour force working on the mining sites. A joint venture heads of agreement (HoA) between the parties was drawn up and signed, allowing a two-month due diligence period. Unfortunately, the project did not proceed past the HoA for several reasons.

Description

The proposed development was a three-star hotel and serviced apartment complex managed by an internationally recognised hotel brand. The existing tavern, which had a restaurant, provided catering and room service to the proposed hotel rooms and serviced apartments.

The complex would have a fully equipped gymnasium, a pool and decking area, outdoor BBQ areas, a business centre, a secure gated community, and car, boat and trailer parking. The proposed accommodation would include 198 serviced apartments, 96 hotel rooms and staff accommodation of 18 rooms.

A residual valuation was completed during the due diligence period. It found that the land price needed to be $10 million to make the project viable. But the landowner wanted $12 million plus control of the catering services.

JV legal structure

The landowner provided a subdivided portion of their land for the short-stay accommodation and sold it to the hotel operator at $12 million. The transfer and land settlement would be paid only when the new buildings were completed. The hotel developer was to finance the land, buildings and additional utility services, and manage the hotel and serviced apartments. The landowner would also provide catering services to the new hotel and serviced apartments exclusively.

Lessons learned

The JV ended after the due diligence period. The landowner would not budge on his asking price of $12 million even though the residual analysis showed it should be $10 million. Being a residential developer who sold whatever he developed, the landowner did not understand how commercial developments were structured.

The landowner also wanted to be the exclusive provider of catering services and not have the quality and standards of their brand controlled by the hotel operator. It would not work as it would cause conflict between the parties.

The critical lesson here is that sometimes JV partners' agendas conflict. This was not a win–win structure, and it was best to walk away. In hindsight, it was fortunate that the hotel operator did not proceed as there was a mining downturn soon after.

CONCLUSION

A clear and pragmatic agreement is essential for building a successful joint venture relationship. Here are some additional tips to ensure that your JV runs smoothly.

Communication

Good communication is an essential element of building a healthy relationship. It can be achieved by arranging regular, face-to-face meetings with all the key people involved in the JV.

SWOT analysis

Before proceeding with a JV, the parties should review their business strategy to see if a JV is the best way to achieve your goals. Then they should undertake a SWOT analysis to see if the partnership is a good match.

Sharing information

Information, especially on financial matters, should be shared openly. Honesty and trust are vitally important in a JV relationship. They will prevent partners from becoming suspicious of each other.

Key performance indicators (KPIs)

Establishing KPIs will help measure performance and provide the JV with an early warning of potential problems. Everyone must know what they are trying to achieve with their JV goals.

Be flexible

When two parties are making decisions, matters can become complicated, even with simple projects. The parties should have a flexible arrangement to ensure the smooth running of the project. It will also help to review areas of the JV that could be improved and determine whether some objectives should be altered.

Find solutions to disagreements

All business relationships have disagreements from time to time. It is wise to approach any dispute positively. Look for a win–win situation rather than scoring points off each other. Most JV agreements should set out agreed dispute resolution procedures for when parties cannot resolve their differences.

■■■

Forming a JV can be challenging, but if done correctly it can be worth the effort, especially when the parties complement each other. For example, more significant real estate developments require the collaboration of several parties to ensure the project's success.

CHAPTER 3
DEVELOPING WITH MINIMAL CASH

Developers are visionaries, promoters, entrepreneurs, but not all are financial geniuses or accounting specialists. The most common problem for developers is a lack of cash and cash flow. Most have their capital tied up in other properties. Developers who are just starting out in the industry may not have any money at all. People tend to believe that becoming a real estate developer is impossible unless you have a substantial amount of money in your bank account. However, there are strategies that enable you to get started with only a small amount of cash.

Most financial institutions require at least 25 to 30 per cent deposit or equity before advancing any loans for a development project. So how do cash-poor developers overcome this problem? This chapter introduces some examples of developing real estate using only a small amount of your own cash. Of course, these examples are just that. There may be many more solutions, but new solutions require creative and lateral thinking.

Your goal as a developer is to develop properties using as little of your own cash as possible. You can find articles or YouTube videos whose authors claim to have financed real estate ventures without a cent of their own money. In my career, I have yet to see this work. You will always need some cash at the start. Besides, any potential investors will want to know what skin you have in the game.

The techniques and strategies presented here will show you how to minimise your cash injection. Not all will work, as their success will depend on several factors, including the developer's experience and understanding of the models, and even then not all parties will accept these proposals.

Understand the fundamentals

To better understand the strategies presented here, you need to know how the process of real estate development works and how projects are financed. If you have some experience in the real estate industry, these strategies will make sense. If you are a novice, it will be necessary to educate yourself or gain experience. Here are some pointers.

Understanding the principles and process

Real estate development is a complex process that can be lengthy and risky. It can take years to bring a project from the initial planning stage through construction to completion, and there are likely to be plenty of obstacles along the way. Yet development projects can also be highly profitable investment opportunities.

Real estate development provides many opportunities for an intrepid entrepreneur, especially one who understands fully what it takes to deliver a successful project. Executed well, a development project can be a runaway success on a scale that cannot be matched by other investment assets. Understanding the principles and process of a typical development, and applying some lateral thinking, can be financially rewarding.

The fundamental building blocks of a successful development include *market analysis, location and site selection, planning and design, project feasibility, financing option,* and *marketing and leasing.*

Familiarising yourself with the development process will give you a broad understanding of what steps to take to ensure the smooth flow of your project. Although the process will vary slightly from project to project, all real estate developments must go through the following stages:

1. vision

2. pre-purchase

3. concept

4. purchase

5. town planning

6. working drawing and documentation

7. pre-construction

8. construction

9. completion and post-construction.

Understanding development funding

The structure of funding is critical for any new development. The strategic use of financial instruments such as loans and investments is key to every development's success. Understanding the underlying principles and their variations will help you find a solution to your project's funding.

The elements that make up a funding solution may include *seed capital, equity, senior debt finance, mezzanine finance* and *loan interest.*

Understanding free equity

Equity is the hard-earned real money you invest in a property or asset. *Free equity,* also known as *sweat equity,* is money created or built up over a period. It is free equity that all real estate developers target. The more free equity you create in the early part of a project, the less risk you will encounter and therefore the less cash you will need to find for the property's deposit.

If you have a career connected to the building industry, you certainly have an advantage in real estate development. As an architect, builder, engineer, bricklayer, plumber or carpenter, you will be able to provide the cost of your job on your project for free, which will create free equity. As a non-member of the building fraternity, you can still generate sweat equity through the following channels.

Skilled negotiations

You can generate sweat equity as a skilled negotiator. Lenders have guidelines that determine a property's fair market value. Whatever you negotiate below this assessed market value can be viewed as your sweat equity.

Finding distressed sellers

It takes time to find properties whose owners are in financial difficulty and forced to sell. With a quick sale, the price is usually below market value. These opportunities allow the developer to purchase a property well below its market value, creating instant equity.

Management and administration

The manager's role in a development project is to find the development, negotiate the deal, coordinate the development team and strategise the marketing. It all takes many hours of work on the manager's part. If the project is your own, you can include some of these costs as sweat equity.

Understanding leveraging

One of the most significant advantages of real estate development is using the financial method of leverage. In finance, *leverage* is a general term for any technique to multiply gains and losses. In real estate, leverage allows you to achieve a much higher return on investment than you could without it. In addition, real estate will enable you to use leverage when you develop. Using leverage in your real estate development therefore can affect your returns and equity position significantly.

For example, if your total development project cost is $10 million and your targeted profit is $2 million (20 per cent), the lender will provide $7 million finance, requiring a $3 million equity injection, then your return on equity is 66.6 per cent ($2 million over $3 million). If $4 million equity is needed, the return on equity is only 50 per cent ($2 million over $4 million).

However, maximising leverage carries risks if you intend to hold the asset. There is the risk of interest rate increases, which could affect your income. Developing with a clear exit on completion could reap a more substantial profit margin on the equity invested.

SUMMARY

If your strategy is to inject a minimal amount of your own cash, or if you're a novice developer with limited cash at your disposal, it is vitally important that you understand the fundamentals of the development process. After all, if you have a shortfall in the required equity of a project, you will be approaching other people with cash. These people will be reluctant to part with any of their hard-earned money to a person who lacks knowledge of these critical fundamentals.

Increasing your equity and value

Developing real estate can be a complicated and expensive process. A vital aspect that all real estate developers should understand is the importance of how equity and leveraging works in real estate. Comprehending these features will place you in a strong position when it comes to minimising your cash injection into a development.

Real estate development is a staged process that increases in value when certain milestones are accomplished. It is worth noting that equity increases in value during the process, and the principal debt is required only when the project proceeds to construction. The pre-construction stage allows developers to increase their free equity and the balance from other sources.

Increasing your equity in a staged process

Property development is one of the few businesses in which enterprising entrepreneurs are rewarded exponentially for their added value efforts. Developers take the most significant risk in creating new property and should receive the most significant rewards. The art of utilising the least amount of capital through one's vision, expertise and commitment can create substantial returns for equity participants.

Following is a staged process to increase your equity value during the development process on a project you initiated. The strategy demonstrates how you control the process at each stage and sell a percentage of your shareholding only after adding value to the project.

Stage 1: Land purchase

I have already stated a well-known saying in the development industry: 'Developers make their money when they buy the land.' Buying and settling on a development site carries risk, especially if you have not secured a development approval (DA) for your intended project, and other factors may affect a sale with this condition in the contract. There are alternatives, such as securing development rights or establishing a joint venture with the landowner. Each of these options has its idiosyncrasies and should be evaluated accordingly. However, if the aim is to secure and control the land with a minimum of your own capital, the strategy would be to secure the land at a lower value and secure a DA that increases the property's value before inviting in other investors.

Stage 2: Predevelopment approval

Once you have control of the land, the next step is to raise seed capital for the documentation required for the DA. The seed capital required is generally around 1 per cent of the development cost. There are several sources where seed capital is raised, but what can be offered in return? Adopting one structure, a convertible loan entitles the lender to convert the loan to equity after approval of the DA. As a DA application is still risky to the lender, they will expect a much higher return on their money, ranging from 20 per cent per annum to 5 per cent per month. Security can be provided by way of a caveat over the development property or some other asset you can provide. Some lenders may ask for a personal guarantee on top of the additional security provided.

Alternatively, Class A preferred shares can be converted into ordinary shares after the approval of the DA. The value of Class A shares varies and depends on the type of project, the risk and the projected profit. For example, if the seed investor provides 1 per cent of the development cost, then they will typically be looking at a 5 to 10 per cent share of the development company.

Stage 3: Post-development approval

Securing a DA removes one of the main risks from a proposed development and adds value to the project. As a result, equity investors will be more comfortable investing. Evaluating the percentage of the development company you are prepared to part with for the additional equity required will depend on new valuations. If you have done your numbers, and they show a good return on the project, then you should be able to demonstrate to the investor the return on their cash invested rather than the actual return on the total development cost. Table 3.1 gives a theoretical example.

Table 3.1: possible shareholding structure in a development

Total development cost	$10 000 000
Profit margin on development — 20 per cent	$2 000 000
Equity required — 30 per cent	$3 000 000
Return on equity — 67 per cent	($2 000 000 / $3 000 000)
If additional equity is required for the project	$2 000 000
Expected return by an investor — minimum of 30 per cent	$600 000
Therefore, investor's shareholding — 30 per cent	

Using this table, based on the $2 million investment of the $3 million equity required for the project to move ahead, generally one should be offering a 60 per cent shareholding. As the developer has spent time and effort finding the opportunity, it is reasonable to offer a shareholding based on return on equity rather than equity against equity. However, it must be pointed out that this shareholding concept may not appeal to all investors, especially sophisticated investors.

When assessing these values, use a good accountant or lawyer with property development knowledge and expertise. They will be able to structure the shareholding of the development company and explain to the equity investor the justification of their shareholding.

SUMMARY

Knowing where value and equity are created through a development process will assist you in how and when you can create free equity with a minimal outlay of your cash. It also enables you to justify, with reasons, why you deserve the free carry of shares within a development company undertaking the project. In each of the strategies explained later, you will understand and validate the value you are bringing to each type of strategy.

Find an equity partner

Should you need additional money that you cannot obtain on your own to develop a property, you might want to consider finding a partner who can cover the shortfall in the form of cash. You will in all probability have to share up to half the profits, but keep in mind that half the profits is much better than nothing at all.

If you are serious about developing property, you need to cultivate partner relationships. There will always be times when you find yourself financially stretched. Aim to have at least four or five partners whom you can approach when the need arises. If you prove to be successful with your development ventures, you are unlikely to find yourself short of partners. Best of all, you may never have to use your own capital for future developments, because you can rely on other people to provide all the development capital you will ever need.

Dealing with an equity partner

Many people have substantial money in savings accounts earning low interest. A developer need only convince them that investing in their development will bring them higher returns. Many investors are motivated by greed and are always looking at avenues to get a better return.

While it is easy to convince people to become partners, these friendships can come unstuck if some basic rules are not followed. Hold on to the following principles, and you will have fewer problems down the track.

Form partnerships only when necessary

Partnerships must be formed only when necessary. New partners should provide whatever the developer lacks (usually funds). A partnership functions better when people complement each other and work together as one.

Be selective with partners

If developers source partners from among their relatives, friends and business associates, they should be very selective and ensure their personalities do not clash. Preferred partners understand the property industry. If the development does not achieve the expected returns, there is nothing worse than having to deal with a partner who does not understand the issues involved and accuses the developer of recklessness.

Define the role of each partner early

If a developer's role is to manage the development because of their knowledge, then the partner's role is to provide or raise funds because of their financial standing. These roles should be defined before the partnership is formalised and signed off.

Define early how the profits are to be split

If a project is profitable, the developer should negotiate a fair arrangement for both parties related to their roles. Several models can be used. For example, the finance partner can be offered an annual percentage return on the capital injected with the balance of the profit split, say, 50:50.

Reduce your partner's fear

If your partner is putting up the money, it is essential to ease their fear of losing it. This can be resolved by placing the property in joint names or setting up a company with agreed shareholding. Also, decide on how the development should be managed and what fees should be paid to the manager.

Maintain control of the partnership

It is crucial for the developer who found the project and knows how to deliver the development to retain control. If the partner is found to be incompatible and is limiting the progress of the development, it is best to dissolve the partnership as quickly as possible.

Maintain a partnership with one property at a time

Each development project should be assessed on its own merits. At the end of the project the profits should be split and the partnership dissolved. Following this rule allows flexibility when another property development opportunity arises. From the outset it should be clearly understood that the partnership is temporary and applies only to a specific development.

Establish a procedure to follow if the partnership is forced to dissolve

Not all partnerships work out successfully. There could be a personality conflict or misunderstandings along the way, or perhaps even the death of a partner. The situation can be worse when the development is in progress. For example, it must be decided at the beginning what procedure should be followed if for whatever reason one partner decides to sell out.

SUMMARY

When developing property with minimal cash based on one's knowledge and expertise, it is vital to build credibility and trust. Treat partners fairly and don't abuse the relationship, because word will spread fast and it won't be easy to find future partners.

Secure seller finance

Secure seller finance is also known as vendor finance. It is a simple concept. A developer buys a potential development site. The landowner agrees to sell the land and is prepared to wait to be paid only when certain milestones are achieved. These milestones can include development approval or secured total development funding.

How does seller finance work?

The value of the land is agreed upon between the landowner and the developer. The developer pays a small deposit to the seller and makes repayments over an agreed time. These repayments may or may not include interest, but the purchase price or the repayments are typically higher than a standard loan.

Depending on the individual agreement, the developer will have the option of paying instalments until it is paid off in full, or making the repayments until the developer can raise funds from investors or qualify for mainstream development funding. Should everything work according to plan, as soon as the last payment is made the developer assumes ownership of the property.

Benefits to the vendor

Not every seller will look at this type of proposal as they may require the funds to purchase another property. Still, those who can finance the developer will benefit by:

- receiving a fair sale price as they are providing vendor finance

- achieving a better interest rate on money offered by the bank

- setting a repayment from the developer higher than their current mortgage repayments

- passing on the responsibility of paying for maintenance and repairs to the developer when the developer agrees to sell or occupy the property

- being reimbursed by the developer for outgoings such as council rates, water rates and insurance premiums

- retaining the property title in their name as security until the developer pays the total price.

Benefits to the developer

The developer will benefit by:

- obtaining a loan that does not require standard qualification

- securing an interest rate and terms that are usually better than the bank would offer

- having an approval time quicker than the bank's

- structuring repayments to suit the developer's development program

- being able to start the development process as soon as the parties sign an agreement

- having an option to improve the value of the land and time to secure other development funding or investors.

Points to consider with vendor finance

When negotiating a vendor finance opportunity, consider the following aspects before committing to the agreement in writing.

Legal fees and taxes

Be aware that the exact fees and taxes are payable with seller finance as with a traditional mortgage bond. However, there is more legal work and higher costs with the additional complexity.

Interest rates

Try to negotiate a better rate below the standard offered by financial institutions. If possible, secure an interest-only loan, with the final payment after the development is sold or at the end of an agreed term. Delayed payment of interest will assist cash flow during the construction phase.

Repayments

You will need to ensure that you have enough funds to meet the monthly repayments. If in doubt, use the services of an accountant or financial adviser to ensure you're in a solid financial position to service the repayments.

Terms and conditions

If possible, try to secure a longer-term loan that will allow you enough time to achieve the required milestones. However, if the term is shorter, negotiate an option to renew. Also, include a clause stating that there are no penalties if the loan is paid off before the maturity date.

Types of vendor finance

Following are three types of seller finance that a developer can consider when negotiating with a landowner.

Traditional vendor finance

With traditional vendor finance the landowner agrees to sell their land to a developer and gives time to the developer to secure funding for the full payment. With this structure, the developer owns the property outright along with the direct profits of the development.

Share of profits

An alternative structure sees the seller leaving the land as equity in the development and sharing in the development profit like other investors. The developer does not make as much profit with this option.

Wholesale product

Under this arrangement, which applies mainly to residential developments, the developer agrees to sell a residential unit or two to the landowner, at cost or wholesale, when the project has been completed. If the sale is lower than the land value, the developer pays out the balance to the landowner. If the cost is higher, the landowner must pay out the balance to the developer.

SUMMARY

Seller financing is ideal for developers who cannot secure a mortgage to purchase a property until total development funding is secured, either from investors or from banks. Another benefit is that when development approval is granted and the land is revalued, the developer may find that there is enough free equity that part or all of the seller's finance will no longer be required. They can therefore raise the necessary finance to pay the seller.

Generate your own fees

If you are an experienced and well-qualified developer, you will be spending a great deal of your own time and knowledge in researching and evaluating potential development opportunities. You will also be responsible for managing and supervising the project from inception to completion. For all this effort you should be rewarded in the form of a fee payment.

This fee should be factored into the development as an outgoing. Various management fees can contribute to the development cost, including any overheads such as administration, rent and overhead costs. Following is a range of management services that can be treated as equity if not paid out during the development process, depending on your specific role.

Site procurement fee

This fee is paid to the manager for their initiative in finding a viable project. It can include using their time to research the market, networking with various people within the property industry, creating the vision and structuring a deal with the landowner. The fee for this service is usually based on a percentage of the development cost or a fixed figure. Fees can vary from 2 to 3 per cent of the land cost.

Development fee

This fee is paid to a developer for their initiative in finding a viable project. It can include the time to research the market, networking with various people within the real estate industry, creating the vision and structuring a deal with the landowner. The role also includes dealing with accountants and lawyers and, more importantly, securing debt and equity funding for the project. The fee for this service is usually based on a percentage of the development cost or a fixed figure. Fees can range from 2.5 to 5 per cent of development cost depending on the size, scale and complexity of the proposed development.

Project management fee

A project management fee can be mistaken for a development fee. A development management fee is for initiating the development and managing the project on behalf of the ownership group. By comparison, a project manager is a contracted party given the task of supervising the project to ensure its completion within budget and on time. The fee for project management is usually based on a percentage of the overall development cost or the construction cost (excluding land). Of course, it will depend on the role and scope of work the project manager is undertaking. The percentage fee for this service can range from 1 to 3 per cent of construction cost.

Performance fee

A performance fee is an incentive fee paid to a development manager to achieve a high profit level. For example, in a typical development project, an equity investor invests $3 million in a $10 million project that earns a $2 million profit after two years. Out of the $2 million profit, the investors are paid 15 per cent per annum of their investment, which equals approximately $900 000 (30 per cent of $3 million). The balance of $1.1 million is split between the developer and the investors. Depending on the arrangement set in an agreement, the developer's share can range from 30 to 50 per cent of this surplus profit.

Construction management fee

If you have experience or have some qualifications in the building industry, you could undertake the management of the construction of the development. In effect, you contract as the general contractor to oversee the construction management. Alternatively, and depending on the size of the project, you could undertake the management and coordination of subcontractors and building materials. This fee can be based on a monthly retainer fee, a percentage of the construction cost or a predetermined set fee.

Marketing or leasing fee

A developer who undertakes the marketing and leasing of the development should be paid accordingly. Fees are based on industry standards and the going market rate. Unless a developer is geared to do the job and has the marketing expertise, it is wiser to employ the services of a third party who has the proper credentials to concentrate on developing.

Fees for managing a real estate syndicate

We covered syndications in chapter 1 and provided a fee structure for managing a syndicate. For ease of reference, I think it is worth reviewing the fee structure again here.

Development stage

The manager will spend a great deal of their time and knowledge researching and evaluating potential developments and managing the development process, as outlined in table 3.2.

Table 3.2: fee structure during the development stage

Project procurement	This fee is paid to the manager for their initiative in finding a viable project.	Based on a percentage of the land cost, it can vary from 2 to 3 per cent.
Development management	The fee is for managing and arranging finance during the development stage.	Subject to project size, fees can range from 2 to 5 per cent of development cost excluding land.
Syndication fee	This fee covers creating the syndicate, working with investors, negotiating debt finance, and setting up the management and accounting systems.	The fee can be either a flat fee or based on a percentage of the equity raised in the range of 2.5 to 5 per cent of the monies invested.
Performance fee	This payment is made to the manager for generating positive returns.	Any excess over a targeted investor return is split between the investors and the manager, generally 70:30 or 50:50.
Director's fees	If there is a board of directors, they will be compensated for their time.	The fee is agreed to upfront by the board.

Operation stage

Should the development be held as a medium- to long-term investment after completion of the project, the cost and fees outlined in table 3.3 might apply.

Table 3.3: fee structure during the operation stage

Asset management fee	The manager may charge for managing the property on behalf of the syndicate members.	A fee of 1 to 2 per cent of gross asset value is usual.
Performance fee	Like the performance fee under the development phase, the performance fee under operations may be based on offering equity investors a preferred return.	If an expected return is 10 per cent and the investors' preferred return is 6 per cent, for example, then the 4 per cent balance would be split between the members and the manager.
Refinance fee	This fee is for refinancing the current mortgage of the syndicated property.	A refinance fee of 1 to 2 per cent of the refinance loan amount may be applicable.
Loan guarantor fee	If a manager is a guarantor, then a guarantor fee applies.	The fee may be 1 to 3 per cent of the loan amount or just a flat fee.

SUMMARY

The various fees outlined in these tables are only a guide. There are no set standard industry or association fees. They can be higher or lower depending on the scale and complexity of the project. A higher fee may be charged based on the developer's track record and the number of successful projects concluded. If you are a novice developer, therefore, it would be difficult to charge or justify a fee for services rendered.

Rezoning properties

If you have studied and researched your development of interest, you will know most current council zonings and future town planning proposals. For example, these new proposals could increase residential densities in a specific zone of a growing suburb or convert a corridor along a major arterial road from residential to commercial.

Some property sellers will not know of these new proposals and will sell their properties under their present zoning. Here a confident developer can take advantage of the situation by placing an offer on a property 'subject to rezoning' or by taking out an option allowing a reasonable time for council approval. If the rezoning is approved, the property's value will increase significantly, and the developer will have created their free equity.

The same strategy can apply where a proposed town planning scheme amendment changes zoning from residential to commercial. Generally, these scheme amendments take place on busy arterial roads where traffic volumes have increased and are not conducive to residential living. However, scheme amendments also occur when councils decide to create their own 'city centres'. It is worth keeping an eye on new scheme amendments in the area you intend to develop.

CASE STUDY 1:
TOWN PLANNING SCHEME AMENDMENT

In researching certain suburbs, I found a precinct in a suburb where the zoning change was about to occur. The rezoning proposed was amending an R20 (20 dwellings per hectare) to R40 (40 dwellings per hectare). I found a 1000 square metre property within this precinct. I placed an offer for the total asking price of $500000 subject to the scheme amendment being approved.

The property had only one existing dwelling, which would allow me to develop four houses on the site. I paid a deposit of $10000 and another $10000 on development approval. After approval, the property was valued at $700000. I could have sold the property and made a quick $200000. But after securing DA, the development was valued, with each dwelling priced at $600000, or $2400000 for the total project.

A loan of 70 per cent of the end value was offered, which came to $1680000. With a construction cost of $250000 per unit plus $50000 in soft cost, the total development cost came to $1200000. This allowed me to pay the $480000 balance to the seller, and I had the $1200000 loan to complete the development. In the end it cost me around $20000 of my own cash.

CASE STUDY 2:
REZONING FROM RESIDENTIAL TO COMMERCIAL

When developing shopping centres, I found a 1.8 hectare site zoned residential. Three roads bordered it, one a major highway, another an arterial road and the third leading into the residential area. The site was for sale at $2 million, and I placed an offer for the total asking price subject to rezoning from residential to commercial within six months and also provided a bank letter of approval.

The rezoning application took nine months rather than six. After the rezoning approval was granted, I had the property revalued, and it came in at $4 million. I sold the property within three months to another shopping centre developer for $4 250 000, a significant windfall with minimal cost other than time and professional fees.

These opportunities do not come around very often. And you need to understand how commercial real estate works and the process of rezoning a property so your offer to purchase is tailored accordingly.

Subdividing property

Subdividing semi-rural lots into new suburban lots or suburban lots in older suburbs into smaller green title lots can create substantial financial opportunities for a residential property developer. As illustrated by the previous case studies, studying the local town planning scheme and looking for the growth areas will undoubtedly give you an advantage when new properties come onto the market. Here again, when an opportunity arises, place an offer on a property conditional on subdivision approval by your State Planning Commission, but allow a reasonable amount of time for the approval. The approval time can be checked with a town planner or land surveyor.

CASE STUDY 3:
SUBURBAN LAND SUBDIVISION

A client of mine made a financial windfall in a suburban subdivision. He offered to purchase an established home on a 960 square metre lot in a corner location. Upon checking with the local council, he found that he could subdivide the property into three separate lots, each with a minimum size of 250 square metres. He realised too that if he could acquire an additional 40 square metres he could create four smaller green title lots. So he approached the adjacent owners and persuaded them to sell 50 square metres of their site, which could be amalgamated with the house he had offered to purchase. The additional 10 square metres was insurance, and his offer was again conditional upon amalgamation and subdivision.

The subdivision was approved, and my client was now the owner of four green title lots. And what did it cost him? A small deposit, time, effort — and knowledge! The sale price of the house was $450 000, the additional 50 square metres cost $50 000, the subdivision cost plus purchasing cost and demolition $50 000. With capitalised interest and contingencies of $15 000 for six months, the total cost was $565 000. After approvals, the valuation came in at $180 000 per green title lot, totalling $700 000. This gave my client an increase in equity of $155 000, representing 22 per cent of the new land value.

Secure development rights

Development rights are also known as a *development lease*. In this case, the developer negotiates a deal with a landowner to develop residential units on his land. The developer provides the expertise, erects the buildings, markets the residential units and pays the landowner for the portion of the land with accrued interest when each residential unit is sold. These deals are not ordinarily available to a novice developer, as a landowner would be sceptical of the developer's experience. Experienced developers with a track record are looked at more favourably.

Developments rights are covered more extensively in chapter 5, and appendix III has a sample development rights agreement. But it is worth providing a brief overview of this concept here as a strategy in developing with minimal cash.

The benefits

A number of benefits accrue to the developer:

- The developer does not have to outlay large sums of capital or borrow funds to purchase the land.

- The developer's cash is not at risk.

- Savings on settlement fees, stamp duty and the like will reduce the development cost and increase the profit.

- There is no pressure to build immediately, and the correct planning can occur, compared with borrowing funds and feeling the pressure of the landholding cost.

Several benefits accrue to the landowner too:

- The landholder does not have to wait for a buyer and pay a sales commission on the sale.

- The landholder receives a higher interest rate on equity than if the money was in the bank.

- If the developer defaults, the landholder still retains the land along with the title.

Preliminary considerations

In formalising a development rights agreement, both parties should consider the following aspects to prevent any misunderstanding during the period of the agreement.

The value of the land

An agreement should be reached on the land's actual market value, and a sworn appraisal by a property valuer will help in this regard. The land cost per unit should also be assessed and agreed upon. For example, if the land value is $800000 and eight residential units are to be built, the land value per unit should be $100000. Therefore, the developer should negotiate a better price. At the same time, the developer must undertake a comprehensive feasibility study to ensure there is a reasonable profit margin relative to the development risk involved.

The terms and conditions

Depending on the scale of the development, the area of the proposed project and the prevailing market conditions, a time will be set for the development to be completed. The developer should aim at a more extended period, as unknown factors may delay the project. There should be enough time for completing feasibility studies, planning approvals, development finance approvals, building approvals, construction, marketing and the conclusion of each unit's sale.

The interest rate

Try to negotiate an interest rate with the landowner below standard bank rates with interest only. More important, try to set the start date of the interest—for example, after approvals and outstanding conditions have been met or, better still, from the first drawdown of the construction development loan. Allow for a six-monthly review in case there is a general drop in rates while capping the rate at a reasonable level.

The development finance

The development finance will cover constructing the units and the site infrastructure such as internal roads, sewerage, water, electricity, gas and phone lines and any other incidental costs to complete the development for sale and occupancy. The landowner or another financial institution can supply these funds. If external funds are to be used, there will be a mortgage over the property, and the developer will be the loan's guarantor. In some cases, the landowner will borrow the development finance, but they will charge a higher interest rate to the developer.

The distribution of funds after the sale of units

After the development is completed and successful sales concluded, the allocation of funds will be calculated, as illustrated in table 3.4.

The sequence would be, first, paying out any money owing to the bank financing the development cost, then paying the landowner plus their interest. The balance would be the developer's profit on the unit.

Table 3.4: an example of the distribution of funds after the sale of units

Net sale of a unit	$500 000
less development cost/unit	$300 000
less land value per unit	$100 000
less interest to the landowner	$10 000
Profit to developer	**$90 000**

Utilise options

Most developers are not inclined to purchase a development site that involves an immediate sale. Instead, they prefer enough time to undertake due diligence and feasibility studies. Options are an ideal method of delaying the purchase. They also enable developers to get their foot in the door without costing them significant capital, and they can create a substantial return on investment.

What is an option?

An option to purchase a development site is simply a contract to buy a property at a specified price during an allotted period. Depending on the market and the property, an option can benefit both the seller and the developer. While options are not suitable for every situation, property developers should be familiar with the transaction's basics. A sample option agreement is provided in Appendix III.

Advantages to the developer

Securing an option offers several advantages to the developer:

- The developer can acquire the property without competing with other potential buyers.

- The developer does not have to manage the property or pay rates, taxes, insurance or other associated expenses during the option period.

- The developer is committed only to paying their option money and is not responsible for a large mortgage and the associated interest repayments.

- The developer has time to complete a comprehensive feasibility study, arrange finance, invite partners or simply to sell the property to another developer for a higher price.

- If the developer fails to exercise the option, all that they lose is their option money. They cannot be sued for damages, as in an offer to purchase contract.

- It gives the developer time to find the best financing arrangement.

Items to be taken into account

For these advantages, the developer pays the cost of the option, which is usually a tiny portion of the total purchase price. If the option lapses, the property owner usually keeps the option fee. Thus, the seller is compensated for taking the property off the market during the option period.

Granting an option

Generally, granting an option does not constitute an immediate taxable event for the landowner or the developer. The landowner receives cash or other payment but does not report taxable income. Similarly, the developer makes a payment with no immediate tax consequences. Granting an option is a non-taxable, open transaction that remains open until the option either is exercised or expires. An option payment will be assessed as ordinary income regardless of whether the option is exercised or expires. It must be reported as taxable income in the year it is received.

Option money

It is not always beneficial to place the minimum amount of option money on the table, as the landowner may not consider a developer's offer a serious one. Depending on the option's circumstances, it may be better to offer more money but better terms to the development's benefit. Once the property owner agrees to the terms of the option, they cannot change their mind. It is wise, therefore, to structure the option with as many benefits to the development and not necessary on the cash amounts. In addition, it provides an avenue to sell the option to a third party if required.

Exercising an option

Once the developer exercises the option and purchases the property, the option money paid is included in the amount paid for the property. The option agreement should recognise that the option money is part of the property's selling price. Accordingly, the option money and the purchase price are included when calculating the amount realised on the sale.

Extension of time

Consideration should be given to what will happen at the end of the option if more time is needed or if the funding for the land is not in place at the end of the option term. There should be a provision in the option agreement for these eventualities. It should be written into the agreement that the option can be extended for another year or whatever extended period is required. In some cases, an additional payment amount may be agreed upon by the seller.

Types of options

There are three types of options that can be used by a property developer and are applicable in various circumstances.

Standard option

A standard real estate option is a specific contract between a developer and a seller of a property of interest. The developer offers the seller an option to purchase the property for a specified period at a fixed price and pays a non-refundable option fee. In the option agreement, the developer has a specified period in which to purchase the property or not. If the developer decides to exercise the option and to buy the property, the seller must sell the property to the developer according to the contract terms.

Staged option

This option is used predominantly in land transactions where a land developer does not want to buy a large tract of land at once, as the initial capital cost and interest could make the development unviable. Instead, the developer negotiates to buy the first stage or portion of the land with an option to purchase the other sections at a higher price later. If the project turns sour, then the developer is not obligated to exercise the options they have on the balance of the land. They will lose their option money but will look at better opportunities.

Lease with an option to purchase

Using this option technique, a developer can lower the option money and take out a lease with an option to purchase. The only investment the developer will have in this situation is time to find a tenant to cover the cost of the monthly lease arrangements. The benefit of this option is that it secures a property without a large capital outlay, and the developer can decide when is the appropriate time to exercise the option and develop the property.

Where options can be used

Although some money must be paid for the option, these amounts can be recouped in the second financing round. Securing an option and converting a property to better use and, at the same time, increasing its value, can be financially rewarding. Here are some circumstances in which options can be used.

Amalgamation of sites

If you are contemplating a substantial development such as a retirement village or a shopping centre, you will require some smaller residential sites that can be amalgamated into one. Most residential sites in older suburbs range from 750 to 1000 square metres. If a retirement village is contemplated, you will require at least five to 10 adjoining sites. In this case, the best way to obtain options on each property is to organise a general meeting with the owners of the properties. It allows you to present your project and answer questions. When making such a presentation, you should invite essential members of your development team and especially your solicitor and property valuer. Be sure you have the option agreements ready so the owners can take them away and discuss the proposal with their solicitor.

Preparation of a feasibility study

Comprehensive feasibility studies take time, and by securing an option, you are buying a reasonable amount of time to undertake research and market studies without due pressure. This pressure can come from a real estate agent advising you that several other purchasers are interested in the property.

Pre-selling off the plan

Securing an option for a residential unit development, then immediately preparing architectural designs, will allow you to start the marketing process a lot earlier. If the units are sold off the plan conditionally, and before you must exercise an option, your chances of securing 100 per cent finance are improved. In many instances, financial institutions require a percentage of the development to be pre-sold before granting the development loan. Of course, there are several conditions on the option agreement, including the pre-sale contract. By law, you cannot contract to sell a residential unit unless a development approval is granted. Consult your lawyer before adopting this strategy.

Extension on a more significant development

You have undertaken a project and are halfway through the development, and you find there is considerable public interest. There are also adjacent sites that could accommodate a similar development. Be sure to secure options on these. If other developers hear of your successful development, they will rush to secure these sites and develop right next door to you, thus competing for the same slice of the market. Alternatively, you may find that demand is slowing and you are able to sell your option to your competitors at a higher price, thereby reducing your risk and making a quick profit.

Future rezoning

By understanding and researching growth areas in your city, you will be aware of zoning changes in the locality of your development interest. These zoning changes may not take place for a year or two, but if you have options on properties over this length of time or more, you can secure good financial rewards. If you need additional time to exercise the option and the property owner is not happy giving a further period, offering the seller a lease-type option will provide them with more comfort. However, ensure that you will be able to lease the property to a third party for an equal amount or more than the rent you will be paying.

Infrastructure change

In larger capital cities in Australia, there are always infrastructure changes due to rapid population growth. These changes can include, for example, new freeway systems, road tunnels, shopping malls and entertainment areas. Knowing the infrastructure changes well in advance, the intelligent developer should secure options in well-located areas close to these changes, as the surrounding land will always increase in value.

SUMMARY

Options are excellent tools when buying a development site, especially for a developer, as they can minimise their risk. However, options are not easy to find, and it takes a great deal of time to research the property that will increase in value in the short term. In addition, it is usually difficult to convince a property owner to give you an option on their property.

Raising investor funds

When starting a project using the least amount of your personal capital, you will invariably need assistance from other investors. To attract investors, you need to foster investor relationships. In order to develop property with minimal cash by relying on your knowledge and expertise, you must build credibility and trust.

To target and pursue suitable investors, the developer must understand their investment strategy and preferences. Developers tend to be over-optimistic about their projects, but this confidence may not be shared by the investor. A developer needs to understand how investors think to communicate successfully with them. Investors will evaluate you and your project based on what they see as its business and financial merits. Learning investor language and demonstrating sound business skills will place you in a stronger position.

Pitching to investors

When presenting your project to potential investors, consider the following factors.

Effective communication

When seeking equity for a development, it's easier to gain the confidence of potential investors if you understand each investor's requirements and background and, more important, listen more and speak less. The biggest obstacle to good communication in this context is the one-sided nature of overselling. To determine what will motivate the investor to part with their money, it is far better to listen than to talk.

Body language

Communication is not just about the words said. We all communicate more through gestures, posture and facial expressions—also known as body language—than through speech. Taking notice of the potential investor's body language will signal if they are interested in the project and guide where negotiations are heading.

Prevent any misunderstanding

During negotiations any misunderstandings must be prevented at all costs. Pay close attention to prospective investors' responses. Their responses will not only clarify what they are saying but signify what they are thinking.

Selling trust

Developers who successfully sell themselves as trustworthy and credible when dealing with prospective investors for the first time have half the battle won. Be frank and answer all questions professionally, even if some may be intimidating.

Introducing your project

At the first meeting, developers may have less than three minutes to introduce their project. Investors are busy people and do not have much time, so the introduction will make or break the opportunity. A developer must be professional and well prepared for this meeting, with a brief, thorough oral presentation that will have an impact. Following is a list of crucial information that should be clearly presented on a single page:

- the development project
- the development's potential and returns
- the market research undertaken

- the marketing strategies planned

- the key managers and consultants, and their backgrounds

- the amount of financing you require and how you will use it.

If the investor is interested, they will probably ask for the feasibility study or the investor package.

Negotiate and close the deal

Developers should be flexible, as most investors prefer to structure deals themselves. The investor may propose a funding package that contains various forms of finance. The funding package is complex but vitally important, so it is worth consulting an attorney beforehand. Intelligent investors will continue to evaluate a proposed development project carefully. They compare this with the required rate of return to decide on the type and level of investment they are prepared to make in exchange for a percentage of equity proportional to the risk.

CONCLUSION

The ideas and strategies outlined in this chapter illustrate how real estate developments can be created with little capital outlay, but knowledge and expertise are essential prerequisites to pursuing these opportunities. In addition, if you are asking others to invest in your project, you must be able to prove that you have been successful in past projects.

This means you will need to inject some of your own cash into your first project, study the pitfalls and learn from any mistakes along the way. Only through such experience will you be able to persuade an audience of would-be investors of your knowledge and expertise. Investors must be confident that you are the right person for the project.

CHAPTER 4

SECURING LOW-COST DEVELOPMENT LAND

In chapter 3, I explained the basics of developing real estate with minimal cash outlay. In this chapter I describe some different techniques of applying this concept. Your objective is to secure potential development sites by leveraging your time, skills and knowledge into equity without committing too much of your cash. We study techniques around development rights, government land, leasing development land and land assembly. Of course, these opportunities are not marketed on public platforms such as realesate.com.au or domain.com.au. You will have to spend time searching for them or finding a network that can offer you such opportunities.

Development rights

I introduced a broad overview of development rights in the previous chapter. Here I provide more details of this strategy in relation to government land. A sample development rights agreement can be found at the back of the book as appendix III.

Securing rights to develop a property without having to spend too much of your cash is an ideal scenario for a developer, but such an opportunity does not come easy. Landowners willing to offer their land are cautious. They will only work with experienced developers with an excellent track record. The main benefit to the developer is that less capital is required to buy the land. Also, they save on interest payments, rates and taxes, and possibly on stamp duty too.

Where to find development rights opportunities

Development rights opportunities can be found in several ways.

Private landowners

An enterprising developer can approach private landowners who own large tracts of land in the outer suburbs, such as small market gardeners. As the city expands, they may find themselves surrounded by new homes on smaller lots after a zoning change. In these circumstances a developer can sometimes negotiate a deal with the landowner to develop residential units on part of their land. The developer provides their expertise and erects the buildings, and the landowner is paid for the land with accrued interest when each residential unit is sold.

Government land

Another source of opportunity is to look out for government-owned land and take note when a government entity opens a development tender to qualified developers. In many instances, payment for the land is not the government's priority, which is focused mainly on certainty and community benefits. So they are willing to provide development rights to the selected tenderer, and the land is paid for only at project completion. Some governments are eager to offer land for a small cash payment or other nominal consideration, sometimes called a 'peppercorn rent'.

What is a development rights agreement?

In a *development rights agreement*, also known as a *development lease*, a landowner grants a developer the sole rights to design and construct a new building or buildings on the landowner's land. A development rights agreement is used in the following three types of arrangements.

Sale of private land

Selling land to a developer under a development rights agreement means the landowner is paid when the building or residential units are sold to a third party or refinanced on completion. The developer assumes all the development risks. It may or may not have a profit-sharing component.

Joint venture

In a joint venture between a landowner and a developer, the landowner provides the land and the developer undertakes the construction. The profits are shared according to an agreed share structure when the building or units are sold.

Sale of government land

In this arrangement the government provides the land and the developer assumes all the development risks. The land is paid for after the building is refinanced or sold to a third party.

Motivation behind a development rights agreement

Most development rights agreements are commercially motivated. There is no set structure, and each aspect of the agreement is open to negotiation between the parties. The final agreement adopted will depend on the negotiations between the parties.

The developer's motivation includes:

- minimising any upfront costs and therefore minimising initial funding

- sharing the development risk with the landowner

- reducing the chance of incurring environmental or other land-based liability

- minimising stamp duty and other taxes, and timing those liabilities to coincide with the receipt of income.

The landowner's motivation includes:

- maximising the return on the sale of the land

- sharing in the development profit

- assuming little or no development risk

- incurring little funding risk.

Government entities will sometimes sacrifice some profit to decrease the risk and increase the certainty of the development. Their primary goal is to provide a positive outcome for the community or adjacent areas. They want certainty in both the built form and the financial outcomes, and are averse to carrying any development risk at all.

A common thread running through this sort of agreement is that the landowner will exercise control over what is to be developed, but the level of this control varies with each agreement.

Advantages to the parties

There are several advantages to the developer:

- The developer does not have to outlay large amounts of capital or borrow funds to purchase the land.

- The developer's own cash is not at risk.

- Saving on settlement fees, stamp duty and other taxes will reduce the development cost and increase the profit.

- There is no pressure to build immediately, and the correct planning can take place with borrowed funds. Also, there is no pressure on the landholding cost.

Advantages to the landowner include the following:

- They don't have to wait for a buyer or pay a sales commission on the sale.

- They receive a higher interest rate on their equity than had they sold and placed their money in the bank.

- They retain the land if the developer defaults, as they still hold the title.

Development rights with private landowners

When negotiating a development rights agreement with a private land-owner, specific parameters must be set to ensure success. This section focuses on residential developments rather than more complicated commercial developments. First, some guidelines.

Value of the land

An agreement should be reached on the land's actual market value; a sworn appraisal by a property valuer will help here. Land cost per unit should also be assessed and agreed upon. For example, if the land value is $500 000, and eight residential units can be accommodated, the land value per unit should be $62 500. The developer should negotiate a better price. Simultaneously, undertake a comprehensive feasibility study to ensure a reasonable profit margin is achievable relative to the development risk involved.

Terms and conditions

A completion date should be set for the development. This will depend on the development scale, the area of the proposed project and the prevailing market conditions. The developer should aim for a more extended period, as unknown factors may delay the project. Adequate time should be allowed for completing feasibility studies, planning approvals, development finance approvals, building approvals, construction, marketing and the conclusion of the sale of each unit.

Interest rate

If possible, try to reach agreement with the landowner on a zero-interest rate on the value of the land. Failing this, try to negotiate an interest rate below standard bank rates with interest only. More important, set the start date of the interest after all approvals and special conditions have been met or, better still, from the first drawdown from the construction development loan. Allow for a six-monthly review in case there is a general drop in rates, but cap the rate at a reasonable level.

Development finance

Development finance is used for constructing the units and the site infrastructure such as internal roads, sewerage, water, electricity, gas and telephone, and any other incidental costs to complete the development for sale and occupancy. The landowner or another financial institution can supply these funds. If external funds are to be used, there will be a mortgage over the property, and the developer will be the loan's guarantor. In some cases, the landowner will borrow the development finance but charge a higher interest rate to the developer.

Distribution of funds after the sale

After the development is completed and several successful sales have been concluded, the distribution of funds can be calculated (see table 4.1).

Table 4.1: an example of the distribution of funds after a development is sold

Sale of each unit	$500 000
less development cost/unit	$300 000
less land value per unit	$100 000
less interest to landowner	$10 000
Profit to developer	**$90 000**

The process would be to pay out any money owing, first to the bank who financed the development cost, then to the landowner plus interest. The balance would be the developer's profit.

Development rights with government

Securing a development rights agreement with government can be initiated through the following methods.

Government tender

Both local and state governments are focused on stimulating the economy within their jurisdiction. Periodically they will place offers of tenders to sell or seek developers to develop their land. Seasoned developers, who are always looking for these sorts of opportunities, will express their interest. It should be noted that developers may spend both time and money submitting proposals that are not always successful.

Unsolicited bid

If a developer finds a development site that belongs to the government, they can submit an unsolicited bid. Not all local and state governments have legislated this process, however, so it is important to check if this avenue is available in the area you intend to develop. Where unsolicited bids are legislated, governments consider a unique proposal that provides a value-for-money solution.

Types of government development rights agreements

Government development rights agreements are lengthy and complicated legal documents, and can take various forms.

Sale of land

Where a government has created a new precinct or an industrial estate on their land or a site that could be improved, they will offer the land for sale at a price or through a tender process. Some of these offers will include a development rights agreement stipulating that the land can be paid for on completion.

Public–private partnership

In a public–private partnership (PPP), the government pays the private sector to deliver infrastructure and related services over the long term. The private provider (in this case, the developer) will build the facility and operate or maintain it to specified standards over a limited time. Although most PPPs are used for infrastructure work, in some cases the government owns land in public areas such as a beach or riverfront. Here they would retain ownership and would offer a land lease agreement and development rights.

Structuring an agreement with government

Following is a broad outline of the critical elements of a government development rights agreement. Most government agreements are lengthy and complicated, and there are no standard contract forms. Instead, a government-appointed solicitor generally draws up a bespoke agreement after a negotiated process with a developer and their lawyer. These are some of the areas to consider.

Background

Background paragraphs explain the agreement. They should address the 'who, what, where, when and why' of the agreement. Paragraphs will include a statement of ownership or control, a statement of status and a statement of purpose.

Body of the agreement

Although agreements may differ, they generally include a project description and a timeline. A project description includes the number of buildings, a breakdown of the estimated square meterage of various uses, the number of parking spaces and any other relevant items related to the proposed development. A project timeline will include a breakdown of project phasing and identify key milestone dates.

Public infrastructure

Where the government or the developer is responsible for any public improvements such as roads, water supply or drainage, this should be clearly defined.

Project mitigation

Mitigation relates to things the developer must do, at their own expense, to alleviate potential negative impacts of the project on the site and its surroundings.

Public benefits

Public benefits can be defined as contributions from the developer towards programs or improvements that benefit the community.

Government actions

The government will outline activities it will undertake in support of the project. Some actions can be taken via executive authority or a commitment by a department.

Default and remedies

A default is a failure by one party to do something promised in the agreement. Remedies may include mediation involving an independent third party. Should this fail, an arbitration process will be initiated.

Financing

Any funding by either party should be clearly defined. The agreement should specify what the developer or government is paying. It should also describe how the developer will fund the total development.

Roles and responsibilities

The agreement summarises what may have been outlined earlier regarding the parties' roles and responsibilities. It should articulate specifically what each of the parties will be responsible for and when.

Suspensive conditions

If there are any suspensive conditions, these should be included. Most suspensive conditions are finance related. Even though the developer may be granted funding for the project, most lenders have suspensive conditions, which should be considered. A timeline should also be included.

■■■

These items are the more notable ones. The developer should work closely with their solicitor and add other relevant items after negotiations with the government.

Commercial development rights

Most commercial buildings are held as medium- to long-term investments and sold to a third party only after a few years. The developer will therefore need to refinance the building and pay the landowner when the building has been completed (see table 4.2).

Table 4.2: an example of the distribution of funds after a development is completed

Assume land cost	$2 500 000
Assume development costs (loan)	$7 500 000
Assume end value	$15 000 000
Assume long-term loan of 66.6 per cent of end value	$10 000 000
Distribution of funds	
Pay out development loan	$7 500 000
Pay out landowner	$2 500 000

This example illustrates the concept in principle. Several other factors must be considered when using a development rights agreement to undertake a commercial project. For example, additional investors may be required to pay out the landowner if there is a shortfall.

SUMMARY

A development rights agreement is an excellent instrument for a developer, but not many landowners find the structure appealing, as it is a complex arrangement, and generally they would prefer cash in their hands. However, the structure can be negotiated where government land is concerned.

Securing government land

Securing government land is another strategy for starting a development project at minimal cost. Government land may be owned by government at federal, state or local level. Government agencies or government-sponsored organisations may manage these assets.

Government-owned land is disposed of when it is surplus to government needs or when it can be better utilised in the interest of the government if in private ownership. The sale and transfer of land should be in the community's best interests and provide the best financial and non-financial results for the government and the community. Proceeds from the sale of surplus government land are reinvested in essential new infrastructure such as schools, hospitals and public transport.

Sales are conducted through a public process — a public auction, a public tender or by registration of expressions of interest — unless circumstances justify an alternative method of sale, such as sale or exchange by private treaty or unsolicited bid. Generally, government disposes of unused land by way of a traditional public sale, public tender, private sale or leasehold land.

Traditional sale

Government can sell land by public auction or through a contract of sale. They will appoint a real estate agent to market the land and deal with potential purchasers.

Auction

A reserve price is determined, and a licensed valuer undertakes a valuation. After the selling agent's report has been received, the auction will take place. Usually, the reserve price is not less than the market value; it should be set before the auction and remain confidential. If the auction fails, it must be passed in for negotiation with the highest bidder and offered for sale to that person at no less than the reserve price. Should the land remain unsold following negotiations after the auction, it will be left on the market for private sale at no less than the reserve price for an appropriate or reasonable period as determined by the government.

Contract of sale

In some states, government agencies act as land developers. They master-plan estates such as an industrial area or a residential community. The sale would include individual lots with a set price and be offered to private developers. Generally, there are no negotiations on the sale price, although conditions or terms can be negotiated. Interested developers would then place an offer through the government-appointed real estate agent using a commercially transacted offer to purchase. The sale would proceed as a typical transaction until settlement.

Private sale by government

In some circumstances, the government may decide to sell land by private treaty or through an unsolicited proposal. In both cases, the sale will be conducted privately rather than through a public process.

Sale of land by private treaty

The nature of the land will determine how the proposed sale is initiated. It may include rear laneways, rights-of-way, closed roads or an allotment in a land subdivision. Prospective purchasers may include owners of adjacent properties, developers, community groups or other parties with a specific interest in that land.

The government's view of the land's value may differ from that of the prospective purchaser. The final value is determined by considering the nature of the land and public perceptions of the transaction. The process involves the highest standards of probity and transparency.

Unsolicited bids

Unsolicited bids were outlined briefly under development rights. Here I will explain it in more detail. In an unsolicited proposal or bid, a developer brings an innovative development proposal directly to the government. Most state governments have guidelines covering unsolicited development proposals. The following points are applicable to this method of sale.

THE CRITERIA

An unsolicited proposal:

- must be unique, with an outcome that could not be obtained through a competitive process

- must have a significant beneficial impact on the economy, community and environment

- must offer the government value for money

- must be both technically and financially feasible

- must align with relevant government policy.

THE PROCESS

An unsolicited proposal typically progresses as follows:

1. A first meeting is held with the Department of Lands at which the developer presents an overview of the proposal.

2. Following the initial meeting, a formal proposal can be submitted.

3. The department will conduct a preliminary assessment, ensuring the formalities have been complied with, and submit a recommendation to the Minister for Lands.

4. The minister will then decide whether the proposal should proceed to the detailed assessment stage.

5. Cabinet will make the final decision on recommendation of the minister.

6. If the proposal is successful, the department will negotiate the land sale or lease on an exclusive basis.

Tendering for government land

The tendering system is used mainly for larger development projects. The state or local government has an area or zone that they are trying to promote to developers for economic reasons. At times private landowners may also offer their property for tender. They may want the best possible outcome for their land in terms of price and design, or just a better price.

Winning a tender, especially a government offer, can be financially rewarding for a developer. However, as with all tenders, there is no guarantee of success. The process involves both time and money, which a developer should be prepared to lose if they are not successful in their bid. However, there are strategies to improve one's chances of success.

The government's public tender of land falls into one of two areas: sale of land by public tender or registration of expressions of interest.

Sale of land by public tender

It should be conducted in the following manner:

- Tender documents must outline the process for the sale and relevant timelines.

- Documents should also outline the objectives, how tenders are received and assessed, and how any tender negotiations will be conducted.

- The government should appoint a probity auditor to oversee the tender process.

- The reserve price must be established before the tenders close. It must remain confidential to ensure the sale process's integrity.

- Tenders must be lodged with the government or its legal representative.

- Tenders submitted by electronically-signed document or email, or submitted late, are not accepted.

- Tenders should be opened only by an appointed panel comprising government representatives or its legal representative.

- A conforming tender at or above the reserve price should be accepted.

- If no conforming tenders are received at or above the reserve price, the government may commence post-tender negotiations as per its predetermined strategy.

- If the land remains unsold, it will be passed in, and all tenderers will be advised. The land will continue to be marketed for an appropriate or reasonable period, as determined by the government.

Sale by public registration or expression of interest

This method of sale is handy where a council wishes to expose land to the market without the assistance of an agent. In addition, it can be used as a public marketing process alternative to an auction or tender. This approach is appropriate if the government wishes to control the land's future use or development in addition to selling the land.

Potential developers are invited to provide details of a design concept or agree to develop the land under the government's brief. Interested developers may also be required to provide details of their performance ability and history of achievements. Registration of expressions of interest may or may not be binding on either party.

The reserve price should be set before receiving offers and must remain confidential to ensure the sale process's integrity. The marketing of the land should be undertaken in the same manner as sales by auction or tender.

How to secure a government tender

If you participate in a tender, you must understand that you are competing with other tenderers. It is essential that you have the right attitude and the ability to be a strong contender.

ASSESS WHETHER YOU HAVE THE CAPABILITY

It is pointless entering a tender if you do not have the capability and resources to compete with other tenderers. Therefore, it is essential to find out who the other potential tenderers could be. Also, consider the following questions:

- Do you have the financial resources to pay for consultants to assist with the submission?

- Do you have the proper credentials? If not, can you find a partner who does?

- Do you have the experience and past projects to prove your capability?

If your answer to these questions is negative, do not waste your time and money participating in the process.

BE CLEAR ON WHAT IS REQUIRED

Before submitting a tender proposal, you must be prepared. Look at what is required in the tender documents. Missing any small part of the requirements can disqualify you. Here are some pointers:

- Read the tender document in full, understand the tender conditions and make sure you meet its requirements.

- Attend all briefings and information sessions, and ask any questions you need to clarify the requirements.

- Allow enough time to complete the tender, and be aware of all deadlines.

- Ensure that you can satisfy all the tender requirements if you are selected as a preferred proponent. That includes your financial capability and the right development team.

- Make sure your capability statement is relevant to the scope of the tendered works. It will also help if you provide references of your past successful projects.

- Address all the requirements and complete all documents, schedules and attachments, following the tender template format if provided.

- Once the submission documents have been completed, ask someone else to proofread the submission to check for errors.

WILL YOUR PROPOSAL STAND OUT?

If you are confident that you have the capability and experience to compete with other tenderers, you should make sure your submission stands out from other tenders. Make your tender proposal unique by highlighting something special that other tenderers may not be able to offer. Prepare a professional presentation document. The adjudication panel will be reviewing several proposals and not you in person. A professionally prepared report will always stand out. Also, abide by the rules and scope of the tender while at the same time keeping your proposal simple and easy to read.

Developers need to understand that tenders are not necessarily awarded to the lowest price, but their capability and value for money must be demonstrated in their submission. In addition, it would help to describe how your development team would manage and deliver the work.

Where to find government tenders

If you are looking for tenders, there is no single marketplace where you can access both government and private tendering opportunities. Every year federal, state and local governments present thousands of tender requests to supply goods and services to the private sector. Following is a guide to some of the leading websites you can use to find information about government tenders.

FEDERAL GOVERNMENT TENDERS

The federal government publishes all tender opportunities, annual procurement plans, multi-use lists and contracts on its centralised Austender website, tenders.gov.au.

STATE AND TERRITORY GOVERNMENT TENDERS

It is also worth considering tender opportunities advertised by state and territory agencies:

- New South Wales: tenders.nsw.gov.au

- Victoria: tenders.vic.gov.au

- Queensland: qtenders.hpw.qld.gov.au

- South Australia: tenders.sa.gov.au

- Western Australia: tenders.wa.gov.au

- Tasmania: tenders.tas.gov.au

- Australian Capital Territory: tenders.act.gov.au

- Northern Territory: nt.gov.au/industry/procurement

LOCAL GOVERNMENT TENDERS

Finding local government tenders requires work. There are hundreds of local councils in Australia, though not all of them will be putting out tenders. Depending on your location of interest, it is best to look at the council with jurisdiction over the area and to register your interest if they offer this service.

COMMERCIAL TENDER WEBSITES

Several commercial websites can be used to identify relevant government tender opportunities. Some provide dedicated consultancy support, access to templates and checklists to support tender development. These can usually be accessed by paying a fee for service. Commonly used commercial tendering websites include Tenders.Net, TenderSearch, Tenderlink, Australian Tenders and ProjectConnect. This is not a definitive list, and you may find other commercial tendering websites.

Networking

Attending business events, tradeshows, exhibitions, seminars and conferences is an excellent way to find out about potential tenders and a great opportunity to network with relevant government officials. In addition, networking with people in your industry and other sectors can give you a different perspective on the market and potential opportunities.

Government leasehold land

Leasehold land is a landholding leased to a person, company or developer by a state government. (A *land lease* of freehold land is not leasehold land as the land has a freehold title.) Generally, under a lease the lessee is granted the right to exclusive occupation of the land. Leasehold land tenure can typically be summarised as a:

- **term lease.** The term will generally be between one and 50 years, and it will be for a specified purpose.

121

- **perpetual lease.** A lease in perpetuity may be used only for the specific purpose.

- **freeholding lease.** Where approval has been granted to convert a lease to a freehold, the lessee elects to pay the purchase price in instalments.

Leasing land, whether government or private, for development is explained in more detail in the next section.

SUMMARY

While there are some significant financial advantages in securing government land, the process can be long and arduous, which can result in a loss of opportunity in finding other potential development sites. In addition, the government's bureaucratic structure means some processes can take six months or more, if the land is not purchased outright.

Leasing land for development

Developing a leasehold property takes the massive land capital cost out of the equation, and can therefore provide a healthy return. There are several drawbacks, however. First, it will only suit certain asset classes, such as entertainment centres and public or communal facilities, so the development strategy would be to view it as a typical commercial project. The key is to establish a solid rental return, paying off the project's capital cost earlier, and enjoying a passive income. Of course, if there are still several years left on the lease there is also the opportunity to sell the completed project to a conservative investor.

What is a leasehold property?

Leasehold refers to a property's tenure. One party buys the right to occupy the property for a given time (anywhere between 25 and 50 years). Usually, a government authority remains the landowner of leasehold land. It provides the land to a developer to develop on a leasehold basis.

Ground or land leasing is more likely to occur when land costs are high or a prime land parcel is involved, such as a beachfront or waterfront lot.

These locations are generally government-owned land or Crown land where ownership remains in government's hands. The private sector also offers leasehold opportunities. A landowner who does not want to take on the development risk would still like to receive an income from the leasehold arrangement.

In summary, a land lease is a type of financial structure in which land is leased rather than sold to the developer and the land and buildings are owned independently. Some local governments lease rather than sell land, especially in public areas like a beachfront. As a result, a developer can develop facilities for public access such as restaurants and entertainment or shopping precincts. A land lease contract can run for between 25 and 50 years. When the lease term ends, and depending on the agreement, the lease can be renewed. Rents for the land are paid monthly or quarterly.

Advantages and disadvantages of a land lease

A ground lease can have pros and cons for both the lessee and the lessor.

Tenant benefits

The ground lease allows a tenant to build on property in a prime location they could not find to purchase. A ground lease does not require the tenant to have a deposit for securing the land, as a typical freehold land purchase would. Therefore, less equity is involved, which frees up cash for the development and improves the yield on the completed building.

Any rent paid on a ground lease is tax-deductible, which reduces the tenant's overall tax burden.

Tenant disadvantages

Any changes made on the property require the landlord's approval, so there may be more restrictions and less flexibility for the tenant.

It is challenging to finance the development if the landlord does not want to subordinate (agree to a lower priority of claims than a senior lender).

Landlord benefits

The landowner gains a steady income stream from the tenant while retaining ownership of the property. And they receive rental increases through escalation and eviction rights should the tenant default on the lease agreement.

There are tax advantages to a landlord who uses ground leases. If they sold the property instead, they would have to report any capital gains. A landlord may also retain some control over the property, including its use and how it is developed. This means the landlord can approve or veto any changes to the land.

Landlord disadvantages

Landlords who do not include the correct provisions and clauses in their lease agreements stand to lose control of developing tenants. Both parties should have their leases reviewed by their solicitors before signing.

Depending on where the property is located, a ground lease may have higher tax implications for a landlord. Although they may not realise a capital gain from a sale, the rent is considered income. So rent is taxed at the standard rate, which may increase the tax burden.

Subordinated vs unsubordinated ground leases

A ground lease tenant such as a developer will often need finance for their project, so the landlord must understand the requirements of the tenant's lender.

We will now look at the difference between a subordinated and an unsubordinated ground lease.

Subordinated ground lease

In a subordinated ground lease, a lender will prioritise claims on the asset. For example, when a construction loan or a permanent loan is used to finance a development, the senior lender will require a 'first in line' in the hierarchy of claims on the asset, which is collateral for the loan. As such, a senior or 'first' lender will require any other lenders or claims on the property to be subordinated to its primary interest. It is worth noting that for this arrangement, the landowner may negotiate higher rent payments in return for the risk taken under a subordinated ground lease.

Unsubordinated ground lease

Under an unsubordinated ground lease, the landowner retains the priority of claims on the property if the tenant defaults on the loan. As the lender may not take ownership of the land if the loan goes unpaid, lenders may be hesitant to extend a loan for a new development. As the landlord retains ownership of the property, they typically charge the tenant a lower rent amount.

Lease agreement structure

Most ground lease agreements will have standard lease terms negotiated. However, your priority as a developer would be to ensure that the ground lease agreement allows debt finance for your project. This means that the agreement should include 'subordination' of the landlord's interest with provisions to protect the lender from certain risks that could arise if the developer defaults on the loan. Following are other terms to consider in the lease to ensure that a loan can be approved.

Fixed rent

Lenders will want to know that the rent is either fixed at a specific rate or predictable with only limited escalation. If they are forced to take back the property, they will need to analyse the associated risk of the required rent.

Long term

The ground lease term is significantly longer than the duration of the loan. A lender will want a sufficiently extended period if the developer defaults to recover their investment in the property. Ground leases with a relatively short term can be problematic.

Option to renew

For the same reasons, lenders will want to see an 'option to renew' clause. In addition, the lender will want the right to exercise any options to renew even if the lessee is in default or has failed to exercise the renewal options.

First right to purchase

A lender would also like to see a clause permitting them to exercise any first rights to purchase the property should the lessor decide to sell.

No sublease clause

The lender may require that the ground lease does not have a sublease clause, as it can create more complexity. On the other hand, the lender may impose more security or protections and assurances if the ground lease is a sublease.

Use clause

A lender will want broad rights to use the property without undue restrictions. For example, after taking possession through default, the lender may need to change the property's use to facilitate the sale, lease or disposal by other means, or to enhance revenue.

Limited liability

The ground lease should hold the lender responsible only during their period of ownership. Their responsibility would cease after its sale or the assignment of their interest in the property in the event of default by the developer.

Right to mortgage

The lease should include an express right for the ground lessee to enter a leasehold mortgage, pledging security against the ground lease interest in the land, and their interest in the improvements.

Waiver of landlord's lien

The lender would also want to see a waiver of any landlord's lien that might otherwise be available to the landlord under applicable law.

■■■

These points represent a brief overview of specific basic conditions that a lender will consider before providing a loan on a ground lease. A developer should negotiate these terms upfront. There are other essential conditions, and it might be worth discussing these with a lender before signing a formal ground lease.

Viable developments with leased land

A ground lease's significant benefit is that less upfront capital is required than if developing on purchased land. However, a ground lease is not viable for all developments. For example, a strata residential apartment would be complicated to market to homebuyers in Australia. Besides going against the traditional norms of freehold ownership, financing the apartment by the buyer would face some challenges.

Viable developments with leasehold land look more favourable within a rental or commercial structure. As the land does not belong to you, but the buildings do, it may be better that the buildings are designed so they can be moved to (a) another site as a transportable modular building and (b) a lower building cost structure that can be paid off in the short term, leaving you without debt and with a better return for the remaining lease period. Following are some development examples that can be viable for ground leases.

Lifestyle centres

With a lifestyle centre such as a retirement community, manufactured or transportable homes are paid for by the retiree, but the retiree pays rent to the developer for the small portion of land where the home is placed. While the developer pays a land rent to the landowner for the whole village, the developer installs all the required infrastructure suitable for a lifestyle centre and subleases smaller portions of land to retirees.

Caravan parks

Similarly, a caravan park developer provides the necessary infrastructure and communal facilities such as washrooms and restaurant or café, and rents out allocated serviced lots to caravan enthusiasts.

Low-density resorts

Like the previous two developments, a low-density resort would include transportable chalets that would be rented out to tourists and holiday guests. Again, the location for this type of development will be critical.

Entertainment centres

Entertainment centres with food and beverages, primarily located on the beach or riverfront, are ideal for ground lease developments.

Housing cooperatives

Under this model, the homes built on ground-leased land belong to a single cooperative entity. The cooperative will build the houses and communal facilities then rent or sell the individual homes to homebuyers under a purple or company title.

■■■

These are some of the better-known developments for ground leases. Others include industrial warehouses and solar farms. Whichever type of development you are considering for a ground lease, it is crucial to base its viability on whether the buildings can be leased at a higher rental, relocated or, if they are permanent structures, paid off in the short term.

How ground leases are valued

Commercial lease terms generally range from 20 to 50 years. Depending on the location and the surrounding economy, lease rates typically range from 7 per cent to 10 per cent of the property's value. However, reaching an agreement on that value can be challenging. Here are a few ways to get a valuation.

Third-party valuation

Most landlords will look for higher value but may not have considered that leasehold land is different from freehold. Besides location, there are other factors to consider. These include bulk utilities to the land, rates and taxes, and land taxes. Land leases are not common in residential real estate, where homes together with the land are sold to third parties, whereas with commercial real estate the value is determined by the income of the property. If an agreement cannot be reached between the landlord and the tenant, it is better for both parties to seek an independent valuation from a professional.

Residual land valuation

Another way of assessing the land's value is to research the going and acceptable rent for the type of building to be developed. Then, taking the gross rental income and capitalising this income against a cap rate of similar types of buildings will provide the value of the end product. Finally, deducting the construction cost, professional fees, interest and other development costs will provide a residual land value.

Whatever value or rent is agreed between the landlord and the lessee, it is essential to remember that the income on the completed development comes from third-party tenants. So there should be enough for the developer to pay off the capital cost and rent to the landlord. On the other hand, if the ground rent is too high and the lessee does not make any money, the lessee will not have a tenant, which will lead to foreclosure and a loss in rent for several months before the matter is resolved.

Assembling land for development

With the continuing increase in urban populations, government planners are under pressure to increase densities in older suburbs close to the CBD. The changes to these zonings present an exciting opportunity for developers to assemble a group of properties to create a super lot for new development such as a shopping centre. However, packaging these sites is often a challenge, and the difficulty increases exponentially with the increased number of landowners.

What is a land assembly?

Land assembly means forming a single site from several properties to create a significant development to suit growing market demand, for example a new shopping centre or a mixed-use development with apartments. Sellers who participate in a land assembly will generally receive a much higher price than they would on a one-off sale to an individual buyer.

Careful preparation, research and intuitive savvy when working with landowners who are reluctant to sell are essential to a successful land assembly. Developers who understand this challenging process can appreciate an expert's value in site acquisition. The site acquisition expert could be a solicitor or an experienced real estate professional, or a combination of the two.

Pros and cons of land assembly

The main advantages of this strategy are the relatively low capital cost and higher returns, and that the increased value provides a strong equity position.

Low capital cost for higher returns

The cost of assembling parcels of land is low when one places this against the amalgamated lots' final value. Depending on its zoning and the type of project that may be approved, the land's value could be three times that of each of the single properties.

Increased value provides a strong equity position

The increased value of the single super lot significantly enhances the developer's equity. They can then sell the property to another developer, create a syndicate or partner through a joint venture.

■■■

The two main disadvantages are that it is a long-drawn-out process and that one reluctant seller can scuttle the whole project.

A long-drawn-out process

Dealing with several owners takes considerable time and patience. It could take several months of negotiation before all the owners agree to sign their acceptance.

One reluctant seller can jeopardise the development

There may be just one owner who is unwilling to participate. Either they are looking for a higher price or they simply do not want to sell for personal reasons. If their property is strategically located in the middle of a group of sites, this can create a significant obstacle.

Strategy

From a developer's perspective, the strategy is to tie up each property for as long as possible without paying anything unless the proposed development goes ahead. The carrot to dangle in front of the owner is that they may potentially receive a lot more money for their property than the current market value.

There are several initial steps to take before starting the process of a land assembly.

Build a team

Land assembly requires an experienced and competent team who can work together throughout the process. The team should include an experienced real estate lawyer, a capable buyer's agent, a local town planner and an architect experienced in the type of project you intend to develop.

Research

As with any development, research is vital. This includes checking the local town planning structure plan if the zoning of the targeted land is in place or if the area is to be rezoned. Also research the market for your intended development.

Study real estate market prices

Verify the current market price of the properties you intend to assemble, as this figure will be presented to the current owners. Also, undertake a preliminary feasibility study and a residual land analysis to gauge the maximum price you are willing to pay for each property.

Establish a budget

Assembling land comes with a cost, and a developer must draw up a budget to pay for consultants, legal agreements and, if required, any deposits for securing the targeted properties. Except for refundable deposits, any money spent during the process cannot be recouped if the operation fails.

The process

Land assembly is a challenging process that requires lateral thinking, excellent negotiation skills and intelligent problem-solving. The process involves the following steps.

1. Finding suitable sites

When appointing the site acquisition expert or buyer's agent, establish the site selection criteria based on your proposed development. All or any of the following should be considered:

- What and where will the proposed development be best located?

- What is the land area size required to make the project viable?

- What is the maximum price per lot that the development can accept?

- What is the cost of the additional utilities?

- Is there a developer's contribution due to change or increase of use?

- Are there alternative options if the first assembly does not work out?

With this information, you and your team can create a systematic market assessment to identify suitable locations and properties. A range of resources are available to help you complete the evaluation, including mapping tools, online aerial photography from Google Maps or local government and planning departments, and site visits.

2. Meeting the landowners

After you have compiled a list of potential sites, it is time to open communication with the landowners. The following preliminary questions will help you determine their views on selling their property.

- Is the landowner interested in selling, and if so, at what asking price?

- Who owns the land? Is a syndicate or company the decision-maker?

- Do they understand the real estate sale process?

- Have previous offers to purchase been made?

- What are their critical concerns about selling?

In most cases, these properties are not on the market, and your agent must approach landowners directly. Owners who are reluctant to sell their properties present a challenge.

3. Pricing and negotiations

After establishing landowners' pricing motivations, you can start to prioritise sites based on which group of properties appears to be in your price range. The next step is to create an offer price and terms for each parcel. The final price will range between the offering price and the maximum amount you are willing to pay based on your project's budget, comparable sales and the owners' market value expectations.

Each sale transaction could take months to complete. Ensure that you allow sufficient time for due diligence in the initial offer, and record the progress or delays. Complications multiply as the size and scope of a project increases. You and your team may find yourselves in the situation of negotiating an extended due diligence period with each owner. Several issues can delay the project's progress and warrant further extensions.

Another decision in the acquisition process is whether to disclose your name and the nature of the project. A proposed project plan can be a successful selling tool. Still, some developers are reluctant to identify themselves for fear that one or more landowners will attempt to extract an unreasonable price for their properties.

4. Dealing with reluctant owners

When a selected property is not on the market, the landowner must decide whether to sell and at what price. Often, owners do not know what the property is worth or have unrealistic expectations of its value. The best way to move the process forward is to establish a dialogue, increase the owner's comfort level, find out their actual objections and work to overcome them. Although there is no standard procedure to follow, your agent must understand the owners' current and future situation, recognise their motivations and present a proposal addressing their concerns.

If an owner will not sell, usually the reason is the timing of the offer or unrealistic price demands. Uncovering these barriers to purchase before the actual assembly process begins saves valuable time. But if it becomes apparent during negotiations that a contract cannot be finalised, you should cease discussions and focus on another site. Sometimes knowing the buyer has moved on will spark interest from a reluctant property owner.

5. Other points to consider

Although the strategy is to pay no money upfront, there may be cases where the properties are strategic to your overall development. Therefore, to demonstrate your seriousness in the negotiations, you may consider placing a refundable deposit of 5 to 10 per cent of the market price, with conditions that will suit your intentions.

In most cases, a new development will not be built for a year or more after the successful conclusion of the land assembly. In this situation, the house may be liveable during that period. Therefore, you may negotiate free rent for a year or more while the seller finds another place to live. Also, provide a sublease clause. If the seller finds another property to buy or rent, they can sublease it to someone else and keep the rent as part of their remuneration.

■■■

There is no standard formula for success as the circumstances vary from site to site. Ultimately, successful completion will justify all the challenges and the time and effort invested.

Land assembly fund

Another strategy that can be used in a land assembly is to create a land assembly fund. This involves creating a development entity, such as a limited liability company, to control the assembled properties. The idea is to invite the property owners to participate as investors. Following are some key elements.

The fund's strategy

The purpose of the fund is to secure the parcels of land and to demon-strate the end value of the super lot. The value is calculated when the amalgamation process is complete or, better, when development approval has been granted. Participants in the fund will benefit from the increased value and can exit when the proposal is sold to another developer for a profit. Alternatively, the fund could develop the property, showing a higher value for the assembled land.

Property owners

Property owners choose either to sell their land at an agreed price or to participate in the fund. If they decide to participate, they will receive shares in the fund and benefit from the future increase in value.

Investors

The purpose of the introduction of investors is to accrue sufficient funds to purchase the properties of owners who prefer to sell rather than become shareholders in the fund. Investor funds will also assist in preparing all legal matters in the amalgamation and paying for any cost in securing development approval for the proposed development.

The creation of the fund may take longer and entail many meetings with property owners and investors. However, it does assist the developer, who is no longer taking all the financial risk in the process. Of course, the developer in this case must be credible and demonstrate their success in past developments.

CONCLUSION

The techniques outlined in this chapter for finding development sites at lower cost and minimal cash outlay have made many intelligent developers very wealthy. It is not easily done, however. These developers have worked hard to learn, test and understand how these processes work. Above all, they understand the concept of leveraging their hard work and expertise into equity wealth, equity that is then grown further by inviting other investors into the project and using debt from third parties.

If you want to follow in the footsteps of these successful developers, you first need to understand the full spectrum of real estate development, from residential to commercial, and to fully utilise leveraging strategies as a pathway to success.

CHAPTER 5

ALTERNATIVE SOURCES OF DEVELOPMENT FINANCE

Traditionally, banks have been the primary source of funding for developments. In recent years, these banks have tightened their lending due to the credit crunch and have introduced stringent criteria when lending even to experienced developers. However, there are alternatives, which we explore in this chapter. These alternative funding methods should be treated cautiously as some funds, such as private lending, can prove to be more expensive.

With the big banks creating a 'capital vacuum' through their restrictive lending, developers are forced to look for other sources and techniques and become creative in looking at ways to fund their projects. Technological advances have opened up new means of organising and collaboration, as exemplified by the rise of crowdfunding and other alternatives such as social impact bonds. At the same time, some developers have created their own funding sources through development funds. Before pursuing one of these alternative funding sources, you need a broad understanding of all of them, as each has its own nuances and peculiarities.

Understanding these wide-ranging options will lift your knowledge on financing your development to another level. During my career I have used several of these options. For example, when I was developing shopping centres, I would pre-sell the project before starting. The sale would be to an institutional investor. Under their investment policy, these investors would not take on development risk but were happy to own an income-producing property with a guaranteed return. Because I had a buyer of this financial standing, the banks provided the finance with little equity required.

Private lenders

Since the Australian banking commission report most banks have taken a cautious approach when providing loans to real estate ventures, whether for investment or development. However, expanded regulation and increasing rates and fees have taken the banking sector's conservative underwriting of real estate financing to an unprecedented level. As a result, developers are now seeking private lenders with the tight lending criteria of conventional bank lenders in the real estate market. While private lenders' interest rates and fees are higher than banks, their terms and conditions may not be as onerous as the banks'.

Private lenders vary in their offerings. While some offer similar loans to banks, others specialise in mezzanine finance or seed capital such as bridging loans. Following are loans that banks do not provide but that are available from private funders.

Bridging loans

Depending on a developer's finances, bridging loans may be required in the conceptual stage of new development. This relatively small initial finance is needed to cover consultants' costs and disbursements for the initial design and submission for development approval.

With bridging loans, the interest rates are a lot higher than for other loans due to the higher risk stage of the project. They are considered high-risk loans and can be obtained in exchange for an equity stake in the project.

Mezzanine loans

Mezzanine loans are debt capital that gives the lender the right to convert to an ownership or equity interest in the company if the loan is not paid back in time and in full. This loan is often a more expensive financing source for a developer than secured debt or senior debt.

Developers often use mezzanine loans to secure additional funding for development projects where the senior lender requires a shortfall of equity. It is generally subordinated to a senior debt provided by a bank. This type of loan is advantageous because it is treated as equity and may make it easier to obtain standard bank financing.

The higher cost of capital associated with mezzanine financing is the result of its being an unsecured, subordinated (or junior) debt. It means that the mezzanine financing is repaid only in the event of default after all senior obligations have been satisfied.

In compensation for the increased risk, mezzanine debt holders require a higher return for their investment than secured or more senior lenders. Therefore, it is priced aggressively, with the lender seeking a return in the 20 to 30 per cent range.

Preferential equity

Preferential equity (PE) is a hybrid of debt and equity. It is essentially a debt that gives the lender the right to convert to ownership and control of a project in the event of a prolonged default that cannot be rectified. It may include the loan not being paid back in time or due to an extended unresolved problem.

PE is generally used to fill the gap between what the bank will fund and what the developer can contribute towards a project. The main advantage of PE is that, unlike to mezzanine debt, it does not require a registered second mortgage or a deed of subordination to the senior lender such as a bank. For example, a bank funds 70 per cent of the total development cost (TDC). PE lenders will top this up to 90 per cent TDC. The 20 per cent PE is subject to the development's viability and a clear exit strategy for the

PE lender. It leaves the developer to provide 10 per cent of their equity. This equity enables developers to spread their cash equity across more projects while maintaining a healthy equity return.

PE is often considered an expensive funding option. However, many of Australia's largest and most successful developers use PE to improve their return on equity. The PE return pricing is generally calculated on a risk-adjusted return on a capital basis. It must achieve a minimum internal rate of return (IRR). This means PE's returns are fixed, reducing potential conflict in calculating the project's profit. In addition, it gives developers the opportunity and the incentive to make an additional profit if the project achieves gains beyond those forecast initially.

Blended first mortgage

Private funders generally offer a blended first mortgage. Primarily, a private lender provides a loan with a high LVR and a higher interest rate, as the lender is pricing their risk in the project. This loan works effectively for residential projects. It is used when (a) pre-sales achieved are well below what the bank requires, such as 100 per cent net debt cover, and (b) the equity falls short of a bank's requirements.

Developers are often offered a development loan from private lenders without pre-sales requirements. However, the cost and rates are much higher than the banks'. It works well if you are confident that your project will sell as soon as construction starts and that you will achieve a higher sales value for your project.

SUMMARY

As seen from these various offerings, private lending can be expensive, ultimately costing the developer's profit margin. However, the developer may have no choice but to accept these high costs because of the tight lending from traditional banks. Therefore, the developer must understand the private lender's offer terms. Use their finance offer wisely by ensuring that you have an exit strategy to clear their loans in the shortest period possible.

Joint venture funding options

Joint venture real estate development funding is an arrangement between two or more parties who agree to combine their resources for a specific project. Developers will typically join forces with another party to compensate in areas in which they fall short, such as development finance. A developer who cannot fund a potential project will look for an investor to bridge the gap between their equity level and the capital needed to start the project.

There are various options for a joint venture funding arrangement. Funding can come from potential partners such as private equity funds, real estate funds, finance companies, corporate or private investors, and builders.

Joint venture finance

Under this arrangement, the joint venture partner provides 100 per cent of the required development finance. In addition, several arrangements can be structured under the joint venture from a split of profits, fees and other incentives.

In some joint ventures the lender provides all the development funds required, and profits are split on a 50:50 basis, with lenders charging interest on funds drawn down. Other structures include a developer's management fee, a minimum targeted return to the JV lender on their funds and the balance of 50:50 or 70:30 in favour of the investors. The latter structure is usually incorporated under a funds management arrangement.

There is no fixed or standard joint venture structure. Instead, the joint venture arrangement is negotiated with each project based on the partner's roles, their value in the partnership, the type of development and many other factors.

Builder's design, construction and finance loan

In this JV structure, a builder with a significant balance sheet can offer design, construction and financial loans to approved developers. A joint venture may not be necessary, however. Some builders would provide funding like a private lender and not share profits.

Before the builder makes this type of loan, they will require an unconditional bank guarantee that all the costs they pay will be repaid at completion. The advantage for the developer is that they do not have to fund the total equity required by a commercial bank, especially if the equity required is 30 per cent or more. The developer has to finance the land and development approval cost plus the running and overhead costs.

The disadvantage with the type of loan is that the builder will add a margin over their own bank's interest to cover the risk of providing the finance to the developer. In some cases, this could be higher than the currently available rates.

Before entering such a loan contract, the developer should have an independent quantity surveyor verify the builder's cost and ensure it aligns with the current construction rates.

SUMMARY

Joint venture funding is generally available for larger projects and where the developer has a credible track record of completed projects. In some instances, when there is not much construction work around, a residential builder may consider financing a small residential unit development.

Crowdfunding

Crowdfunding is using an online platform to fund a project or venture by raising small amounts of money from many people. The digital funding concept has supported many entrepreneurial ventures such as creative projects, medical expenses, community-oriented social entrepreneurship projects and real estate investing.

Through social media outlets like LinkedIn, Facebook and Twitter, it reaches out to an audience of potential investors. The crowdfunding strategy is that more people are willing to invest a small amount of money than more significant sums. As a result, it opens doors for businesses to a new range of investors.

The current crowdfunding model

Opportunities to purchase properties through Australian crowdfunding platforms are currently limited to residential properties. Most real estate crowdfunding offers involve equity investments. Investors are shareholders in a specific property, and their share is in proportion to their invested amount. As a result, returns are derived from a share of the property's rental income less service fees paid to the crowdfunding platform. Investors are also paid a percentage share of any appreciation value if the property is sold.

Crowdfunding for real estate development

Equity is often most difficult for newer or smaller developers. Real estate crowdfunding platforms can benefit real estate developers looking for additional sources of capital from qualified investors. There is also a cost advantage. Online platforms have lower overhead costs than banks, which translates into less fees and lower interest rates for borrowers. An alternative solution is to create a platform where investors can lend money to the developer for real estate development purposes. The loan agreement obliges the developer to repay the loan principal and interest and costs over an agreed term (see figure 5.1).

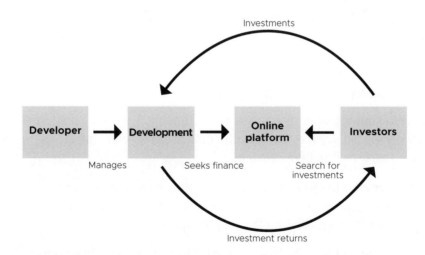

Figure 5.1: real estate crowdfunding

As crowdfunding grows, more real estate developers use crowdfunding sites to solicit high-net-worth investors' investments. Success so far has been low due to several factors, including the size of investment offered and lack of trust and transparency.

Types of real estate crowdfunding

The two common types of real estate crowdfunding are equity and debt investments.

Equity crowdfunding

Equity crowdfunding investments give investors an equity stake in commercial or residential real estate, effectively making them shareholders. Dividends are generally the rental income of the property. The investors will benefit from their equity investment's capital growth when the property is sold. It is an excellent option for developers seeking equity for their development projects.

Debt crowdfunding

In debt crowdfunding, investors act as lenders to real estate developers. Investors receive a fixed rate of return based on an agreed interest rate. This interest is usually paid either monthly or quarterly. As this is a loan, crowdfunding investors have priority when the property is sold. There is no additional income when a property is sold, as the investors do not own a share of the property. It can be an excellent option for developers looking for alternative finance other than banks.

How does crowdfunding work?

Several online platforms promote crowdfunding. Look for a platform that has completed a real estate crowdfunding project. Following are the main steps in a crowdfunding campaign.

1. **Create a project profile.** A compelling crowdfunding profile of the real estate project will include a pitch video, supporting documents, project images and explanatory graphics.

2. **Set an achievable funding goal.** The campaign will be funded once contributions exceed the stated goal. No contributions will be collected if the funding goal is not achieved.

3. **Market to the crowd.** Marketing is critical for a crowdfunding campaign to work successfully. It will require proper forward planning and strong execution during the campaign.

4. **Collect funds.** If the funding goal is achieved, money is transferred to your account from the promoters on the platform, minus any applicable commission.

The campaign does not stop after receiving the required funding. The developer must keep investors informed of the real estate project's progress through monthly or quarterly reports.

Pros and cons for investors

What are the pros and cons of crowdfunding for investors? Simply, it comes down to risk for both sides.

Pros

- Investors can access the real estate market with small amounts of money.

- Investors can work directly with sponsors and developers and have a voice in the process.

- Investors choose which real estate projects they want to invest their money in. They have access to multiple projects, so choice is not a problem.

Cons

- The investment risks are the same as for any real estate investor. If the market declines, an investor can lose money.

- There is the potential for default by a real estate developer, as with a REIT.

- In the absence of a secondary market, a lack of liquidity restricts investors from selling their shares.

Pros and cons for sponsors and developers

Sponsors and real estate developers can reap significant financial returns through crowdfunding and spread their risks, but there can be disadvantages too.

Pros

- They can take advantage of the platform's social media impact to reach new investors.

- Most platforms have a vast community of investors, and there is the potential to receive pledges from strangers.

- They can get early feedback on their project through the site's comments section and updates.

- Investor pledges can be used as validation. In addition, this data can be used when further funding is needed.

Cons

- It takes time and money to create an attractive project page, documentation, reports and videos.

- Significant time is required to market the project, reach out to new investors through social media and be attentive to current investors.

- There is a risk of embarrassment if you fail. However, many creators fail the first time then successfully relaunch their campaign.

Crowdfunding and blockchain

The problem with the current crowdfunding platforms is that they are centralised bodies, charging high fees and influencing the projects. The alternative is blockchain-based crowdfunding, a game-changer because it decentralises the funding model. For example, some existing crowdfunding platforms charge 5 per cent of the total funds received, plus an additional 3 to 5 per cent for processing payments. Blockchain's distributed ledger can remove this third party, saving considerable costs. So how does blockchain crowdfunding work?

It operates like the current crowdfunding platform. The sponsors post their projects and raise funds from a community of interested parties. The difference is that a blockchain platform will create digital currency or tokens to sell to potential investors. The blockchain will account for and keep track of these digital currency tokens, making them immutable and difficult to forge. The tokens represent shares in the development, and like ordinary shares on the stock market they have the potential to go up in value.

Blockchain crowdfunding for real estate investment or development allows a crowdfunding platform to create digital currencies sold to potential investors. It enables the platform to raise funds from early investors. At the same time, the investors can make money if their cryptographic shares' value increases.

Some advocates consider this a superior form of crowdfunding because it removes intermediaries between the backers and the platform. It can also boost new blockchain platforms because it will give the blockchain community a new way to fund its projects.

SUMMARY

Real estate crowdfunding is an investment trend that is starting to take off. Crowdfunding investors can now easily own shares in real estate projects with steady growth and higher net rental yields once available only to the wealthy. In addition, this method of raising capital for their projects is more straightforward and more manageable for sponsors and developers than most lenders' strict processes. Additional information on crowdfunding can be found under Chapter 7 as a FinTech application.

Take-out or head-lease funding

Bankers and lenders of real estate development are always looking for an exit strategy or what underpins a new development. For example, most home units are sold to homebuyers in residential developments such as apartments. Funding is generally granted based on the number of pre-sales before the release of their funds. With a commercial project, though, the two areas that would make a lender more comfortable are a clear exit strategy or a head lease from a credible lessee.

Exit strategies

Two exit strategies can be applied to commercial development: a take-out loan and a take-out through an end sale.

Take-out loan

A take-out loan is long-term financing that replaces short-term interim funding such as a construction loan. Unfortunately, no bank or lender will provide a developer with an unconditional take-out loan. They cannot set aside finance for a development that may only be completed in, say, two years' time. However, the construction loan's lender may provide the take-out loan if they feel that the project is viable.

End-sale take-out

In some cases, and more likely with a larger project such as an office block or shopping centre, a developer may sell the completed project to a large financial institution, such as insurance or investment companies, based on a guaranteed return on the purchase price. To ensure the returns are guaranteed to the investor, the developer can take a percentage of the development profit and place these funds into an escrow account as a top-up mechanism.

Head-lease strategy

With a head lease, lenders will look at the party behind the lease. This party must be financially credible. For example, most lenders will not finance a hotel with a management agreement, no matter how strong the operator's brand recognition in the marketplace. However, they will support a construction loan should the operator provide a head lease or a guaranteed income.

Guaranteed income

Lenders of a construction loan with a head lease or guaranteed income in place will provide a loan only if supported by the lease. For example, suppose the guaranteed income is $1 million per annum and the interest rate is 10 per cent. In that case, the loan amount will be $10 million.

Credible third party

A head-lease strategy could also work by a credible third party signing off a 'Head Lease Agreement'. For example, suppose a $10 million project provides a 9 per cent yield on its rental income but the $10 million loan is at a 6 per cent interest. In that case, the head-lease guarantor offers a guaranteed income of 7.5 per cent, which leaves a buffer of 1.5 per cent to the head-lease guarantor. But, again, this type of structure will appeal more to a not-for-profit development than a commercially driven one.

SUMMARY

The end take-out and head-lease funding models are mainly applicable to commercial developments. Many successful commercial developers have used this strategy and have become multimillionaires for their efforts.

Ethical funds

Since the debate on climate change started in the last century, there have been several incentives created by socially responsible people. So, when it comes to new products, energy, infrastructure and building regulation, it is no surprise that these incentives have led to ethical funds being created. These socially responsible funds target ethical investors. They assist entrepreneurs with finance for projects that seek to preserve natural resources, mitigate the environmental crisis and create a better planet for future generations.

Socially responsible investing, also known as sustainable or ethical investing, a subset of impact investing, is an investment strategy that is focused on creating a positive social impact through targeted investment.

Ethical funds in real estate

In the real estate space, the buildings we live in consume significant resources and produce high volumes of waste. Our built environment is responsible for 50 per cent of all global energy use and half of greenhouse gas emissions. In addition, buildings consume 17 per cent of all fresh water, 25 per cent of world wood harvests and 40 per cent of all other raw materials. Also, construction and later demolition of buildings produce 40 per cent of all waste. No wonder new buildings are coming under increasing scrutiny. 'Green' rating tools are critical for measuring this. NABERS (National Australian Built Environment Rating System) is a government initiative to measure and compare the environmental performance of buildings and tenancies.

Many ethical funds are willing to invest in new projects that have a 'green' rating and comply with the following standards.

Life cycle assessment (LCA)

LCA assesses a range of impacts associated with the process stages from the extraction of raw materials through materials processing, manufacture, distribution, use, repair and maintenance, and disposal or recycling.

Sustainable design efficiency

Any new built form starts with the initial concept and design stage. The concept stage, a significant step in a project life cycle, has the most impact on cost and performance.

Energy efficiency

NABERS' star rating sets standards to encourage reductions in energy consumption. It measures the energy required to extract, process, transport and install building materials, and the operating energy to provide heating and power for equipment.

Water efficiency

Reducing water consumption and protecting water quality are key objectives in sustainable building. Ideas that have been widely implemented include installing water tanks to capture rainwater and greywater for landscaped areas.

Building materials efficiency

Green building materials include timber from forest plantations, rapidly renewable plant materials such as bamboo and straw, recycled materials, and other non-toxic, reusable, renewable and recyclable products.

Indoor air quality

High-quality indoor air flow reduces volatile organic compounds and air impurities such as microbial contaminants. New buildings should be designed with passive or natural ventilation.

Operations and maintenance optimisation

No matter how sustainable a building's design and construction, it can only maintain that standard if operated and maintained responsibly. Operation and maintenance should be part of the project's planning and development process.

Waste reduction

Green architecture seeks to reduce energy, water and materials consumption during construction. Well-designed buildings also help reduce the amount of waste generated by their occupants by providing on-site solutions such as composting.

Reduce the impact on the electricity network

When a sustainable building is designed, constructed and operated efficiently, peak electrical demand and carbon emissions are reduced. Design considerations include orientation, indoor thermal mass, insulation, solar panels, thermal or electrical energy storage systems, and smart building energy management systems.

HOW ETHICAL FUNDS WORK
(COURTESY OF VARNA CAPITAL)

'As an example, a developer is building and owning a mixed-use site for $50 million. We consider the design and energy-consuming technologies for the site (i.e. lighting, solar, metering/embedded network, thermal insulation, glazing performance, energy efficient whitegoods, hot water, HVAC). Varna assesses the ongoing lifecycle cost of these technologies. We then create a package outlining which products have an attractive investment return based on the predicted energy costs. For this example, $5 million is taken out of the project's capital cost and funded using alternate sources specialised in this space (at a meagre rate). It will reduce the developer's CapEx and OpEx, improving cash flow and returning profit. This reduction of $5 million (or 10 per cent) contributes to reducing the project's development finance LVR without using additional equity.'

Social impact bonds

Social impact bonds (SIBs), also known as pay-for-success bonds, compensation-for-success bonds, social benefit bonds or just social bonds, are used to fund social service programs that combine outcomes-based payments and market discipline. They are designed to raise private capital for suitable intensive support and preventative programs to be funded by government.

How does a social impact bond work?

Following are the main steps involved (further illustrated in figure 5.2).

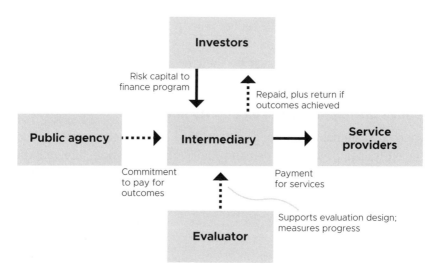

Figure 5.2: social impact structure

1. Identify the problem and possible solutions

The process generally starts when the government detects a problem or challenge in the public sector. Typical difficulties include public safety, health, housing and family support services.

2. Raise funds for the project from private investors

After a potential solution has been approved, the government will attract private investors to the project. First, the parties determine the quantifiable metrics to indicate the project's success. Interested investors then provide the required capital to support the execution of the solution.

3. Implement the project

The project manager or developer uses the obtained funds to finance the project's operations. Finally, the service provider begins the program's implementation.

4. Assess the project's success and pay the project manager and investors

At the end of the fixed term, an independent evaluator completes the assessment of the project's success based on predetermined metrics. If the project meets the criteria, the government pays the project manager or developer, converting the investors' funds into social impact bonds.

How can developers be involved?

Developers in the affordable housing and health sectors could consider social impact bonds as a means of funding. State governments across Australia, along with numerous government bodies and investors worldwide, are moving towards contracting for social outcomes rather than inputs or outputs. This is an important development in social service delivery. For example, government funds are used to support innovative programs to improve housing and welfare outcomes for young people at risk of homelessness, including those supported by specialist homelessness services, exiting the out-of-home care system or existing institutions such as juvenile detention.

With almost 200 000 people on social housing waiting lists across the country, housing experts have found that social impact investment can provide a lifeline to the country's most vulnerable groups.

Public housing stock can no longer meet the needs of the low-income population. Social impact investment and government intervention working with private-sector developers could provide a much-needed boost to affordable accommodation.

Social impact investment in affordable housing internationally accounts for 22 per cent of assets under management. It has yet to take off in Australia. As more Australian landlords are willing to accept lower rent, a growing focus on institutional and superannuation funds offers more ethical investment opportunities. It is only a matter of time.

Government funding

Affordable and social housing has always been a political issue for both federal and state governments. All government levels must assist through grants or act as a vehicle to underwrite the project's risk. Governments could also help minimise the project risk by guaranteeing buyers or tenants for the developed home units. Following are some examples of both federal and state government's involvement in affordable housing.

Federal government's housing affordability fund

The Department of Social Services has established a Housing Affordability Fund, a five-year $400 million investment by the Australian Government to help reduce the cost of new homes for homebuyers. The fund addresses two significant barriers to increasing the supply of affordable housing: (a) 'holding' costs incurred by developers due to lengthy planning and approval times, and (b) infrastructure costs, such as the supply of power, water, sewerage and public transport links.

The fund provides grants to state, territory and local governments. They work with the private sector, reduce housing-related infrastructure and planning costs, and pass savings on to new home purchasers. Two funding rounds have been conducted, and program funding is now fully committed. Seventy-five projects have been approved for financing, stimulating new housing supply and supporting more affordable housing.

State governments

Each state government works closely with developers of affordable housing. They support developers in several ways. These vary from state to state, and some of the government programs change from time to time. Examples of state government assistance to developers include:

- **provision of land.** Offer state-owned government land to affordable and community housing developers.

- **pre-purchase.** Pre-purchase or commit to purchase some of a developer's homes or units when completed.

- **capital grants.** Make grants available for specialised projects such as reducing homelessness.

- **planning bonuses.** Provide additional floor space incentives for affordable housing developments.

- **partnerships.** Encourage community housing providers and others, including private developers, on affordable housing projects.

- **state government fund.** A dedicated fund to support innovative partnerships between the government and private sectors and the not-for-profit and local government sectors.

This assistance varies from state to state, so developers need to do their own research when developing affordable housing.

Real estate development fund

An alternative way for developers to raise capital is to start a real estate development trust (or fund). Real estate trusts may be listed or unlisted. Typically, listed trusts (also known as Real Estate Investment Trusts — REITs) are traded on a stock market (such as the Australian Securities Exchange), whereas unlisted trusts are privately held and there is no public market. This section focuses on unlisted trusts and, more specifically, a real estate development fund.

Listed vs unlisted real estate trusts

Before going into the details of a real estate development fund, it is worth building a clearer understanding of the distinctions between a listed and an unlisted real estate trust in Australia.

Listed property trusts (LPTs)

An LPT is listed on the ASX. Units on the exchange can be bought and sold just like shares. Following are some additional distinguishing features:

- An LPT is called a 'closed-end' fund because the number of units on the issue remains virtually unchanged. As a result, every transaction involves both a buyer and a seller.

- An LPT has a higher liquidity level as investors can redeem their units by selling them on the stock exchange.

- The trustee of an LPT trust is responsible for holding the property and ensuring the trust deed provisions are professionally upheld.

- The LPT manager is a contracted employee of the unitholders. This manager can be forced to resign if the unitholders are dissatisfied with the trust's performance.

- As LPTs are traded on the stock market daily, they can be subject to significant volatility driven by perceptions of their underlying assets along with general market sentiment.

- LPTs are not subject to the 'takeovers' provisions of the Corporations Law, which means control can more easily change hands.

- Another characteristic of an LPT is distributing all taxable income to benefit from the 'tax-exempt' status. However, because LPTs are not tax-paying entities, they cannot benefit from tax deductions such as depreciation.

- The assets of an LPT are typically retail shopping centres, office blocks or industrial properties. Childcare centres, medical clinics and hospitals, hotels and residential properties are other examples.

- Gearing in an LPT can be higher than in an unlisted trust but tends to have more complex investment structures.

Unlisted property trusts (UPTs)

UPTs are often referred to as 'open-end' funds. Investors wishing to purchase units in a UPT must do so through the prospectus available from a fund manager. Following are further distinguishing features:

- UPT units are not quoted on an exchange and cannot be traded at any time. They are generally held for the investment duration (five, seven or 10 years).

- A UPT will generally hold a single asset or a set number of assets. So, for example, it could entail a single shopping centre or a group of shopping centres as a set portfolio.

- UPTs can continuously accept new subscriptions from the public if they issue a recent prospectus.

- If a fund manager feels the UPT has reached an optimal size, it may stop receiving new subscriptions and essentially become a 'closed-end' fund, like an LPT.

- UPT units will not fluctuate in price the way listed shares do because the fund's properties are valued regularly, so they do not display the same level of volatility as an LPT.

- Unlike listed funds, UPTs can also provide a steady income. Again, they have long-term contracts in place, giving investors certainty with income.

- There is less liquidity with a UPT. Investors must submit a redemption request, and the process can take time, which means the units' price may change.

- Some UPTs may require investors to keep money in the fund for a specified time. Redemptions can be frozen if too many investors want to withdraw their money at the same time.

- UPTs tend to have lower gearing levels when compared with LPTs.

What is a development fund?

A real estate development fund is a managed investment scheme (MIS). It allows investors to invest in a significant real estate development through debt financing arrangements or direct equity investments.

Development fund managers secure projects with attractive returns and appropriate risk profiles. The investment capital is used to execute the necessary steps, such as acquiring a site, obtaining development approval, constructing the property, and selling or renting the property on completion.

A development fund allows investors to access an asset class that is otherwise inaccessible without a large capital outlay for land purchase, development applications, planning and construction.

Project development funds (PDFs) can be structured in two ways: (a) for a single development project, or (b) for a diversified portfolio of projects often in different geographical locations.

Most investors in a development fund are sophisticated investors who typically invest a minimum of $50 000. To qualify, they must have a net worth of $2.5 million or have earned more than $250 000 in the past two years.

Advantages and disadvantages of PDFs

There are advantages and disadvantages to establishing a development fund. The advantages may include the following.

Access to a broader group of investors

A development fund structure opens up development opportunities to a larger pool of investors looking for professionally managed investment schemes. While most investors will be sophisticated investors, a PDF structure can also attract institutional investment funds.

Higher fee generation

Due to the substantial amount of money invested and the project's scale, a manager can generate significantly higher fees than if they spent the same time on smaller projects.

Ongoing access to funds

As it is an open-end fund, the manager has access to secure additional funding for new development opportunities if they fall into the same investment criteria as proposed in the initial prospectus.

Professional fund managers

Professional and experienced development fund managers generally manage these funds. They should hold an Australian financial services licence.

■■■

Disadvantages may include the following.

Large capital cost upfront

Starting a development fund requires significant capital upfront. It also requires an extraordinary amount of time researching and finding a suitable development project, then fulfilling the necessary compliance and prospectus requirements. For all that, there is no guarantee that investors will invest in the proposed fund.

Strict regulations and compliance

A development fund is a managed investment scheme (MIS) and is strictly regulated by the Australian Securities and Investments Commission (ASIC). Non-compliance with these rules can attract hefty penalties.

The manager can be dismissed

You may have initiated a development fund and spent both time and money getting it operational, yet there is no guarantee that you will always be in control. In terms of the Act, a fund manager is only contracted to a fund. They can, therefore, be dismissed on reasonable grounds.

Commitment by investors

If the proposed development fund is for a broad, diversified range of projects with a call on commitments when a project fits the PDF's criteria, there is no guarantee that the investors will commit to it. Investors may like the investment criteria of a PDF but may invest elsewhere if the PDF cannot offer a project early.

Development fund structure

Figure 5.3 (overleaf) shows a typical open-end development fund structure for a more extensive diversified development portfolio. The fund is a unit trust that should be registered with ASIC as a managed investment scheme. The fund will own and manage special purpose vehicles (SPVs), which will be utilised for individual investment projects. It will allow the risks and liabilities associated with particular investments to be managed for the benefit of the fund.

Depending on the investment, it is anticipated that a typical SPV, such as a commercial project, will be held as a short- to medium-term investment or sold post-completion. Apart from reducing development and interest rate risk, the utilisation of such entities will provide greater flexibility regarding the disposal of completed projects.

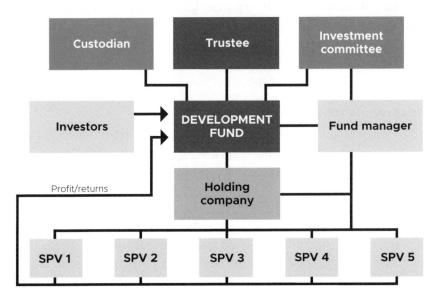

Figure 5.3: an open-end development fund structure

Overview of a development fund

Most PDFs are unlisted unit trusts. An appointed manager is the fund's responsible entity and the issuer of the units offered under an information memorandum. Listed here are some of the key fundamentals that should be included in an information memorandum.

Performance objective

The manager should set out the objective of the fund. In addition, the manager should state the targeted internal rate of return (IRR); for example, an IRR of 15 per cent per annum on investor's equity (before performance entitlement and taxes) to investors.

Type of developments

The fund should stipulate the real estate type and geographical location of properties to be developed in a diversified portfolio.

Development policies

The policies of the fund can stipulate that it intends to develop opportunities that will be benchmarked against defined criteria, which include:

- predictable and stable long-term cash flows

- revenue growth potential

- availability of significant interest or shareholding

- a risk/return profile complementary to the risks associated with such investments.

Investment strategy

An outline of the fund's strategy to achieve its objective can include, for example:

- sourcing opportunities by adding value in providing equity, management and expertise

- sourcing development opportunities to design and construct new buildings

- trading opportunities to undertake refurbishment and expansion of existing properties.

Proposed developments

The fund should include the type of developments that will be undertaken. If the fund is a diversified portfolio of developments, it should specify the sector and asset class that the fund will manage. The range can include any of the following examples:

- *retail*—shopping centres, showrooms, specialist retail outlets and bulk goods stores

- *industrial*—industrial land, warehousing, logistic and industrial parks

- *offices*—office blocks, business parks and technology parks

- *leisure*—hotels and apartments

- *residential*—land subdivisions, townhouses, villas, apartments and student housing

- *retirement*—lifestyle villages and aged care facilities.

Investment criteria

The manager of the fund should define the criteria before the fund commits to investing in a new development project. The requirements can include the following:

a. The manager should undertake thorough due diligence on the proposed development, and similarly, on the joint venture partner where a joint venture is undertaken.

b. The manager should prepare a detailed feasibility study, which an external third-party consultant will review independently to determine if the project can meet the targeted return.

c. It can stipulate how much of the fund's cash will be invested per project; for example, no more than 30 per cent of the fund's assets may be invested in a single development project.

d. The manager should state that it will also perform a sensitivity analysis. The variable factors that should be considered can include the following:

  - current and future sale price, including pre-sales
  - current and future market rents and capitalisation rates
  - project completion program and selling periods
  - change in market demand
  - project cost overruns (potential or existing)
  - interest rates.

Investment committee

A development fund should establish an investment committee to decide on:

- investment project feasibility and budgets

- investment projects before commencement

- related party transactions

- capital management transactions, such as debt facilities and calls on commitments

- distributions.

Compliance committee

A compliance committee should be formed, comprising one internal member and two external members. The compliance committee's role is to ensure compliance with the Constitution and Compliance Plan and the Corporations Act.

Custodian

If the fund targets a number over the ASIC's ruling, then a custodian should be appointed as the fund's custodial agent. Their role as custodian is limited to holding the fund assets as an agent of the fund manager. The custodian has no supervisory role with the fund's operation and is not responsible for protecting investors' interests.

Borrowings

In a PDF, there should be no borrowings at the fund level. Borrowings should be made by special purpose vehicles (SPVs). Also, lenders should have no recourse to the fund's assets other than the money the fund has invested in a specific project under an SPV. A borrowing criterion should be set.

For example, SPV projects can acquire properties using a combination of debt and equity, resulting in ventures having debt levels up to 70 per cent of asset values.

As another example, should the gearing level exceed 70 per cent at any time, the manager must take steps to reduce the gearing to 70 per cent within three months. Alternatively, if the manager considers that this is not practical or in investors' best interests, they will convene a meeting of the investors to seek special resolution approval to exceed this limit.

Size of the fund

The size of the fund in terms of the amount that can be invested should be stipulated. For a single project, the amount can be predetermined. In contrast, for a larger, open-end fund with a broader range of projects it will depend on the number of projects targeted. For example, the fund's initial size will be a minimum of $30 million in equity up to a targeted maximum of $100 million. Should the minimum commitment not be achieved, the manager will not proceed with the fund, and investors will be notified of the cancellation of their commitments.

Life of the fund

The life of the fund should also be stipulated. For example, it can state that it is an open-end fund until 1 March 2032. It is open for ongoing investment in the healthcare sector during this period as long as development projects fit into the fund's investment strategy. The fund can be terminated earlier by the manager following notification to investors or under the Corporations Act. Following termination, the manager is required to sell and realise the fund's remaining assets and distribute the proceeds, less expenses, to investors in proportion to their respective holdings at the time of termination.

Valuations

It should be noted that valuations on the developments will be carried at a lower cost or net realisable value. The manager will value the fund's assets annually, based on the requirements of the Corporations Act, ASIC, International Financial Reporting Standards (IFRS) and Australian Accounting Standards.

Reports and accounts

The manager should provide quarterly updates on the progress of the fund and its associated developments. At the end of the financial year, the manager should provide audited financial statements within 90 days. In addition, the manager should undertake annual unitholders' briefings and conduct separate unitholders' meetings to consider issues requiring the unitholders' approval if such problems are not covered in the annual briefings.

Calls on commitments

Following the initial investment commitment made by investors, the manager will determine the associated requirement to draw down or 'call' on those commitments to fund various development projects during the life of the fund. The manager will issue the calls on unitholders. They will occur primarily based on the number and size of the investment projects undertaken by the fund and the determination of the most suitable funding program regarding the appropriate mix of debt and equity.

Issue of units

At the manager's discretion, applicants will be issued either new units or transferred existing units held by the manager in their capacity. Units may be transferred to an applicant in circumstances where the manager has acquired units. The acceptance of an application for units will be at the absolute discretion of the manager, who may reject an application, in which case the manager will refund the application monies without interest.

Reserve amount

The manager may elect to allocate up to 10 per cent of the investment made into the fund. The reserve amount will be utilised as a part of risk management to provide an additional contingency, above that already provided for in individual financial investment project feasibilities. Such funds may also be utilised to support various financing facilities such as bank guarantees. To maximise returns to unitholders, the reserve amount will generally be provisioned but not drawn from available equity unless required.

Calculation of unit price

The value of units in the fund can change with the fund's underlying assets. Therefore, the unit price paid on an application for units in the fund is calculated as the net asset value of the fund's assets (total assets minus total liabilities) less accrued income earned plus transaction costs, divided by the total number of units on issue. In addition, the unit price is calculated when an investment is withdrawn, except transaction costs are deducted.

Withdrawal of units

Due to the fund's expected asset allocation, the fund is unlikely to be 'liquid'. Therefore, the manager will not be compelled to accept withdrawal requests at any time. However, the manager may elect not to make a withdrawal offer if it is not in the investors' best interests or if the fund's assets are not sufficiently liquid to satisfy a withdrawal. Such a situation could arise because of the nature of the fund's investment activities, with the fund not necessarily holding cash until the realisation of any income. Given the nature of the type of investment activities, a withdrawal offer will not be made for the first 18 months from the commencement date.

Distribution to investors

Investors will be entitled to receive distributions of all income generated by the fund, net of fees, and the fund's expenses. It may differ from reported income due to relevant accounting standards and the requirement to report revenue other than realisation. In general, income distributions will be determined immediately before each new issue of units or units' transfer from the manager. Each investor's entitlement to the fund's distributable income is proportional to the number of units they hold.

Distributions and reinvestment

The constitution can make provision that the fund manager may permit investors to reinvest their distributions to acquire additional units. Applicants may elect to participate in the distribution reinvestment plan. If an investor does not participate, then that investor's interest in the fund would be diluted relative to those who participate.

Investment process

The investment process in a fund is based on seeking to realise returns from achieving the targeted IRR on equity within acceptable risk parameters. Accordingly, the investment process is broadly based on four key activities:

- identification and evaluation of development opportunities

- approval and execution of acquisitions

- delivery of developments

- disposal of developments.

Investment procedure

Figure 5.4 shows a typical investment procedure that requires approval at various stages and before the fund proceeds with a new project.

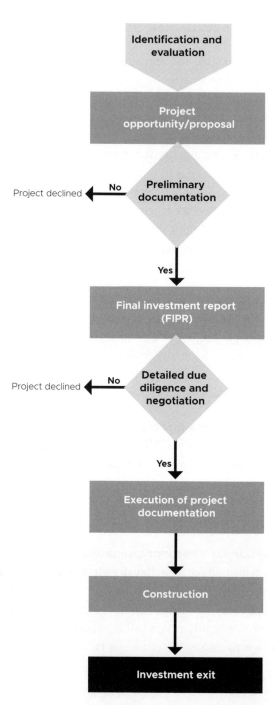

Figure 5.4: stages of an investment

STAGE 1: IDENTIFICATION AND EVALUATION OF DEVELOPMENT OPPORTUNITIES

The manager will be responsible for managing the process of sourcing opportunities and the initial evaluation of such opportunities. First, they determine whether the proposed projects are consistent with the fund's investment objectives and strategies. This initial assessment will filter out many inappropriate development opportunities, reducing costs. If the preliminary analysis is favourable, the manager will seek approval from the investment committee (IC) to undertake a more comprehensive review, including project and financial feasibilities and risk assessment. Once the development's evaluation is complete, consideration will be given to structuring the ownership of the development within an SPV (if required) and the associated financing required. The manager will then seek preliminary approval for the acquisition from the IC.

STAGE 2: FORMAL EVALUATION AND DUE DILIGENCE APPROVAL

Following preliminary approval from the IC, a conditional offer may be made to secure the project, subject to due diligence and final approval from the IC. Following this, the manager will undertake a formal due diligence review. This review may include the engagement of appropriate external consultants to facilitate such evaluations.

STAGE 3: FORMAL APPROVAL AFTER DUE DILIGENCE INVESTIGATION

Following the due diligence process, the IC will be provided with a formal report from the manager. The IC will then unanimously approve or reject the proposal. Following formal approval from the IC, the manager will manage the process of issuing an unconditional offer to acquire the property through an SPV (if required).

STAGE 4: MANAGE DEVELOPMENT PROJECT UNDER AGREED GUIDELINES

The manager will then manage the development process to ensure the development is completed on time, on budget and in line with the investment proposal approved by the investment committee. The manager will meet monthly and continually review all aspects of the development, including specific program issues, design, construction, costs, financing and leasing.

STAGE 5: MANAGE THE SALE OF DEVELOPMENT PROJECTS

The manager will appoint marketing agents or real estate brokers to sell the units in the development project. Brokerage fees should be agreed on before construction and included in the feasibility study. The manager will ensure the sale transactions are completed in a timely and diligent manner by the settlement agents involved.

Regulations and compliance

A real estate development fund is classified as a managed investment scheme (MIS). It enables investors to contribute money that is pooled for investment to produce a financial benefit as defined by section 9 of the *Corporations Act 2001* (Cth). An MIS can be either registered or unregistered. Regardless, all MISs must be operated by a manager with an Australian financial services licence, authorising it to run the scheme.

Registered MIS

An MIS must be registered with ASIC and have 20 or more parties. The scheme is promoted by a party that is in the business of promoting MISs.

Should a scheme be required to be registered, the following requirements must be addressed:

- A Responsible Entity (manager) must be appointed (rather than a trustee for an unregistered MIS).

- The manager must be an Australian public company holding an AFS licence.

- The manager must, as a minimum, have net tangible assets of $50 000 or 0.5 per cent of the value of the scheme's gross assets, up to $5 million if a custodian is appointed. Otherwise, $10 million is required.

- In some cases, custodians must be appointed.

- A constitution that meets the Corporations Act requirements must be lodged with ASIC.

■ A compliance plan must be established and lodged with ASIC, setting out the measures a manager will undertake in operating the scheme in compliance with the constitution.

■ A compliance committee must be created if the manager's board of directors does not consist of at least 50 per cent external directors.

Registered versus unregistered managed investment schemes

Table 5.1 shows the differences between registered and unregistered managed investment schemes.

Table 5.1: registered MIS vs unregistered MIS

	Registered MIS	Unregistered MIS
Product issuer	A Responsible Entity — must be a public company with a minimum of three directors	The trustee — must be a public company or a proprietary limited company
Members	Retail and wholesale investors	Typically, wholesale only (with certain exceptions)
Offer document	Product Disclosure Statement	Information memorandum
Establishment requirements	The scheme must have a constitution with a compliance plan, and lodge with ASIC for review before registration.	The scheme must have a constitution or trust deed. However, the scheme does not require a compliance plan or documents lodged with ASIC.
AFS licence requirements	Required to hold an AFS licence to operate a registered scheme, deal in a financial product and provide advice (with some exemptions)	Required to hold an AFS licence to deal in a financial product and provide advice
Financial requirements	Must meet solvency and cash needs requirement plus minimum net tangible asset requirement. Note: additional requirements are imposed if a custody service is provided	Must meet base-level financial requirements such as solvency and cash needs requirements

Governance	The scheme must have an external board of directors or a compliance committee of at least three members, requiring that a majority of committee members are external.	The scheme does not require an external board of directors of the compliance committee.
Reporting	• Lodge annual audited accounts with ASIC as a minimum • Compliance plan audited annually • Annual reporting to investors • Periodic statements to investors and continuous disclosure obligations	• No lodgement of accounts with ASIC • Fund accounts are not required to be audited • Fund manager determines investor reporting
Custody	• The responsible entity can hold scheme assets if it contains sufficient financial resources ($10 million) and meets custodial standards under ASIC policy. • Typically, an external custodian will be appointed.	• The manager can hold assets but may be required to have an AFS licence to provide custodial services. • Custodial standards must be met but a reduced financial resource requirement ($150 000). • Often a licensed external custodian is appointed. • There is no licensing exemption for custodians if financial products are held.

Fees and expenses

Following is a guide to the fees and costs that can be charged to the fund. Fees may vary depending on the scope of the manager's responsibilities and the type of MIS.

Fee table

Table 5.2 (overleaf) shows fees and expenses that may be charged to the fund and unitholders. The manager may accept lower fees or defer payment of fees for any period. If deferred, the fees accrue daily until paid.

Table 5.2: fee table summary

Type of fee or cost	Amount	How and when paid
Establishment costs: the costs that relate directly to the establishment of the fund.		The manager is entitled to recover all legal, tax advisory and other third-party costs incurred in establishing the fund.
Application fee: a fee for the initial and every subsequent issue of units to a unitholder.	Upfront — 4 per cent (including GST) of application money	The manager is entitled to a fee of up to 4 per cent of the value of funds raised from investors in the fund. This fee is paid in the form of application or brokerage fees. The application fee may be negotiable.
Management fee: the fee for operating the fund, including administration and management fees charged by the manager.	Management fee — 2 per cent	The manager will charge a base fee of 2 per cent of the aggregate of all invested capital. This fee is accrued and paid quarterly in arrears and payable from the fund's successful launch.
Project establishment fee: for the work involved in assessing and sourcing suitable projects for the fund.	Establishment fee — 2 per cent	The manager is entitled to receive a fee of up to 2 per cent of the total amount invested by the fund in each project.
Performance fee: applies to individual projects, where the return exceeds an internal rate of return (IRR) of 15 per cent on equity invested.	Performance fee — 30 per cent of excess return	Where the IRR of each project exceeds the 15 per cent target, the manager is entitled to a fee of 30 per cent of the excess return above this level.

Expense recovery: for expenses or disbursements incurred.		The manager is permitted under the constitution to recover fund-related expenses from the fund.
Transfer fee: charged for transferring units.	A fee of $220 (including GST) per transfer	The buyer's GST-inclusive transfer fee is payable to the manager directly.
Custody fee: annual fee paid to the custodian.	Greater of 0.02 per cent of gross assets or $20 000 for the first year of operation	Payable annually to the Custodian from the Fund.
Expenses: incurred by the manager for the proper performance of its duties in respect of the fund.	Up to 0.3 per cent per annum of the NAV of the fund (e.g. $30 per $10 000 of unit value)	Repayable to the manager as they are incurred on an ongoing basis by the fund. The manager will bear expenses above 0.3 per cent per annum.

SUMMARY

The development fund outlined here is only a guide, offering developers an overview of funding sources available in Australia at the time of writing. The final funding package will depend significantly on the type, scale and targeted outcomes of the planned development project. It will also depend on the developer's financial position or entity.

CONCLUSION

As reiterated many times, you cannot start a project without development funding. Only with comprehensive knowledge of how development funding works and what financial products are out there will you be able to make informed choices from among the various options at your disposal. There are many ways to fund a project, but you will be stuck without knowledge. So keep on improving your financial literacy.

Banks and lenders are continually changing their lending policies, which can also vary from state to state. These changes may pertain to local economic conditions or other factors such as the recent royal commission into the banks' prior operational methods. So it is well worth keeping up to speed with what is happening in the development funding area, or at least working with a credible finance broker. Naturally, it would be best to determine with confidence the best funding arrangement for your project. However, there is no harm in asking your broker whether they have considered any other funding options you picked up in this chapter.

CHAPTER 6

CREATING A PASSIVE INCOME REAL ESTATE PORTFOLIO

Many real estate investors have become extremely wealthy through property investment. Real and faster profits are made through real estate development. The key to unlocking real wealth is developing quality properties and retaining as much of your project product (assets) as you can in your long-term real estate portfolio. Holding these assets as investments enables you to acquire your real estate at the developer's wholesale cost. Holding the asset also increases the capital growth and defers the tax on the development profit until sold.

Instead of waiting for capital to grow over time, as with an established property, you watch your capital or equity grow through your efforts in developing real estate. The money made when the total development cost is deducted from the project's value on completion is called the *developer's profit margin* or *sweat equity*. The value of the equity built during the development will depend on several factors, such as the location, quality, planning and finishes of the project, and on managing the risks such as council approval and the builder's program.

One of the main reasons for building a real estate portfolio is to build up your wealth so you can enjoy financial independence and secure a passive income in your retirement. Creating a portfolio of investment properties is not a short-term project. In the short term, there may be little or no profit from the rent after expenses like mortgage, insurance, rates and maintenance are taken into account. However, in the long term, your real estate investment will show a profit when prices rise and your original mortgage is reduced, increasing your equity position and net worth.

Why have a real estate portfolio?

A real estate portfolio has many benefits for an astute investor seeking financial freedom. By creating a portfolio of properties, spreading capital across different locations with varying asset types can reap significant wealth. Placing money in a bank savings account may protect your money, but growth is likely to be modest compared with the potential profits in the real estate market. Once you have created a real estate portfolio, you can invest in protecting your capital and position your portfolio to earn sizable profits. Following are the main benefits of having a real estate portfolio of diversified real estate assets, with various properties in varied locations.

Passive income

Being financially free means having enough income to support your lifestyle. One way of achieving financial freedom is to create a passive income, which is a regular income produced with minimal effort needed to sustain it. One of the easiest and most popular ways of generating a passive income is through real estate investment. Provided you plan early, and stick to your plan, you can acquire a portfolio of properties that produce a steady income stream.

Leveraging through equity growth

Many intelligent people in Australia own two or more properties. They start building wealth by leveraging their initial investment property. They buy their own home, and after a few years of ownership, they discover their property's value has increased significantly. Instead of selling, they take out another loan from the bank against the increased equity in their home. With this cash, they place a deposit to buy another property. Later they find that both properties they own have continued to grow in value. They approach the bank again for a loan against their properties' equity and buy a third property. They repeat the process until they are ready to retire or continue to grow their portfolio as a hobby.

Direct control over your investment

Unlike investors in shares or managed funds, as a property investor you are the owner of the entire investment, so you have total control over it. When you invest in shares, you will generally need a broker to handle your trades for you, unless you have the know-how to manage the transactions yourself using one of the many software packages on the market. Also, the value of your shares relies on market conditions and other people's actions running that company you have no control over. In real estate, once you have settled property in your name, you own and control the asset directly so long as you can meet the mortgage payments. This means you can influence the property's value by adding value to it through renovations or rent increases.

Pride of ownership

As a tangible asset, real estate can always be viewed by you and others. Having a portfolio of properties should give you a sense of pride when driving by. It also gives you a sense of security as you watch your assets grow over time. Thinking about your portfolio over the long term, you may reflect on and plan the investment legacy you will pass on to your children. Depending on their ownership structure, you can pass your investments on to your children before or after you die. Your portfolio can also be used to raise capital for your children when they attend university or start their own business.

You can use your super

One way of building a real estate portfolio more quickly is to use your superannuation (pension) and the yearly contributions you make to a self-managed super fund (SMSF). This option has been around for some time. Recent changes in the Australian law regarding borrowing within your super fund mean it is now feasible to invest in property via an SMSF.

An SMSF is tax effective as the capital gains tax (CGT) on sale is just 10 per cent, and zero if you are over 60. I advise you to seek professional advice on SMSFs, as each investor has a different income and asset holding profile. In addition, you must abide by the rules, which are quite complex and prone to changes by the Australian Government.

Buying established real estate vs developing

We have looked at the qualitative aspects of real estate development. Now we will turn to how real estate development compares with buying established real estate. What are their respective advantages and disadvantages, and how will they benefit you financially? Of course, most people's decisions will depend predominantly on personal choice. Still, they can involve many other factors, such as their availability of time, their financial situation, timing and location.

Disadvantages of developing

Here are the main disadvantages of developing rather than buying established real estate.

Budget blowouts

When an established property is offered for sale, there is usually a bottom-line price that the seller is prepared to accept. It gives the investor a degree of comfort, knowing they are liable only for additional costs such as stamp duty and conveyancing fees. When building new, developers know the fixed price for the land, but they can find that the building's final cost has blown out beyond their set budget. There are always additional costs that a builder does not include in their price, such as landscaping, fencing, floor coverings, and curtains or blinds.

You cannot 'see' what you are purchasing

Unless you are building a replica of another development, most new buildings start with an idea or concept, which is eventually drawn into a set of working plans. To most people, reading and visualising the built form from architectural drawings is difficult. With an established building, you can walk through, get the feel of it.

Established gardens

Plants and trees take a long time to get established. In a new development, the gardens will look quite stark in the initial years unless you have a generous landscaping budget. If you purchase an investment property in an older suburb, the plants and trees have likely had several years to reach maturity.

Disputes with contractors

Inept builders are always making media headlines, making us aware of unscrupulous work practices and creating a degree of scepticism about the building industry. If disputes with builders delay the project's completion, your holding cost increases, which reduces your profit. These reports are enough to make many people shy away from tackling a new development project. Fortunately, not all builders are dishonest. Indeed, most have a well-established reputation for quality work and excellent client relationships.

Immediate return

When you invest in an established property, especially if it already has a tenant on a long lease, you can immediately assess the value of your return. On the other hand, when you develop a new property, your return can be evaluated only when the building or buildings have been completed and fully leased, and this can take many months.

Advantages of developing

Here are the main advantages of developing rather than buying established real estate.

Free equity

If you are a good negotiator, there is always an opportunity to purchase land below market value and negotiate a better price. On the other hand, if you are an experienced developer, you can save money by putting in your own sweat and undertaking some sections of the project yourself. Either way, you create 'free equity', which is the difference in value between the total cost of the land plus building and the market value after the building has been constructed.

Design to suit the market trends

Depending on the building's age, some investment properties may outlive market needs. Perhaps the rooms are too small, there is no family room, the kitchen is poorly designed, or the bathrooms look tired and dated. A new development is designed to suit current market trends.

Exciting

Watching your plans unfold as the architect presents the design and following the various construction stages can be exhilarating. The same cannot be said of purchasing an established building, though there is always the thought of renovating to suit the present market.

New design and materials

Architectural trends and building materials constantly adapt to meet consumer tastes and as our lifestyles continue to evolve. Most established buildings reflect the period in which they were built, but updating an older home through renovation can be costly.

Longer life span

All older buildings will show a certain amount of wear and tear and require ongoing maintenance. Before buying an older building, engage a building consultant to examine and uncover any structural defects, electrical faults, roof leaks and other issues. A younger building constructed to quality standards is less likely to require maintenance in the short term.

Tax benefits

A depreciation schedule calculates the proportion of the cost or the book value of a building that may be deducted annually as a legitimate expense. It is usually determined by the building's original price against the life of the building. With new buildings, the depreciation allowance can span 40 years or more. Established buildings may have exhausted their depreciation allowance.

Less upfront capital required

Most property transactions are financed, with a deposit or similar equity of around 20 to 30 per cent required. With a development, the deposit required when purchasing the land will be lower than that for an established property that includes both the land and buildings.

The decision

The financial decision on whether to invest in an established property or to develop your own will be a personal choice based on the factors listed. However, if you are prepared to go through the process of negotiating a land deal, working on the design with your architect, selecting and negotiating with a builder, and experiencing some significant stress during construction, there is nothing to beat the excitement and stimulation of creating a new development and reaping the financial benefits.

Ten steps to creating a real estate portfolio

The success you achieve as a real estate developer and investor depends on your planning and preparation before purchasing and developing the property. The key to success is implementing a calculated, action-oriented real estate development and investment strategy, as outlined in the following 10 steps.

Step 1: Review your financial position

Before making your first purchase, undertake a complete analysis of your financial position and your current and potential future income to establish how much you can afford to spend. List your assets, including income, and work out your expenses and liabilities, to determine how much cash you can afford to invest. If you need assistance, speak to your accountant.

Step 2: Set your goals

After establishing your financial position, set out your goals and how you mean to improve your financial situation. First articulate in writing your goals for the next five to 10 years. More important, you need to set a deadline for achieving these goals. Suppose your goal is to own four or more properties in 10 years' time. To cover a small deposit and acquisition costs, you may need around $50 000 in savings or accessible equity to purchase and develop your first property. That means you need to save around $30 000 to $50 000 each year, or your current real estate portfolio needs to grow in value by that amount. After working out your financial goals, you can calculate how to achieve them.

Step 3: Study real estate development

Suppose you see real estate development as a way of achieving your financial goals in a shorter time. First it is essential to have a good understanding of the development industry. Furthermore, to succeed as a real estate developer, you need to recognise potentially lucrative opportunities and be able to predict market trends. Following is a broad outline of how to become a real estate developer.

1. **Educate yourself.** Learn all you can about real estate development. And undertake a course in finance, business management, construction or building design.

2. **Gain experience.** Work for an employer in the real estate business, or find a job that allows you to deal with buying, developing or selling property.

3. **Understand finance.** Read as much as you can on finance so you fully understand how borrowed money works in development and in building a real estate investment portfolio.

4. **Understand building construction.** Visit construction sites or work with a building company so you develop a better understanding of how a building is constructed.

5. **Establish a company.** As real estate development carries financial risks, it is wise to establish a business entity that protects you from liability.

6. **Research.** Research market trends and learn how to project rises and falls in real estate prices so you buy when prices are low and sell when prices are high.

7. **Understand commercial real estate.** It is also wise to gain an understanding of commercial real estate, as it deals with larger cash values and is where successful real estate developers make their money.

Step 4: Set out a 10-year strategy plan

If you want to build a lucrative real estate portfolio, it is essential to make sure your actions match your goals, and having a 10-year strategy plan will help you achieve them. For example, you may want to own three investment properties within five years, or you may want to retire on your real estate portfolio in 10 years. You need to know the necessary steps to turn these goals into reality. It helps to write down your plan, including the milestones or short-term goals you need to achieve as part of your 10-year plan. Your 10-year plan should be a flexible working document, like a business plan. It should be a document that can be changed and updated to reflect your lifestyle and changes in your financial situation.

Step 5: Start small, learn and grow

Developing real estate is not an overnight get-rich-quick scheme. Savvy developers and investors minimise risk by starting with a small project and learning from it before venturing into a larger one. Great things almost always start small, so you must learn to walk before you can run. Before starting with your first project, consider the following aspects:

- **Understand your attitude to risk.** Having a good understanding of your risk profile is a must. The level of risk you are comfortable with will depend on your experience and confidence in the project you intend to undertake.

- **Research and ask.** To build confidence, take time to research and talk to people in the industry. The more information and knowledge you have, the more comfortable you will feel making decisions.

- **Create investment criteria.** Once you have a good idea of what type and size of project suits your risk profile and the information you have gathered, you can set out your investment criteria.

- **Research your finance options.** Discuss your objectives, investment strategies and risk profile with your bank or a finance specialist to find an appropriate finance product and process for your purchase.

- **Form a partnership.** Starting your first project can be daunting. It is therefore wise in the first instance to find a mentor or even a partner with development experience.

Step 6: Start with a first project

The next step is to commit, but before you do so, here are some further items to consider and action:

- **Select the location.** Do your research on the suburbs of interest. Physically go out and see what the market is doing in the area where you are looking to buy, and check the area's demographics.

- **Choose the proper ownership structure.** It may be held in your name, or as tenants-in-common, or in the name of a company. Choose ahead of time, so when it comes to purchasing, you know which structure best suits your situation now and into the future.

- **Have your finance in place.** As the project will be a development, you need to ensure that you have funding for both the land and the construction.

- **Undertake due diligence.** When sourcing a property to develop, pay attention to the title documents and town planning regulations, where you will find any restrictions on the property and its zoning.

- **Pay the right price.** Market research and checking comparable properties are essential to ensure you buy at a sensible price. Remember the first axiom of real estate development: you make more money when you buy the land than when you sell.

- **Timing is important.** But don't rush into buying a property. Don't be pressured by agents who insist you will be missing out if you don't buy now. Instead, spend time getting to know your market and the area. However, once you have found a suitable property in the right location, move fast. The quicker you can turn a property around, the better. The sooner it is finished, the sooner you can realise a return on your investment.

- **Consider the rental yield and return.** If you intend to develop and rent, knowing the rental yield is essential; therefore, analyse the return on investment if you find you must sell due to unforeseen circumstances.

Step 7: Find a good development team

Your development's success depends on having a great development team who can provide you with correct and professional advice:

- **Select the right consultants.** Real estate covers a broad and diversified range of buildings and land, and this has created specialist consultants who operate in specified areas.

- **Decide on the number of consultants.** The number of consultants required will depend on the type and scale of the project.

- **Negotiate the consulting fees.** Most professional consultants have a standard guide for fees set out by their association or institute. These fees are negotiable, however, depending on the level of service.

- **Ensure your consultants have professional indemnity insurance.** Mistakes can happen on any building project, so the consultants you employ must have current professional indemnity insurance in place.

- **Build a team of professional advisers.** You should feel comfortable with your team of advisers. The consultants are serving you to the best of their ability. You can call on them anytime when a problem arises.

Step 8: Find the right marketing agent

If your strategy is to sell part of your development to reduce the debt on the units you will be holding in your portfolio, one of the first tasks will be finding the right project marketing real estate agent who can sell off-plan. The following are a few essential factors to consider before you choose the agent to sell your project:

- **Professional experience in your market.** Most real estate agents focus on a specific neighbourhood or region. Selecting an estate agent who knows your suburb can make a world of difference.

- **Credentials and references.** When checking the real estate agent's credentials, you need to find out how long they have been working in the field and their sale success rate in project marketing; references are essential.

- **Comparative market analysis.** Another factor to research is the history of sale prices for comparable units in your area. Again, good real estate agents will be able to provide you with a comparative market analysis.

- **A solid marketing strategy.** You need to determine how the agent intends to market your project. There are many ways to advertise real estate in today's multimedia market. You do not want to choose an agent who limits your buyer pool with a narrow approach.

- **Negotiation skills.** One way to get a sense of how a real estate agent will handle negotiation is to observe how well prepared they are in your first meeting with them. First, look at their marketing material by asking them for print-based and online marketing samples.

- **Agent fees, commission, fees and contracts.** Commission, fees and contracts should be discussed early with any potential real estate agent. It is essential to remember that the lowest commission does not necessarily provide the best and most efficient service from an agent.

Step 9: Find a good property manager

Managing a property is not as simple as it sounds. If you consider self-managing your investment property, there are some things to think through. Do you have the time to devote to it? There is a lot involved in the process, such as finding suitable and reliable tenants, collecting rent, holding property inspections and being on call at any time for emergencies and repairs. Selecting the right property manager for your investment is an important task. Before contracting a property manager, be sure to do the following:

- **Obtain referrals**. Talk to real estate agents and other property owners in your area, and ask them which property managers they use or have used.

- **Do an online search**. Before spending too much time interviewing a property manager, check out their company's reviews on sites like Facebook.

- **Check their advertisements.** Look at some of the property manager's current rental advertisements to see if they are professional, compelling and free of discriminatory statements.

- **Check out properties they manage.** Review the properties that a property manager manages and check if they appear to be clean and well maintained.

- **Interview several managers**. Like anyone you employ, you should interview several property managers or management companies to find the one you are most comfortable with looking after your property.

- **Check their licence**. All Australian states and territories stipulate that a property manager have a real estate broker's licence or a property management licence.

- **Examine their management agreement**. A typical property management agreement will clearly define the property manager's roles, responsibilities and landlord obligations.

Step 10: Enjoy the process and stay focused

Starting a real estate development portfolio is an exciting experience. However, more thought and creativity are needed than buying an established property. The great thing about this strategy is that your profit margin is your manufactured equity, which means that should the value drop in the short term, you have a buffer. It is also a great way to increase your portfolio faster. Here are a few areas to think about when building your portfolio.

Stay focused

Ensure you stay focused on the goals you have set out. Be clear about what you want to achieve. Set target dates for the achievement of specific goals. Identify the milestones you need to reach to achieve your ultimate goal.

Take a long-term view and manage your finances

Remember that real estate is a long-term investment. The longer you can afford to commit to it, the better. As you build up more equity, you can start to consider your next development project.

Budget for emergencies

Unlike shares or managed funds, you cannot just sell part of your investment property if you need money in an emergency. So you need to budget for a buffer against bad times and possible threats to your livelihood.

Don't give up

In building your portfolio you will undoubtedly encounter challenges along the way, but don't give up. Imagine in 10 years' time, if you continue to buy suitable properties to develop, you could be sitting back, feeling happy and secure.

Types of real estate investments

Before building a real estate portfolio, it is essential to analyse the type of real estate you plan on investing in. First ask yourself which real estate type will best suit your investment strategy. Each has a different set of drivers influencing its performance.

In broad terms, real estate investment can be broken down into two main categories, namely residential and commercial. One of the significant differences between residential and commercial properties is how they are appraised or valued. With residential, the value is generally based on a sales comparison with similar properties or market approaches. In contrast, with commercial properties, the value is based on their income; they are not compared to other similar commercial properties. With the latter, no matter how expensive it is to build or how shabby the building looks, the commercial real estate's value derives from its actual income.

Commercial real estate investment will suit investors who are willing to take more significant risks for bigger returns and who appreciate a hassle-free long-term tenant. On the other hand, a residential investment might deliver lower returns and more demanding clients, but it is safer. Before buying commercial or residential real estate, consider the advantages and disadvantages of each.

Residential real estate

Residential properties can be defined as houses, villas, townhouses, apartments or holiday homes rented out to third parties. Length of tenancy is based on the rental or lease agreement.

Advantages

The main advantages of investing in residential real estate are as follows.

VACANCY

Residential real estate is less likely to stay untenanted for long periods. Residential leases are shorter than commercial ones, but are generally easier to rent due to the larger rental market.

MORE SIGNIFICANT RENTAL MARKET

With the high turnover in housing, you can usually count on a significant pool of potential tenants, regardless of the economy. Most people like to live and rent in areas close to their friends, families, work or educational institution.

EASE OF FINANCE

Financing residential real estate is usually fairly straightforward. A smaller deposit is needed, which can be crucial, especially for your first investment property. Depending on your credit rating and income, you can sometimes borrow 100 per cent of the purchase price. Interest rates on residential mortgages also tend to be lower.

CONSISTENT CASH FLOW

Investing in rental properties also guarantees available cash flow, given that they are easier to rent. When a tenant leaves, there are always new tenants coming in. Most residential tenants pay their rent weekly or fortnightly.

EASE OF SELLING

If needed, it is easier to sell houses than commercial buildings because buyers in the housing market are more numerous than commercial buyers, who are mainly investors.

LESS COMPLICATED LEASES

Rental leases are relatively standard, short and easy to understand. Landlords and tenants should not have difficulty understanding these documents.

CAPITAL APPRECIATION

Historically, residential properties tend to double in value every seven to 10 years, whereas the commercial real estate market can be less predictable.

LAND VALUE RATIO

Residential properties have a higher land-to-building ratio than commercial properties. They usually offer higher capital growth because as land values go up, buildings depreciate.

Disadvantages

The main disadvantages of investing in residential real estate are as follows.

LOWER RETURN

Due to the competitive market, residential properties typically deliver a lower yield when compared with commercial properties, which, depending on their location, may enjoy a monopoly, especially if demand increases.

OUTGOINGS AND MAINTENANCE

With a residential property, all maintenance costs and repairs are the landlord's responsibility. An older property may require more repairs and maintenance, which will affect the returns from the property.

MANAGEMENT

Residential properties usually require much hands-on management. Landlords can receive a call or complaint at any time, day or night, so it is best to employ a property manager who specialises in residential leasing—it is certainly worth the money spent.

LATE PAYMENTS

Some residential tenants fail to pay their rent on time. If you are on a tight budget, this can affect your repayments to the bank.

BAD TENANTS

If tenants are not carefully screened, you could end up with a bad tenant who, when given notice for non-payment of rent, will refuse to leave, making the eviction process difficult.

Commercial real estate

Commercial real estate is used by businesses such as retail outlets, offices or industry. Generally, commercial investment involves stricter lending conditions and a more substantial deposit than residential real estate.

Advantages

The main advantages of investing in commercial real estate are as follows.

OUTGOINGS

Commercial tenants are generally responsible for outgoings such as rates and taxes, insurance, water rates, land taxes and other third-party costs, whereas in residential real estate these are the responsibility of the landlord.

GREATER CARE

Commercial tenants are likely to take better care of the property as its look and condition are often essential to the success of their business. Indeed, some tenants will make improvements that will enhance your property.

LONGER LEASES

Commercial leases, which could be for anything from three to 20 years, tend to be much longer than residential rental agreements and are often secured by bank guarantees. This translates into guaranteed long-term cash flow. Five-year leases with built-in rent escalations and options to renew are not universal but are certainly quite common.

FLEXIBLE LEASE AGREEMENTS

Another advantage of commercial leases is that you can add clauses and conditions, when necessary, which can benefit both you and the tenant. Commercial leases are also robust when it comes to leasing payments. Unpaid rents can result in penalties and ultimately eviction.

BAD TENANTS

Both residential and commercial real estate owners can experience bad tenants, although in the latter the landlord has a stronger hand. If it should reach the eviction stage, the landlord has the right to remove the tenant by performing specific actions, such as changing locks and seizing the premises per the lease document.

ESCALATION AND RENT REVIEWS

In most commercial leases, rent is escalated annually by the CPI or by 4 per cent, whichever is higher, and reviews every three to five years keep it in line with current rental values in the area.

HIGHER RETURNS

The return on invested capital on commercial properties ranges between 7 and 10 per cent net after all costs. Residential returns are 5 per cent or less, and investors must pay all outgoings and other expenses.

LESS MANAGEMENT

Hands-on management is less onerous than with residential properties. Most commercial leases are written to include the tenant's responsibility for interior repairs, maintenance, glass breakage and the like.

TENANT FIT-OUT

Depending on the type of space, such as retail and higher-grade offices, the tenant generally will fit out the area to suit their requirements. Some landlords may give a one-off fit-out allowance or a period of free rent to attract a tenant.

CREATING VALUE

A commercial property's value is based on its income stream, so an investor can create value by enhancing that income stream. This means the investor does not rely on general market appreciation to increase the property's value but can take steps to improve its value by renovation or redevelopment.

Disadvantages

The main disadvantages of investing in commercial real estate are as follows.

STRICT LENDING CRITERIA

Financing commercial real estate can be more complicated than residential, so lenders apply more stringent borrowing criteria for commercial properties. Most banks are willing to lend around 75 per cent or more for residential real estate, whereas commercial real estate starts at 60 per cent or less.

MORE EXTENDED VACANCY PERIODS

Commercial properties can be vacant for long periods, particularly in tough economic times. Commercial leases typically require that a tenant exercise an option to renew anything from six to 12 months before the lease expires so the landlord has ample time to look for a new tenant.

LONGER LEAD TIMES

The process of leasing commercial space can take longer compared with residential. After a tenant is found and basic terms are agreed upon, it is usually necessary for the landlord's and tenant's lawyers to negotiate the lease's terms and conditions. The cost and complexity can vary depending on whether you are dealing with a local or national tenant.

COMPLEX LEASE AGREEMENTS

Usually, commercial lease documents are long, with many more clauses than a standard residential contract, which will be provided by a residential property manager or bought online.

ECONOMIC DOWNTURN

As most commercial tenants run their premises for business purposes, a drop in the economy can result in loss of income and eventually even loss of the business. When this occurs they vacate or are forced to go, leaving the onus on you to find new tenants. So commercial vacancies can cost an investor a lot more than residential.

KNOWLEDGE AND CASH RESERVES

Investors in commercial real estate need greater experience and knowledge of the commercial real estate industry, plus cash reserves to sustain any extended vacancies.

■■■

Most real estate investors start investing in residential before stepping up into the commercial sector. Each has its strengths and weaknesses, and you should not necessarily conclude that one is a better investment vehicle than the other. Be sure to analyse and assess each opportunity according to your investment criteria, based on your current financial situation and personal goals.

Why develop and hold?

If you are seeking financial independence, I recommend that you endeavour to hold on to as many of the properties you develop as you can and create a significant asset portfolio. Whether you hold these real estate assets under your name, in a family trust, or in a self-managed super fund (SMSF) is entirely up to you and will depend on your financial circumstances. Following are additional benefits of real estate development.

Creation of free and faster equity

The time and effort you put into real estate development creates free or sweat equity. Your profit is additional equity when valued at completion. Depending on the project's scale, this equity can be created within a year or two. Purchasing an existing investment property could take five years or more to achieve the same result.

Tax deferment

The profit you make in a development project is taxed only when sold. If you hold the property as an investment under the same ownership entity, you are not liable for any tax on the profit. When valuing your real estate portfolio, this 'profit' is added to your equity position if the property is not sold. When applying for additional finance, this increased equity position puts you in a healthy financial situation.

Tax-free refinancing proceeds

An increase in free equity and capital appreciation allows you to take advantage of this equity build-up to refinance another development. If a property is refinanced for more than the existing debt, the proceeds are funds the investor can spend on another project. Also, since this money is obtained through refinancing, these funds are not currently taxable.

Security

Banks and mortgage lenders love real estate as security. It is real and they understand the value of this form of security against the money they lend to you. In addition, the bank's approval process is so entrenched that when presented with increased equity value in your real estate portfolio, additional security for a new purchase falls within their lending policies.

Develop-and-hold strategy

Develop and hold is a powerful wealth creation strategy. The development profit that should be made when you sell plus your initial equity injection should place your project in a favourable cash flow position. But, of course, the outcome depends on the scale, type of project and end valuation. With most development projects such as residential duplex, townhouses and apartments with several units, there is always the opportunity to sell some units to reduce debt and place the holding investment units in a favourable cash position.

Depending on the risk profile of development and location, developers generally target at least a 20 per cent return on a residential project and a minimum of 25 per cent on commercial development. Here is a hypothetical example.

You develop a duplex of two villa units. The total development cost is $800000, including land at $300000. The bank will lend you 70 per cent of the development cost, which is $560000, requiring you to inject $240000 of your cash as equity. The two units' market value is $960000, including a 20 per cent development profit of $160000. With the end value being $960000 and a new equity position at completion of $400000 ($240000 cash equity plus $160000 profit), most traditional banks will lend against this as the LVR is 58 per cent loan and 42 per cent equity. If the units are rented out at, say, $400 per week, this will produce an annual income of $41600 ($400 × 2 × 52), which after allowing for outgoings, management and vacancy periods of 22 per cent ($9152) will provide a net annual income of $32448. If you secure a long-term interest-only loan of $560000 at 5 per cent, then your repayments will be $28000 pa. This exercise (as shown in table 6.1) places your investment in a favourable cash flow position of $4448 ($32448 less $28000).

Table 6.1: sample of a develop-and-hold analysis

Item	Cost ($)
Land purchase (including stamp duty and conveyancing)	300000
Development cost (construction, professional fees etc.)	500000
Total development cost	800000
End value at completion	960000
Development profit on TDC 20%	160000
Initial cash equity required for development 20% on TDC	240000
Total equity position at completion	400000
Gross annual rental	41600
Less outgoings, management and vacancies (22%)	9152
Net rental income	32448
Interest only loan @ 5% $560000 ($800000 – $240000)	28000
Positive cash flow	4448

Bear in mind that in this example when you complete your development, the $160000 profit is not taxed until you sell the units in the future. If you intend to hold the units 'forever', in theory you can defer your taxes for as long as you like. Also, if you ever decide you need to access that equity for another property purchase, you can simply refinance the property to tap into that equity without incurring any tax liability. This is far more intelligent than selling your development, paying 30 per cent or more in taxes.

It should be noted, however, that some banks might consider the above investment a higher risk to them when it is under one ownership. This is because if anything happened to you, they would have to sell both units together instead of individually. Therefore, they would consider this a 'one-line' investment and discount the lending by 20 per cent.

Develop-and-hold analysis

Before adopting the develop-and-hold investment concept, it is important to analyse your various options, such as holding the total project as a long-term investment or selling part and keeping the balance. By comparing the options, you will find which option best suits your investment strategy and personal financial circumstances. To better understand the various proposals, the following case study steps us through the numbers.

CASE STUDY 1:
COMPARING DEVELOPMENT OPTIONS AT THE FEASIBILITY STAGE

Four years ago, my co-directors and I purchased two older suburban homes. These homes fell under the government's Urban Infill Development policy. The two sites were recently zoned R30, which allowed four units per site. After analysing the development economics, it made sense to amalgamate the two properties, create a central driveway and create eight villa units. During our feasibility stage, we looked at three options: (1) develop and sell (table 6.2), (2) develop and rent (table 6.3, overleaf), and (3) develop, sell 50 per cent and rent 50 per cent of the units (table 6.4, overleaf).

Option 1: Develop and sell

Table 6.2: sample of develop-and-sell analysis

Development cost ($)		Projected sales ($)	
Total cost of land purchased	838 400	Sale of 8 villas @ $450 000 each	3 600 000
Total construction cost	1 585 500	Less GST	327 273
Total consultant fees	79 275	Less sales commission	90 000
Total authority fees	54 764		
Total management fees	95 482		
Total marketing, legal fees	63 655		

(continued)

Development cost ($)		Projected sales ($)	
Total finance cost	9000		
Total interest cost (loan $1.83 m)	62707		
Development Cost incl. GST	2788782		
Less GST	171590	Net sales income	3182727
Total development cost (TDC)	2617192	Net profit	565535
Return on TDC	22%		
Return on equity	139%		
The issue with this option is that after paying company tax, our cash position was $395875 and with no holding assets, as shown with other options outlined in table 6.3.			

Option 2: Develop and rent

Table 6.3: sample of develop-and-rent analysis

Investment cost ($)		Projected rent ($)	
Total Development Cost	2617192	Value of villas at completion	3600000
Property management 5.5%	9838	Annual rent 8 villas @ $430 pw	178880
Outgoings (allow 12%)	21466		
Vacancy rate (allow 5%)	8944		
Interest on loan (allow 7% fixed)	128100	Total annual income	178880
Total operating cost	168348	Net income	10532
Loan at completion	1830000		
Equity position	1770000		
Rental return on TDC	7%		
Note: The net rental income is marginal with this option. Any movement on interest rates or unforeseen circumstances would require additional cash injection.			

Option 3: Develop, sell 50 per cent and rent 50 per cent

Table 6.4: sample of develop, sell and rent analysis

Development cost ($)		Projected sales ($)	
Development cost incl. GST	2788782	Sale of 4 villas @ $450000 each	1800000
Less GST	171590	Less GST	163620
Total development cost	2617192	Less commission	45000
Loan after sales	238620		1591380
Investment cost ($)		**Projected rent ($)**	
Property management (5.5%)	4919	Annual rent villas @ $430 pw	89440
Outgoings (allow 12%)	10733		
Vacancy rate (allow 5%)	4472		
Interest on loan (allow 5% fixed)	11931	Total annual income	89440
Total operating cost	32055	Net income	57385
Value of existing 4 villas	1800000		
Equity position	1561380		

Note: This option's net rental income is better, especially with lower debt. We could borrow additional funds to purchase another development property with a strong equity position.

From this analysis we can draw the following conclusions:

1. Option 1 is not viable after the tax profit has been paid. The returns are too low for the risk involved.

2. Option 2 would have to inject more funds should interest rates increase or unforeseen circumstances occur.

3. Option 3 looks like the better solution as we could keep at least 50 per cent of the units without too much exposure. Even with the vacancy factor, the monthly shortfall is more manageable.

Long-term investment analysis

Unfortunately, rather than adopting a 'develop and hold' strategy, we sold all eight units. If we had followed option 3, we would have enjoyed a comfortable outcome. Based on the following data, the long-term analysis is shown in table 6.5.

Value of the balance of units = $1 800 000

Outstanding loan = $1 830 000 less $1 591 380 = $238 620

Equity position = $1 800 000 less $238 620 = $1 561 380

Assume interest only at 7 per cent

Repayments = $72 863

Assume growth of 2.5 per cent per annum

Reduce loan from surplus income after tax

From table 6.5, the following list of assumptions can be made. It should be noted that these are only assumptions and will vary based on research undertaken. Such a spreadsheet should be reviewed annually.

Table 6.5: spreadsheet of long-term investment

Year	Value ($)	Loan ($)	Equity ($)	Loan ($)	Net rent ($)	Rent surplus ($)	Net after tax ($)
1	1 800 000	238 620	1 561 380	16 703.40	57 385	40 682	28 477
2	1 845 000	210 143	1 634 857	14 710.00	58 820	44 110	30 877
3	1 891 125	179 266	1 711 859	12 548.63	60 290	47 741	33 419
4	1 938 403	145 847	1 792 556	10 209.30	61 797	51 588	36 112
5	1 986 863	109 735	1 877 128	7 681.48	63 342	55 661	38 963
6	2 036 535	70 773	1 965 762	4 954.10	64 926	59 972	41 980
7	2 087 448	28 793	2 058 656	2 015.49	66 549	64 534	45 173
8	2 139 634	–	2 139 634	–	68 213	68 213	47 749
9	2 193 125	–	2 193 125	–	69 918	69 918	48 943
10	2 247 953	–	2 247 953	–	71 666	71 666	50 166

■ In year eight, the loan would have been paid off, providing a passive income from the existing villas.

■ After year two, there is enough equity to pursue another development project, if the opportunity arises.

Creating a portfolio faster

These examples illustrate how real estate development can create a positive cash flow investment if done correctly. The profits made through this process increase an investor's equity position faster than buying existing or completed buildings. An additional tool can improve this equity more quickly through leveraging. By accessing this equity and using leverage, you can springboard into another real estate development and start to create a valuable real estate portfolio. And the process can be repeated several times, thereby increasing your wealth exponentially. Here is an example of how leveraging could work for you.

A develop-and-hold strategy

Your goal is to develop a duplex project every second year for 10 years. At the completion of each development, you sell one unit and retain the other. You use the equity gained from the sale plus your initial equity to develop the next project.

Assumptions

The following assumptions are used in this exercise:

Total development cost (TDC) = $800 000 ($400 000 each half)

Equity required for development = 30 per cent of TDC

Construction debt = 70 per cent of TDC

Targeted profit margin on TDC = 20 per cent

Capital growth on portfolio each year = 3.3 per cent (CPI)

Assume interest-only financing = 5 per cent

Leveraging on initial equity of $240000

Using these assumptions and financing the development with equity and debt to develop a duplex project every second year over 10 years (meaning five small projects), the strategy for each project is to sell one of your units and retain the other. The total development cost (TDC) is $800000 (2 × $400000) with 30 per cent equity of $240000 and construction debt of $560000. The targeted profit margin is 20 per cent, showing the 'as complete value' of $960000, or $480000 per unit.

The exercise assumes a modest 3.3 per cent per annum, well below the average long-term growth rate of 5 per cent shown historically in most Australian capital city markets. In year one, you had two units worth $960000, of which one is sold for $424320 net ($480000 less GST and sales commission of 2.5 per cent), leaving you with the other unit valued at $480000. The debt is also reduced by the sale, which now stands at $135680 ($560000 less $424320), leaving you with an equity position of $288640 ($480000 less $135680).

By the following year the first unit held in project 1 is now valued at $495840, reflecting 3.3 per cent growth, with the debt reduced to $125824 ($135680 less surplus income $9856). Project 2, a new duplex, is undertaken, this time with a TDC of $853671, 30 per cent equity at $256101, construction debt at $597570 and an end value of $1024405 with a 20 per cent profit margin. To secure the 30 per cent equity for this new project, the debt on project 1 is increased to $384997. This process is repeated several times over the next 10 years.

Figure 6.1 is a graph showing your equity position, starting with $240000 cash equity leveraging off the equity created without further capital injection. It shows that you could potentially make a $3.21 million real estate portfolio with $1.87 million debt, $1.34 million equity and a $17134 positive cash flow after 10 years.

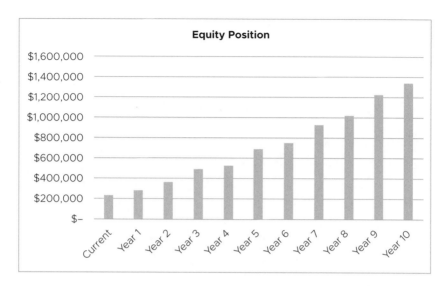

Figure 6.1: equity position starting with $240 000 equity

Leveraging initial equity of $240 000 plus top-up

The second exercise demonstrates that you could accelerate a portfolio by topping up with additional cash equity and using the previous project's equity. The top-up equity is ideal for a self-managed super fund (SMSF). If you use an SMSF, you must get professional advice on the structure and the entity that will hold the investment asset.

You use the increased equity to purchase another property for development, similar to the example above. But instead of waiting for the equity to increase every second year, you inject additional equity cash so you can develop every year. Finding additional equity every year can be tricky unless you use part of your superannuation input as fresh equity. Use this strategy with the initial equity of $240 000 and top-up equity of $41 320 to $53 575 (total $425 000) over nine years, and you could build a real estate portfolio valued at $6.4 million and an equity position of $2.9 million. After paying the annual interest, you still have a surplus cash flow of $48 364 per annum.

You can now see how leveraging, good cash flow real estate and proper planning can fast-track your financial future. Also, conservative figures have been used in these spreadsheets. Suppose history repeats itself, and property values continue to double every 10 years (as they have in

Melbourne for the past 30 years at the average annual growth rate of 7 per cent). In that case, your portfolio could grow even faster, as shown in figure 6.2.

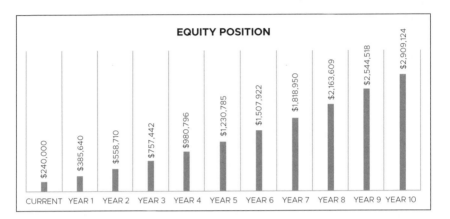

Figure 6.2: equity position starting with $240 000 equity plus top-up

These are theoretical examples using a duplex project as a model for developing, selling and holding. However, a lot will depend on your expertise, experience and cash position. Getting that initial deposit for that first development is usually the hardest. You need to save before getting started.

Benefiting from tax and gearing

Investment in real estate has long been a popular way for Australians to build wealth due to the potential tax advantages of well-managed real estate investment. One of its great benefits is leveraging then taking advantage of negative gearing, tax deductions and depreciation allowances, and hoping that the property's value will grow over time. However, while there are many potential tax benefits of real estate investment, there are also some pitfalls to avoid as an investor. Here we explore these tax benefits and their potential drawbacks.

Leveraging

Leveraging, also known as *gearing*, means using debt to fund a property investment. No other type of investment allows you to leverage borrowings as efficiently as real estate. For example, some lenders will give you a loan with only a 10 per cent deposit. If you take out a loan to purchase an investment property, you can offset interest on the loan and most real estate expenses against rental income for tax purposes. Provided your property is available for rent, the interest charged on the money you have borrowed for the property is tax-deductible. It also includes cash used to purchase the property, undertake repairs and improvements, or deal with tenant-related issues.

The type of security put up for the loan does not affect the interest's deductibility. For example, if your home secures your investment property loan, it does not change the tax deduction available on the interest. However, the tax deduction is available only to the extent that the borrowed monies are used for income-producing purposes such as rent. If the funds were applied for both private and income-producing purposes, then apportionment of the interest would be necessary to determine the tax-deductible portion. For example, if a loan is drawn down to purchase a home and a rental property, only the interest attributable to the rental property is tax-deductible. Similarly, suppose a loan was taken out to buy a single property used partly for rental and partly for private purposes. In that case, only the rental portion's interest will be deductible.

In most circumstances, people would purchase their own home first. Then, when the equity portion of their home has grown over the years, they will take out another loan to buy an investment property. If they are smart, they will maximise the loan on the investment property to take advantage of the tax deduction on the interest charged over the investment property.

Negative gearing

Negative gearing describes the situation when your investment's annual cost is more than your return (income) from that investment. You borrow money to acquire an investment. The interest and other costs you incur are more than the rental income you receive from the property (so you make a cash loss). This cash loss is offset against income from other sources, which reduces your taxable income—that is, the amount of tax you must pay (compared with the tax you would pay without the investment).

As already noted, the government allows you to deduct your property's costs from your gross income. Say your income is $75 000 a year but your property costs you $20 000 a year. Your taxable income will then be $55 000. Under these circumstances, there are tax advantages. Your investment is still making a loss, but you hope the loss will be more than made up for by the property's increasing value (capital gain). Unfortunately, you probably will not see a return on your investment until you sell the property, and only then if you get a much better price than you originally paid.

The term *negative gearing*, used extensively in Australia, is somewhat ambiguous. Most banks would not grant a loan of a greater amount than the value of the asset being acquired (plus other security). So it is unclear in what respect gearing itself could ever be negative. The only 'negative' item in negative gearing is net income, which could be negative without borrowing. Nevertheless, for decades, negative gearing has made it easier for investors to accumulate properties and watch them grow in value over time.

In Australia, negative gearing has been around since the 1930s, when the Commonwealth Parliament passed the *Income Tax Assessment Act*. The Act makes no mention of negative gearing, but it does establish the principle across all types of business and income-earning activity where the taxable income and the expenses earned in assessing that income are deductible from that income. When this principle is applied to real estate investment, the situation known as negative gearing occurs.

If you decide to negatively gear your investment property, it is vital that you do your research and carefully select the location. Invest in areas with good capital growth potential. Investment property with capital growth will more than make up for a short-term cash loss. Also, ensure that you are willing to accept wealth in the form of non-spendable capital gains (or future profits) in the short or medium term.

Tax deductions

Whether you are negatively geared or are enjoying a positive income stream from your property, you can still claim expenses relating to your rental property for the period it was rented. The following costs can be claimed:

- advertising for tenants, agent's fees and commission
- interest payments, loan fees and bank charges

- council rates and taxes and strata fees

- depreciation of items such as stove, fridge and furniture

- repairs, maintenance, pest control and gardening

- building and landlord's insurance

- body corporate fees and charges

- legal and accounting fees and expenses

- government land tax

- stationery and postage

- travel undertaken to inspect or maintain the property or collect the rent

- water charges

- capital works and improvements (refer to the next section).

This is not a complete list of what you can claim. I strongly recommend you get professional advice from a tax expert before submitting your return. Bear in mind that there are also expenses for which you are not able to claim deductions, including:

- acquisition and disposal costs of the property

- expenses you did not incur, such as electricity charges paid by your tenants

- expenses unrelated to the rental, such as those connected to your use of a holiday home

- borrowing expenses or interest on the portion of the loan you use for private purposes, such as buying a new car.

Depreciation

In addition to the tax deductions listed above, many real estate investors forget about claiming depreciation, especially in older properties. Tax depreciation (also known as *property depreciation*) recognises that the value of real estate assets declines over time. It is a legitimate deduction against assessable taxable income generated by a residential or commercial real estate investment. Different items in a rental property have different rates of depreciation based on the item's practical life. The Australian Taxation Office (ATO) provides a comprehensive guide on what it considers appropriate. These depreciation benefits can be calculated by engaging a qualified quantity surveyor to prepare a depreciation schedule upon your purchasing the property. Quantity surveyor's fees are 100 per cent tax-deductible.

The preparation of a Tax Depreciation Schedule should include a site inspection by the quantity surveyor. The report will put a value on each item of plant and equipment within the property that qualifies. It will include the construction cost when the building was built and a projection of the deductions claimable by the owner per financial year over 40 years.

The ATO recognises that the value of capital assets gradually declines over time as they approach the end of their practical life. For example, if you own an investment property (new or old, large or small), two depreciation areas apply: (a) plant and equipment, and (b) capital works on the building.

- **Plant and equipment.** The ATO has identified several removable assets that depreciate faster than the building itself. Depending on the size, age and condition of the property and fittings, as much as 35 per cent of the property's construction cost can consist of plant and equipment, and they will often form a sizable part of a depreciation claim.

- **Capital works.** The materials of any building depreciate over time. Therefore, this value loss is tax-deductible, including the structural elements and any permanent fixtures.

Claiming tax depreciation allowances on a real estate investment increases its value by giving investors a higher return on their investment. In addition, depreciation allowances, combined with additional negative gearing factors such as interest on a mortgage, repairs and maintenance, can help investors reduce their taxable income, pay less tax and improve cash flow.

Risks and pitfalls

While the potential for wealth accumulation from tax benefits through real estate investment is appealing, you must be aware of the risks involved. The risks to consider are: (a) if the value of the rental property declines, the potential tax implication is that your losses might exceed your profits from other sources, which will result in a net loss, and (b) if the property is vacant or tenants do not pay the rent, your financial situation will be affected. There is also a liquidity risk if you want to sell your investment property. If your property doesn't have a buyer when you are ready to sell it, you will have to hold on to the investment or potentially reduce the purchase price to attract a buyer, thus incurring further losses.

One of the most significant risks in real estate development is personal circumstances that could affect your real estate investments. The use of negative gearing as an investment strategy can be a factor. Your financial circumstances could change as a result of losing a job or a business or through ill health. Over the years, I have seen many real estate investors incur significant losses, especially during a recession. In my view, positive gearing is a better investment strategy than negative gearing. Positive gearing means that the rental income minus tax benefits and depreciation gives you positive cash flow.

Capital gains tax

If you decide to or are forced to sell one or more of your investment properties, it is essential to understand the implications of capital gains tax (CGT). CGT is the tax payable on the disposal of an asset acquired after 19 September 1985. You only have to pay tax on capital gains if they exceed your capital losses for the year.

There are adjustments for capital gains—for example, depreciation you have claimed, agent's commissions charged and improvements made to the property. If you have held a property for at least 12 months, any gain is discounted by 50 per cent for individual taxpayers or trusts, or 33.3 per cent for superannuation funds. Capital losses can be offset against capital gains. In a tax year, net capital losses may be carried forward indefinitely.

In real estate investments, CGT applies to the sale of any property held as an investment, including houses, apartments, holiday homes, retail shops, offices, factories and land. However, your principal place of residence is exempt from CGT.

The CGT calculation is based on the sale price minus your expenses:

selling price – cost base = capital gain/loss

The cost base is the total sum of the original purchase price, plus any incidentals, ownership and title costs minus any government grants and depreciable items.

cost base = purchase price + incidentals + ownership cost + improvements – depreciation claimed

where:

- *incidentals* include stamp duty, legal fees, agent fees, and advertising and marketing fees

- *ownership costs* include rates, land tax, maintenance and interest on the loan

- *improvements* include replacing kitchens or bathrooms, or any other improvements you have made on the property

- *depreciation claimed* is the amount claimed annually during the ownership of the asset being leased. This amount is adjusted by any depreciation that has not been previously claimed.

Once you have worked out the capital gain, the figure is then adjusted according to several variables, including:

- any percentage of time when the property was rented out

- if the property was held for longer than 12 months (in which case a 50 per cent discount applies).

If you invest in real estate and create a real estate portfolio, you should be taking advantage of the ATO's tax incentives. Real estate investment has some unique tax benefits over other forms of investment. Taking advantage of the tax offerings to minimise your tax can be a great way to maximise the return on your investment.

Please note that the tax notes and information presented here are only a guide. I highly recommend that you consult a professional accountant on matters referred to in this section.

Mistakes to avoid when building a portfolio

Before rushing out to start your real estate portfolio, you should understand potential mistakes you could make as a new developer investor. Real estate investment should be about increasing your wealth and securing your financial future. Listed below are some of the common mistakes made by new real estate developers and investors.

Mistake #1: not purchasing the right property

This is the most common mistake made by novice developers and investors. When you look at a potential property, you need to view it as a developer with the intent of making a profit and as a long-term rental property. An excellent investment property will be in a good location with transport facilities and social infrastructure such as schools and retail precincts. The property should also have good potential capital growth in the long term.

Mistake #2: not doing your research

By buying a property without doing your research you risk financial disaster. Do not fall into the trap of believing that 'build it, and they will come'. First, you need to look at the local buying and rental markets. Is the buying market made up mainly of owner-occupiers or of investors? Find out who is renting property, how much they are paying for it and whether there is good demand. Next, study the demographic profile of people in the area. Is the area full of students and young professionals who might prefer a large apartment, or is it an area with growing families? Without looking into these facts and figures, you could buy a property of no interest to buyers or tenants.

Mistake #3: not buying at the right price

Developing and investing in property is about ensuring that the project is profitable from both a selling and a rental perspective. Buying at the right price is critical. Thoroughly research what current properties are selling for in the area, and you will soon become good at working out what a property is worth. Never buy in an area that is unfamiliar to you. The 'due diligence' clause in the sales contract allows you to check if the site is suitable for the development you intend to build. You will need to consider planning approvals, engineering and finances before going ahead. Also, ensure that the agent inserts a 'subject to finance' clause in the contract, as your lender will want to undertake a valuation of the property before they provide you with finance.

Mistake #4: not understanding the market dynamics

If you are developing a property, you must follow the market dynamics as a developer and investor. Targeting a market with an oversupply of a product will delay your progress and be less profitable. Reading about property and talking to experts will give you an understanding of the market and where your product would sit. Find out what changes may be happening in your suburb; the local council can often help with this. You will find much independent information from a source such as RP Data, which will provide information on average rents, real estate values, demographics and suburb reports.

Mistake #5: not doing your sums

Real estate development is about making a profit despite the risks. It is easy to make a mistake by underestimating or not allowing for a specific cost to develop the property. It will reduce your profit and manufactured equity, and therefore slow your portfolio's growth. You may have to raise more cash because of the shortfall. Work with industry experts who can provide you with a project's *actual* cost. Prepare a feasibility study and ask an expert to review it to check if you have omitted or underestimated any items. Also, allow a contingency in your feasibility study to cover any excluded cost items.

Mistake #6: not having any spare funds

It is essential to set aside an 'emergency fund' for your development project and investment portfolio. This will cover any extra expenses you have not taken into account. For example, if the property is leased, you may find some expensive repair work is needed. An intelligent way to build your emergency fund is to divert some of your rental profit each month into a separate account.

Mistake #7: believing you know everything

Believing you know everything, not taking advice, trying to do everything yourself, and thinking that in this way you are saving money and increasing your profits can be a huge mistake. It takes years to build up the knowledge and experience to guarantee development profits. Developing an investment property requires more work than you might think. New developers may be tempted to save money by doing everything themselves, but they are setting themselves an almost impossible task. Stretching yourself too thin leads to costly mistakes. So build a team of reliable experts to outsource the work to, so you can focus on the big picture of building your real estate portfolio. Professionals will often know how to save you money.

Mistake #8: rushing into decisions

Entering the real estate development investment market is exciting. It can be very lucrative, but making rash decisions without thinking them through can cost you a lot of money. Be informed and analyse your options before making important decisions. Take the time to research potential properties, get to know the local market and be sure to interview several professionals before appointing them.

Mistake #9: not having a strategy

If your development strategy is 'build and they will come', you are on your way to losing money. Before you commit to developing a property as an investment, you need to have both a short- and a long-term strategy. The short-term strategy will cover the development stage. Think about where you intend to develop, what type of build it will be and your contingency plans if something goes wrong. The long-term strategy will be around whether to develop and hold the property as an investment in your portfolio. Give thought to your long-term goals. Consider what portion of the development you will be selling and what you will be renting, and the tax implications of both.

Mistake #10: developing and investing from a distance

No matter how lucrative a property deal may be, do not be tempted to buy and develop a property a long distance away, in another state or even country, unless you're prepared to travel regularly to the site yourself. Undertaking a development without seeing day-to-day operations is a recipe for disaster. If you decide to buy and develop a property from a distance, make sure you have a reliable project manager or form a joint venture with a local partner you can trust. Also, find a competent property manager. Meeting them in person is also a must, regardless of where they are based.

Mistake #11: ignoring your competitors

Wherever you decide to undertake a development investment, to attract buyers and tenants you must know who your potential competition is. Ensure that your product is better in cost and quality than your competitors'. Do not overlook what other developers are doing in your area. Find out how much they are selling their completed properties for and what they offer in terms of space and finishes. Make a point of researching the advertisements for selling and renting properties in your project area. You can get some handy tips by studying the competition.

Mistake #12: failing to plan ahead

We have all heard about real estate developers and investors going broke and being forced to sell some or all their properties. The reasons can vary from being financially overextended or too highly leveraged, to losing their jobs or income sources due to a slowdown in the economy. These situations can occur at any time. The biggest mistake a developer and investor can make is failing to plan for them. With the proper preparation and risk mitigation strategies, you can protect your investments and ensure you keep moving forward, irrespective of what the market is doing. It is best not to leverage or gear your portfolio too high, and make sure your cash flow is positive even if you must pay more tax.

■■■

Without a doubt, real estate development can yield extremely lucrative rewards. Many novice developers and investors are attracted by stories of self-made millionaires who made their wealth through real estate development and investment. Less talked about are the many failed projects and losses by the less experienced. Things can go wrong—for example, the builder goes bankrupt halfway through construction, planning approval is denied, a loan is called in before it is due, or new regulations increase costs. With careful planning and an awareness of potential mistakes, such events can be prepared for.

CONCLUSION

Building a lucrative real estate portfolio is easier said than done. It requires discipline and a systematic approach. Most important, curb your emotions and stay focused on your goals, both the mini targets along the way and your long-term objectives. If you are a novice in real estate development and investing, be prepared to spend some time and money educating yourself in this field. This game is not purely about investing cash in a property, but also about improving your skills and knowledge in other areas.

Never be overconfident and believe you know everything. This can lead you to make the wrong decisions, which can result in business failure. Instead, surround yourself with intelligent people who are more competent than you, and build an experienced team who know the pitfalls of the development and investment arena.

Finally, knowledge is a never-ending resource for those who seek it. Real estate, and more specifically the real estate development industry, has many aspects to it. Studying them all to perfection could take many years. Nonetheless, successful developers understand that they should never stop educating themselves. So keep learning, because this can only help boost your investment portfolio and smooth your path to a wealthy retirement.

CHAPTER 7

SMART TECHNOLOGY APPLICATIONS

The world is constantly changing, the flood of innovation and accelerating pace of change creating a society in which those who cannot keep up are left behind. We are living longer, but our daily lives have become overloaded. Instant communication and gratification are taken for granted. Our mobile phones control our lives. At the same time, the speed of progress means everything quickly becomes obsolete.

No industry is immune to this pace of change. Any business that is not committed to keeping up with modern technological change will be left behind by its competitors. Someone will always come up with a leaner and meaner business model to disrupt an industry. And we can expect the momentum behind digital transformation to continue to increase. A tough economy will suit those who adapt to leaner, more efficient models. The real estate industry is no different. Real estate developments are starting to use new construction methods that are faster and more cost-efficient.

One of the more exciting developments in real estate investing is the emerging trends of PropTech (property technology), FinTech (finance technology) and ConTech (construction technology). All these technology trends impact real estate development. This chapter reviews the various technologies under each sector and how they can benefit and improve real estate development.

Adopting smart technology

Digital technology has become such an essential aspect of our lives that few businesses are likely to return willingly to more traditional methods. The primary benefits of technology are speed and efficiency. For example, much of the research that once required that developers spend much of their time on the road exploring locations or visiting properties is now carried out on one or several digital platforms. To gain a first impression of a site, the streetscape and the neighbourhood, they need only log on to Google Earth.

Work technology

Modern technology makes it possible to work from a virtual office and communicate directly with businesses and individuals worldwide. With flexible work hours, many tasks and responsibilities can be accomplished from home or while travelling. For example, an architect can have their drafting technicians working from home or contract a company overseas to provide digital perspectives of buildings they have designed. Building information modelling streamlines the design process as more information is shared between the contractor, the architect and other consultants. The integrated design process model allows the architect, contractor and developer to share information digitally to expedite the development process. Cloud services such as Dropbox allow the development team to access files from any location, giving consultants and others the ability to be completely mobile.

Construction technology

Logistics enabled by better and more mobile technology has transformed the construction industry. Information management systems allow a much more precise ordering and delivery schedule, which makes construction much more efficient. Information management facilitates that transition as we refocus development activity on urban places with premier storage and logistics facilities. We are now seeing a different approach to building with more factory construction and on-site assembly of buildings, dramatically lowering costs and shortening construction time. Nanotechnology in building materials and 3D printing concepts will significantly impact the construction of new buildings.

Marketing technology

Social media has had a profound impact on how properties and projects are marketed. Real estate agents and marketers use blogs, Facebook, Twitter, Instagram, YouTube, LinkedIn and rating sites to market and sell. Advertising on these platforms is also much faster and cheaper.

PropTech

Here we examine PropTech and its impact on real estate transformation as a business, beginning with a brief outline of its essential aspects. PropTech will play a significant role in transforming the real estate development industry.

What is PropTech?

Before COVID-19, PropTech was the buzzword. Still the real estate industry sat on the fence, waiting to see it being implemented. PropTech is now rapidly gaining momentum as it disrupts the traditional way business operates in the real estate industry. But what is PropTech and what is its effect on real estate? If you do not know the answers to these questions, you had better start learning or you will be left behind, and your real estate business will begin to decline.

PropTech is part of a broader digital transformation in the real estate industry that embraces both the technological and mental changes taking place in the business, in consumer attitudes, and in movements and transactions involving planning and construction. The term is also applied to start-ups offering technologically innovative products for the real estate industry. Several verticals have emerged within PropTech and can interact with FinTech for the finance industry and ConTech for the building industry. Figure 7.1 (overleaf) helps to illustrate the interaction between the three technologies in the real estate industry.

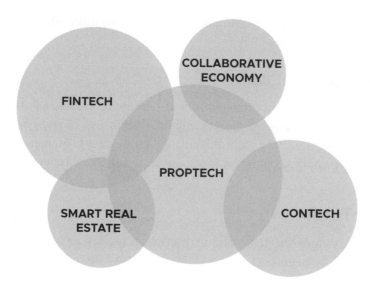

Figure 7.1: interaction between PropTech, FinTech and ConTech

Current trends in PropTech

Following are some examples of PropTech that industry experts currently use.

Big data

Big data is used to assist real estate parties to make informed decisions. It provides information such as the property's history, current value, neighbourhood profiles, mortgage payments and estimated forecast of future valuations.

Blockchain

Blockchain has gained significant momentum. This software is starting to disrupt traditional methods of financial transactions in the real estate industry. This technology is described in some detail later.

Drone technology

Drones are an excellent way of viewing a large property. They allow a neighbourhood tour to be conducted remotely. This innovation assists real estate agents in selling large estates by providing valuable information and different views of the property for the buyers. A drone tour can educate a potential buyer on an area's geographical and cultural traits.

Geolocation

Geolocation technology can convert maps into full-blown sets of critical data. It allows developers to better assess the location and its surroundings, and provides vital marketing information for a development.

Internet of Things (IoT)

IoT refers to the network of physical objects, such as home appliances and other computerised devices and sensors, that are connected to each other and to the cloud. This integrated network is constantly uploading and downloading information. In the future, IoT will offer more comprehensive resources for a homeowner to utilise, such as informing them of an appliance's maintenance history.

Sustainability and greentech

Climate change and sustainable living are not foreign concepts in the real estate sector. Increasingly, responding to consumer demand, architects, planners and builders are working to include technology that makes a home more energy-efficient and sustainable.

Virtual reality (VR) and augmented reality (AR)

Both VR and AR products in real estate have solved the problem of property viewing through 3D digital modelling. For example, a potential buyer located thousands of miles away can view a property or features not yet constructed. AR enables an agent to illustrate and more closely describe the features of a home to a buyer.

Useful web resources for property developers

Some important websites provide continually updated information on the real estate industry, including new market trends and demographics, offering the developer an overview of the residential market. Following is a sampling of these websites.

REIA and subsidiary websites

reia.com.au, reiwa.com.au, reisa.com.au, reiact.com.au, reint.com.au, reiq.com.au, reit.com.au, reivic.com.au

The Real Estate Institute of Australia (REIA) is the national professional association for Australia's property sector. The REIA is an independent organisation that provides research and informed advice to government, MPs, the real estate sector, the media and the public. The REIA and its state counterparts regularly update information on residential market conditions. These websites produce reports examining current market conditions and developments and are a good source for rental yields, capital growth and other suburb data for analysis. Their data helps establish a demand for an area and its market trends.

The Property Council of Australia

propertyoz.com.au

The Property Council of Australia is a prominent promoter of Australia's real estate industry. Members include investors, property owners, developers, professional consultants and trade providers. The organisation is governed by a board comprising key leaders from the industry.

The Australian Property Institute

api.org.au

The Australian Property Institute represents approximately 8600 real estate professionals throughout Australia and overseas. API members include residential and commercial valuers, real estate advisers, analysts, fund managers, lawyers, researchers and academics. The Institute's primary role is to set and maintain the highest standards of professional practice, education, ethics and professional conduct for its members and the broader real estate profession.

Australian Bureau of Statistics

abs.gov.au

The Australian Bureau of Statistics (ABS) produces a vast array of statistics and collected data relating to many sectors, including the economy, the environment, society and many different demographics. The ABS is a valuable source of information for real estate developers. For example, you can find out about the demographics of specific suburbs through historical census data. In addition, it compiles survey data on targeted topics such as housing affordability.

Realestate.com.au and Domain.com.au

realestate.com.au, domain.com.au

These real estate search engines are used by the public to locate real estate listings on the market. As technology has advanced, so has the method of advertising and marketing real estate. Realestate.com.au attracts an average of 18.6 million visitors each month. Australia's two most popular real estate search engines also provide information for real estate analysis. They give a picture of the supply in residential stock and a gauge of market prices and how well they are selling. The site also provides suburb analysis, much like the REIA websites, which helps shed light on the demand factors for the area.

APM PriceFinder

apm.com.au

Australian Property Monitors (APM) and PriceFinder have joined forces. APM PriceFinder is a national supplier of online real estate price information to the banks, financial markets, professional real estate agents and consumers. In addition, APM PriceFinder offers customised research services to private investors and real estate developers, including multinationals and governments.

Property Data Solutions

propertydatasolutions.com.au

The Property Data Solutions group covers everything related to real estate, from individual real estate research for real estate professionals to custom real estate mapping applications for large corporates and government departments. It offers one of the widest ranges of property information on the country's 10.2 million properties.

Residex

residex.com.au

Residex provides a range of real estate information on the housing and finance industries. For example, it supplies automated valuation models to the banking industry. In addition, it provides residential real estate price estimations and trend data to government and private enterprise, propensity modelling to large corporations, and real estate forecasting to institutions and personal investors.

Using online services for real estate information

In addition to general research, a developer may want to find specific information on a property or site they intend to purchase or develop. Such information may include location, neighbourhood, property size and town planning zoning. Following are some of the websites where such information is found.

Google Earth

google.com/earth

Google Earth is a virtual map and geographical information application. It maps the Earth by superimposing images obtained from satellite imagery, aerial photography and geographic information system (GIS) on a 3D globe. Developers can view a potential development site in 3D and even travel around the neighbourhood at street level. However, some of the 3D images may be a few years old. It is always best for the developer to visit the site physically.

Nearmap

nearmap.com

Nearmap Ltd is an Australian provider of high-resolution aerial imagery. It is valuable for developers looking for more updated, higher resolution images of a potential site. A unique, exclusive image capturing, processing and publishing process is used. The provider currently covers 90 per cent of Australia's population, with coverage focusing primarily on capital cities and major regional towns. Imagery is usually updated for 60 per cent of Australia's population regularly, around six times per year for metropolitan areas. Nearmap initially allowed personal use of images at no cost for non-enterprise users. This open access ended in December 2012, when the company modified its business model to user-pay.

RP Data

rpdata.com

RP Data is a paid service that provides a large amount of detailed consumer, financial and real estate information. The resource is commonly used by real estate professionals and financiers looking for details such as historical sales information, property ownership, site specifications, and tools like comparative market analysis and suburb reports.

Council websites

Council websites are vital to the research of a development project. The website's planning section provides the framework and town planning schemes for the area and, in some cases, online mapping tools to assist in finding specific information on the site. This device is particularly useful in establishing lot details and zonings.

IntraMaps

xymapping.com.au

IntraMaps, owned by TechnologyOne Spatial, is an online GIS viewing application. It enables geographic information which can be easily visualised and analysed. Many local councils around Australia use Intramaps to communicate spatial and business data to the public. Developers can access interactive maps from a council's website for details about services and facilities, planning and zoning information, and to explore local topographical information.

Software for feasibility studies

Essential for real estate developers performing feasibility studies for real estate development is the software to calculate and display all the required data to make informed decisions. Several software programs on the market take all the confusion out of a development financial assessment. They are quick to implement and accurate, so long as the developer and team provide the correct inputs. Following are some of the more significant software products on the market.

Microsoft Excel

office.microsoft.com/en-AU/excel/

Microsoft Excel is a spreadsheet application developed by Microsoft for Microsoft Windows and Mac OS. It features calculation, graphing tools, pivot tables and a macro programming language called Visual Basic for Applications. Developers can create their own spreadsheets, from basic feasibility studies to cash flows. Several templates are available on the internet using Excel as their working platform.

DevFeas Pty Ltd

devfeas.com.au

Mark Andrews created this software for real estate developers. The company produces and markets the computer software programs Feastudy 7.0 Professional and Lite for the financial feasibility study of real estate proposals. Devices also provide development feasibility consultancy services.

Estate Master

estatemaster.com

Established in 1991 by Martin Hill, Estate Master has developed a suite of flexible and easy-to-use real estate development, valuation and investment software. Estate Master is used by companies and users across the Asia–Pacific, Africa, Europe, India, the Middle East, the United Kingdom and the United States. Estate Master provides a full range of implementation, support and training services to suit all project requirements globally.

ARGUS Developer

argussoftware.com

ARGUS Software is an international software company that develops products exclusively for commercial real estate companies. Its software includes asset management, asset valuation, portfolio management, budgeting, forecasting, reporting, lease management, collaboration and knowledge management. ARGUS Software is an executive member of OSCRE, the Open Standards Consortium for Real Estate, and an active participant in the world's top real estate trade organisations.

Communicating with the development team

In real estate development, communication between team members is critical. Email has made life a lot easier for professionals. It is quick and easy, and it confirms communication in writing. Circulating large quantities of data and complex plans and drawings via email can be problematic, however, as these files will often exceed the program's permitted file size.

In the past, if an architect wanted to distribute files too large for their email, they could buy web-hosting space, burn a disc or copy the data to a USB drive. Today, many free services offer tons of storage and bandwidth to upload and download files using file hosting, cloud storage, an online file storage provider or a cyberlocker such as Dropbox. These internet hosting services are specifically designed to host user files, which can be accessed by any authenticated networked device. File hosting services include the following.

For more general, personal-use file storage services that offer mass distribution:

- **Box** *box.com*
- **Dropbox** *dropbox.com*
- **Google Drive** *drive.google.com*
- **Minus** *minus.com*

- **SkyDrive** *skydrive.live.com*

- **SugarSync** *sugarsync.com.*

For the corporate context:

- **MediaFire** *mediafire.com*

- **RapidShare** *rapidshare.com*

- **ShareFile** *sharefile.com*

- **YouSendIt** *yousendit.com.*

For architects, project managers, engineers and other consultants:

- **MediaLightbox** *medialightbox.com*

- **iShareDocs** *isharedocs.com*

- **Newforma Project Center** *newforma.com.*

The future of PropTech

PropTech is currently one of the fastest-growing investment sectors globally. Developers and investors increasingly expect tech-savvy companies to add more pace and interest to the conservative real estate business models. However, as with any changes to traditional business systems, capital and incredible talent are required.

The main barriers to the adoption of PropTech applications have been a lack of knowledge and training, associated costs, and uncertainty about the return on investment and the actual benefits. The borders and sub-verticals of PropTech are still being defined.

FinTech

Whether through investment or development, finance plays a significant role in the real estate industry. It is no surprise that there are technology innovations under FinTech (financial technology). FinTech is not new, but it has been under the spotlight recently as business models have challenged existing products, services and processes. FinTech innovations can emerge from both start-ups and established financial institutions. Investors and developers are constantly pursuing financial products ranging from seed capital and equity to construction debt or a mortgage.

What is FinTech?

FinTech refers to the application of disruptive technologies in the financial services industry. It can be described as new technology that seeks to improve, facilitate and automate financial services. It is used to assist companies, business owners and consumers manage their financial operations faster and more efficiently through specialised digital software and algorithms.

Although FinTech emerged at the turn of this century, it was initially applied to the technology used in the back-end systems of financial institutions. Since then there has been a move towards more consumer-oriented services. As a result, FinTech now focuses on different sectors and industries, such as retail banking, consumer goods, investments and real estate finance.

Fintech in real estate

FinTech is the most prominent lending category globally, but it relies on decades-old technology. Traditionally, the real estate sector used manual processes, which made it ripe for technological advances.

FinTech is not going to stop expanding. The COVID-19 pandemic has forced many industries, including the real estate sector, to adopt this technology. For example, users rely on technology and the FinTech industry because easy-to-use banking services have pushed down transactional costs. Here we look at some areas where advances have been made in the real estate sector.

Fintech mortgages

The real estate mortgage industry has benefited from FinTech. Since the 2008 financial crisis a significant number of FinTech-powered mortgage companies have executed responsible and transparent loan agreements on a grand scale. In addition, rather than relying on internal resources, some lenders have entered into partnerships with FinTech innovators.

Today, FinTech mortgages provide the digital infrastructure that helps banks simplify data collection. This enables them to offer a differentiated customer experience while lowering their mortgage servicing costs. FinTech in mortgage lending can assist with better completion rates and faster closings, generating more satisfied customers. We will now look more closely at what a FinTech mortgage is, and the benefits FinTech mortgage servicing can offer consumers and lenders.

Key benefits of FinTech mortgage solutions

While many lenders today use digital front ends, FinTech is more than just a digitising process. A FinTech mortgage helps lenders build better partnerships with borrowers through faster and more streamlined experiences. It speeds up data collection, supports borrowers through better communication and eliminates unnecessary steps along the way. Other benefits include the following:

- **It increases efficiency.** With data-driven workflows, it eliminates unnecessary steps while automating tasks associated with conditions and closing. It supports finance in providing a best-in-class customer experience throughout the lending process.

- **It reduces fragmentation.** FinTech mortgages replace a fragmented, siloed solution with an integrated, end-to-end digital solution. This results in greater productivity and efficiency, shorter loan cycle times and faster closing times.

- **It enables better experiences and higher revenues.** In addition, a faster and more streamlined application process means customers are more likely to complete a given task, which benefits the lender by increasing the number of applications completed and funded.

What is a FinTech mortgage?

FinTech mortgages solve the problem of conventional, fragmented lending practices. A FinTech digital-style mortgage cuts the manual data-gathering steps out of the process, from formal applications to contracts to appraisals and titles. As a result, it allows customers to complete applications more quickly and efficiently. Here's what the FinTech mortgage process looks like:

1. A borrower initiates a mortgage application over the phone, online or in person.

2. When borrowers fill in their applications, they connect directly to their assets, payroll and tax accounts, so there's no need to look for paperwork filed elsewhere.

3. If the borrower stops in mid application, they can conveniently pick up later where they left off, whether online or off.

4. As the borrower completes the application, fields are pre-filled from previous answers and accounts, eliminating more manual steps.

5. If the applicant has any queries, the application interface provides real-time support from a loan officer at any point during the process.

6. Lastly, the borrower can complete and approve the last steps using a digital e-signature.

A FinTech mortgage is more than an online digital process. It is about creating a faster, more efficient application process and providing a more comfortable, pleasant experience for the customer.

Improved reporting solution with FinTech mortgage

With FinTech mortgages, reporting is simplified. Traditional reporting and business metrics look at the percentage of applications submitted, tracking for applications taken and the number of loans closed and funded. While these metrics are important, the FinTech solutions provide a broader perspective. For example, the technology helps lenders understand consumer behaviour and what they report about the application. Lenders can use this information to further refine and optimise the borrower experience.

Real estate crowdfunding

In Chapter 5, crowdfunding was outlined. The subject is further explained as a FinTech application. Real estate crowdfunding is one of the fastest-growing market sectors in FinTech. Crowdfunding is a mechanism of funding a project by raising many small amounts of capital from a large group of people via the internet. A digital platform gives project sponsors access to a vast network of people via social media. This platform is a website that connects investors and entrepreneurs. It can increase entrepreneurship by expanding the pool of potential investors beyond the traditional circle of owners, relatives and venture capitalists. This FinTech method of raising funds has become the champion of small businesses. It is no surprise that it has found a place in real estate funding.

Real estate crowdfunding has grown significantly since the 2008 global financial crisis. When crowdfunding platforms opened to the public, the first-time small investors had direct access to online real estate investment opportunities. As a result, crowdfunding has proven very popular globally and is found in most developed countries.

Real estate crowdfunding platforms offer an online marketplace that connects property developers with potential investors (see figure 7.2). There are two ways of raising finance through crowdfunding:

■ Investors are offered an *equity* stake when investing in a real estate project. In return, they receive a share of the rental revenue generated by the project or its capital profits.

■ Crowdfunding allows investors to invest in *mortgage* loans. These loans are repaid monthly or quarterly, with a small percentage passed to the investor.

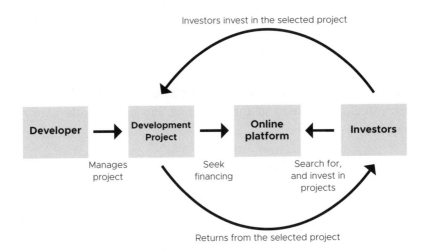

Figure 7.2: the crowdfunding process at work in a real estate project

The advantages of crowdfunding

The benefit of crowdfunding for real estate developers is the funding itself. With so many new projects on the market, raising the money needed to bring a project to life can be complex. A crowdfunding platform can help successful developers to validate their undertakings, and make validation faster and more scalable. Developers are not the only ones to benefit from a crowdfunding platform, however. Investors can examine an investment proposal in depth before risking their money. Real estate developers can advertise their projects to the public and raise funds from a large pool of investors. Investors flock to crowdfunding platforms as the underlying tech gives them three key benefits: lower fees, more diversification and better risk-adjusted returns.

The disadvantages of crowdfunding

Crowdfunding may seem like an excellent option for developers, but it does have some drawbacks. It is a convenient way to raise awareness; at the same time, though, it requires an enormous amount of work, with months of preparation of documents and relationship building with investors. Remember that the developer does not choose their investors, so the boundaries can be unclear. In addition, depending on the platform, developers must pay out between 7 and 10 per cent of capital raised, which must be accounted for in their development cost. Furthermore, crowdfunding platforms usually require reporting and disclosure procedures that must be strictly followed, creating more work for the developer.

The main disadvantage of real estate crowdfunding, however, is its unremarkable success rate. Only about 60 per cent of campaigns make it. If the campaign is not successful, investors' money must be returned. With no clear boundaries between investors and developers, too many regulations, lack of due diligence and, most importantly, a low success rate, crowdfunding is not the answer for many.

Crowdfunding regulations

In most developed countries there are laws that apply to raising capital through crowdfunding. In Australia, the Australian Securities and Investments Commission (ASIC) regulates the number of investors in an investment product. In some cases, investments are open only to sophisticated investors. Furthermore, developers may require a financial services licence to promote their project to potential investors. These regulations are there to protect unsophisticated or non-wealthy investors from putting too much of their savings at risk. With so many new businesses failing, investors face a high risk of losing their investments. Many real estate crowdfunding platforms that have a financial services licence charge a significant fee for using their services.

Fees charged by crowdfunding platforms

Real estate crowdfunding platform fees usually range between 4 and 5 per cent. In addition to the platform fee, campaign creators will be charged a payment processing fee. Most platforms can offer promoters both debt and equity investment opportunities. Typical fees charged by most crowdfunding platforms include:

- funds raised (3.5 to 5 per cent)

- annual servicing fee (around 0.85 per cent)

- annual management fee (1.25 per cent)

- credit card processing fee (3 per cent).

Creating a successful crowdfunding campaign

Crowdfunding offers an alternative channel through which to raise money for a real estate project. However, raising money on a crowdfunding platform requires a well-planned campaign. It involves preparation and a readiness to convince investors that it is worth investing in your project. Preparation, due diligence and effective communication are vital to creating a successful crowdfunding real estate project. The preparation includes documents such as an information memorandum and videos as tools to attract more visitors. As interest in the project grows, the communication with investors and interested visitors should be sustained through regular updates. Following is the step-by-step process of a successful campaign.

STEP 1. RESEARCH THE REAL ESTATE CROWDFUNDING PLATFORMS

Before promoting your project on any of these platforms, research the platforms of interest. Undertake your due diligence and ensure they have the required ASIC approvals and licences. Check out their success rates, fee structure and whether it fits your budget. Consider the following essentials:

- **Credibility.** Is the website well established?

- **Security.** Does it offer secure payments?

- **Accessibility.** Is the website accessible on your personal computer and mobile phone?

- **Functionality.** Does the app function well across various devices?

- **Customer support.** What level of customer support does the website offer?

- **Marketing.** How easy is it to promote your project with the tools provided by the platform and share campaign details across social media networks and email?

- **Fee structure.** What fees, including payment processing fees, are charged if your crowdfunding campaign is successful?

STEP 2. UNDERTAKE A COMPREHENSIVE FEASIBILITY STUDY OF YOUR PROJECT

As with all real estate developments, developers who intend to raise capital for their projects need to undertake a comprehensive feasibility study. This study will help evaluate the total amount of funds required, whether debt or equity. On most crowdfunding platforms, developers are seeking equity investment. They will have spoken to a senior lender and know how much debt or construction loan they can borrow. Once the equity amount is established, the developer will look at what returns they are prepared to offer investors. For example, for a $5 million project, they may require $1.5 million in equity. They would then break the $1.5 million down into (a) 600 shares at $2500 per share, or (b) 300 shares at $5000 per share. If the development is sold on completion, the developer would share the profits with their investors.

STEP 3. PREPARE A DETAILED INFORMATION MEMORANDUM

The next step is to create a detailed IM that contains all the necessary information for a real estate investor. The items covered should include:

- name of the real estate developer

- property location and description (keep it short and add lots of photos)

- description of the development

- architectural plans and elevations

- feasibility study (as above)

- third-party valuation of the property

- analysis of the market, including demographics

- investment type (equity, debt)

- minimum investment and anticipated returns

- profile of the development team and contact details

- the investment offer.

STEP 4. SELECT THE CROWDFUNDING PLATFORM APPLICABLE TO YOUR PROJECT

Most crowdfunding platforms have developed their own format or templates for displaying a developer's project. In most cases, a submission page includes the following information, which is extracted from the prepared IM:

- company profile—the developer's profile, project details, total project value and funding type

- transaction data—the feasibility study, plan of financing request, anticipated returns, anticipated investor-level IRR of the project and the targeted finance required

- contact details—the development team, company name, work email and phone number

- media—some platforms may require that the project's video and website be provided.

The information submitted will populate the project's dashboard. This dashboard provides an overview of investment activities and returns. Typically, it will include:

- active, completed and pending projects

- cash invested

- returns earned

- option to reinvest distributions.

STEP 5. TARGETED FINANCE RAISED

With the above completed, and if the required finance is raised through the platform, the developer will communicate directly with the investors. Should the finance target not be reached, money invested by some investors is returned. However, some platforms have the option that if the targeted finance is not achieved, the developer can retain the funds and pursue other means of raising the balance. For example, if the developer targets $3 million in equity and only $1.5 million is presented, the developer may seek mezzanine finance. Of course, this would require the approval of the senior debt provider.

STEP 6. COMMUNICATION WITH INVESTORS

It is incumbent on the developer to keep the lines of communication open with all investors. This means providing monthly or fortnightly progress reports of the project. All questions, no matter how seemingly trivial, must be answered positively and promptly. Remember, dealing with an increased number of investors is not an easy task, and any changes to the project may require the investors' approval. In this case, the developer is no longer the sole decision-maker.

■■■

Real estate crowdfunding has come a long way since the concept was introduced in 2012. Since then, a new form of crowdfunding using blockchain technology has been created. This new concept is explained in more detail in the next chapter.

Crowdfunding platforms

The US remains the world leader in the number of real estate crowdfunding platforms, followed by the UK. More and more of these platforms are starting up, although most of them are in the US and the UK. In Australia, only a handful specialise in real estate projects, and these are listed below. If you decide to promote your project on one of these platforms, do your research to find the most suitable one for your project. Due diligence is the key to finding the right crowdfunding platform.

POZIBLE
pozible.com

Launched in 2010, Pozible is 100 per cent Australian owned and has raised more than US$100 million across over 15 000 crowdfunding campaigns. It offers extended customer service, with specialised handbooks and options to customise your campaign page with widgets, add-ons and other apps. It is a success-based website, so its fees are applicable only on completion of the campaign. Unfortunately, Pozible is available only in Australia and a handful of Asian markets.

EQUITISE
equitise.com

In 2018 Equitise became one of the first crowdfunding websites to receive an Australian retail crowdfunding licence. Specialising in equity crowdfunding, wholesale investment and initial public offerings (IPO), as of the end of 2021 it had it has raised over AU$39 million across 38 crowdfunding campaigns. Promoters of a project must pay an upfront fee to cover the cost of marketing and creating the offer document.

VENTURECROWD
venturecrowd.com.au

VentureCrowd commenced operations in 2013. By 2015 it had completed the most extensive Australian equity crowdfunding campaign, raising over US$4 million for Ingogo, a taxi booking and payment software solution. As of the end of 2021, VentureCrowd had raised over US$150 million across 67 crowdfunding campaigns spanning retail, wholesale and real estate investment opportunities and attracting over 63 000 investors. It offers diverse investment opportunities appealing to multiple audiences. Promoters must provide a financial allocation as a campaign fee to cover the cost of marketing and promotion.

CROWDFUNDUP

crowdfundup.com

CrowdfundUP is a real estate crowdfunding platform that offers innovative FinTech services that change how you invest in Australian property. CrowdfundUP gives investors with limited capital access to many units or shares of properties, ensuring that they can diversify their portfolios. With its web-based, user-friendly platform, CrowdfundUP allows investors to browse and select property opportunities, complete all documentation, transfer funds and create a personal online property portfolio. In addition, CrowdfundUP's expertise and technology can help real estate stakeholders in other countries enjoy simplified property crowdfunding experiences in their local markets.

The future of fintech

The FinTech trend continues to disrupt many industries, perhaps none more so than those in the lending sector. Using artificial intelligence, big data and even blockchain, financial institutions are turning to technology to solve longstanding issues. Seeing the rise in financial technology, we can say that FinTech has finally made a place in innovating the economy. The future of FinTech seems to be bright. FinTech start-ups will ensure the ongoing development of digital infrastructure.

Surprisingly, the real estate sector has seen fewer innovative FinTech products than elsewhere, even though it is one of the largest lending sectors globally. At the same time, developers can use digital banking and advanced multi-step security solutions to protect themselves from fraud and online hackers. The lending models are limited, and more innovation is needed. The answer may lie in blockchain technology, discussed in the next chapter.

ConTech

Construction is a well-established industry that relies on building methods proven over time. So why change something that does not need fixing? With material and labour costs increasing every year, there is pressure to change practices and procedures. Although industries within the construction sector started to change with technological advancement, the construction industry remained firmly rooted in traditional building practices and unwilling to change.

About 10 years ago things started to change. The introduction of PropTech into the real estate industry and its ever-evolving iterations began to pressure the construction industry to move with the times. With the need to digitalise and optimise the construction business, applying new methods using new technology to the way buildings were designed became paramount. These changes came to be identified as ConTech. But what is ConTech, and how has it become an integral part of the construction industry? And what does it mean for architects, contractors and those who occupy the buildings constructed through ConTech?

What is ConTech?

At its core, ConTech describes the new technologies being applied to transform construction methods used in the construction industry. As in other industries today, technological innovation in construction is progressing rapidly. ConTech can be described as the technology applied to how construction is designed and planned, and how structures are erected. It can also refer to the technology used to manufacture and install components of a building. Unfortunately, ConTech has not always received the same attention as PropTech. Research has shown that only about 16 per cent of PropTech is dedicated to constructing real estate. In comparison, almost 50 per cent is focused on solving sales and leasing issues.

The industry is changing, however, and the focus is indeed shifting towards ConTech and how it can significantly impact the construction industry and, indirectly, the real estate industry too. Aided by ConTech, construction companies are reducing worker injuries, streamlining the construction process, and enabling the construction of more durable and innovative buildings. In addition, ConTech is saving both time and money during the construction process, improving the viability of real estate developments.

ConTech versus PropTech

PropTech and ConTech operate in polar-opposite areas, yet they have in common that they both transact big immobile assets. Both, therefore, require an understanding of the financial aspects, especially around creating liquidity through loans, deposits, working capital management and insuring risks. To understand ConTech, you must understand the management of supply chains; to understand PropTech, you must understand utilisation.

ConTech deals with multiple uncontrolled and active environments, while PropTech focuses mainly on the controlled and static environment. This means PropTech deals with assets that already exist, and it therefore knows the parameters of the asset and its surroundings. For example, property management supply chains are often straightforward and linear, whereas construction supply chains must account for a wide range of factors not under the contractor's control, such as weather and traffic conditions. In addition, it relies on interdependencies such as the timely delivery of materials so subcontractors can maintain their work schedules.

Contech applications

Construction technology applications enable several improvements in the industry. For example, some aim to assist on-site workers to communicate with each other more effectively. Others eliminate the need for workers to perform specific repetitive tasks. ConTech focuses increasingly on virtual reality (VR), augmented reality (AR), wearable technology, construction software, mobile apps, drones, predictive analytics and prefabrication. Other significant ConTech trends include building information modelling (BIM), used by architects and engineers. Here are some of the more exciting types of ConTech applications in use.

Drones

Drones, or unmanned aerial vehicles (UAVs), are replacing traditional land-surveillance methods and rapidly changing how the construction industry works. Drones can provide aerial views of a project, for example, enabling supervisors to detect potentially costly problems before they become unmanageable. Drones can also be used for security surveillance and coordinating the movements of automated vehicles. They can also quickly measure vertical distances that might present dangers to workers. A drone can survey land more quickly than a person on the ground. It can generate a 3D terrain map from the data it collects, giving planners all the information they need prior to construction.

Wearable tech

Wearable construction technology is already assisting construction workers to be safer and more productive on the job. VR and AR headsets give workers an in-depth view of the project they are working on. They can even allow them to see what is hidden, such as wires and pipes behind drywall or insulation. The headset can also show a model of the finished building before construction starts. Here are some of the wearables already used in construction:

- **Eyewear.** Smart glasses can capture pictures, videos and voice, integrated with mobile applications. They can also provide augmented vision to access digital plans and layouts, and identify hazardous materials.

- **Smart helmets.** Smart helmets are superior in strength to traditional hard hats and are designed to protect the technology housed inside them from the dust and grime of a construction site. They also have pull-down visors for viewing plans, 360-degree views of surroundings and direct communication with off-site workers.

- **Smart boots.** Smart boots include embedded sensors that can monitor the real-time location of workers. They can also map hazardous areas, detect pressure changes due to falls or shocks and monitor worker safety.

- **Smart vests.** Safety vests improve visibility on highway and construction projects. Some notable ConTech upgrades can now help track worker productivity and safety in real time. They can also record hours worked, track location and detect hazard zones.

- **Sensors.** A wearable sensor is an accessory that can be clipped to a worker's belt or vest, worn on the arm or attached to a hard hat. They can sense when an employee trips or falls and monitor when a worker may be too tired to perform tasks safely.

- **Exosuits.** Exosuits, or exoskeletons, also called 'bionic suits', are metal frameworks fitted with motorised muscles to multiply the wearer's strength. For example, power gloves can improve a worker's tool grip strength and agility. These suits enable workers to pick up and carry heavy materials without risking injury. Available in many configurations, they can reduce muscle fatigue and allow workers to accomplish more, improving productivity.

Construction software

Modern information technologies and advanced software are transforming all business fields, and the construction sector is no exception. It is easy to focus on the physical machines available to construction workers. However, the software that powers them is equally essential.

Large-scale projects

On large-scale projects, it is helpful to have software that ensures all teams know what is happening at other locations. In particular, supervisors can use the software to ensure everything is running smoothly, even when they cannot visit all the sites in person.

Predictive analytics

New software helps staff at management level. Predictive analytics can recognise patterns in construction data to make predictions about material usage or financial costs, which can help project planners budget more effectively.

Robotics

Construction work is physically demanding and dangerous, and often involves repetitive tasks. Robotic technology provides the construction industry with several advantages. By automating processes and increasing productivity, robotics can get work done quicker, cheaper and with more precision. Robotic technology can also help reduce the amount of waste created during construction. Here are two examples where robotics is being used in construction.

3D printing

3D printing continues to grow in the construction industry. These automated machines make it possible to print complex parts and objects in a layered system used to construct homes and commercial buildings. This technology can also standardise the production of parts used throughout a project, saving both time and money.

Bricklaying

Robotic machines have been developed to increase efficiency in bricklaying. Although residential construction has been slow to adopt technology and change, robotics in bricklaying should be a serious consideration. The process is simple: workers feed bricks into a machine using CAD software, then it is laid out accurately and precisely. The more advanced bricklaying machines can complete an entire home within a few days.

Off-site manufacture (OSM)

I covered OSM in an earlier book, *Australian Residential Property Development for Investors*. If you have not read that text, here is a summary.

One of the key focus areas of innovative building methods is the manufacture of individual elements or modules of a building in a factory before they are transported to the site on specially designed trucks and trailers. The benefit of OSM is that instead of being on-site in all weathers, the tradespeople will work off-site in a controlled environment, where quality control is a lot better. Following are some types of products that can be manufactured using the OSM process.

Prefabricated building components

Prefabrication of concrete and steel has long had a role in construction. Prefabricated steel and glass sections are also widely used for the exterior of large buildings, and small components are conventionally manufactured in a factory then assembled on-site. Now the prefabrication process has taken a big step forward, with almost completed buildings put together in the factory then erected on site.

Flat-pack buildings

Flat-pack buildings, or kit homes as they are known in Australia, are factory-produced building components packaged together, delivered to the site and assembled by skilled and unskilled tradespeople. This is sometimes described as the IKEA building method.

Transportable buildings

Transportable buildings or mobile homes have been around in Australia for a long time. Again, the buildings are assembled in a factory then transported to sites, mainly in regional areas, where skilled trades are unavailable or more expensive.

Volumetric modular buildings

Similar in concept to transportable homes, these mass-produced modular units are designed for apartments, hotels and mining camps. To be cost-effective, identical units are assembled in large numbers. The modular units may form complete rooms or parts of six-sided boxes constructed in a factory before delivery to the site.

Bathroom and kitchen pods

Traditionally, bathrooms and kitchens are both the most expensive areas of a building and the most significant cause of development delays. These pods are similar to volumetric modules, except they house only bathroom or kitchen units. Their most common application is bathroom pods used in hotels and apartment buildings.

Building information modelling (BIM)

ConTech enables consultants and contractors to visualise their projects, collate data and use that information to improve their work. The building information modelling (BIM) process allows the construction team to collate and analyse visual data without spending extensive amounts of time collecting it.

What is BIM?

Building information modelling (see figure 7.3, overleaf), which first emerged in 2002, has increased openness and collaboration in the construction industry. A range of software allows multiple parties to access digital representations of a project's physical and functional characteristics. The modelling evolves in parallel with the actual project to form a reliable basis for decisions during its life cycle, from conception to demolition. BIM is more than a 3D model. It captures a project's geometry, spatial relationships, light factors, building materials data, time and costs. It includes data input from engineers, architects and other experts.

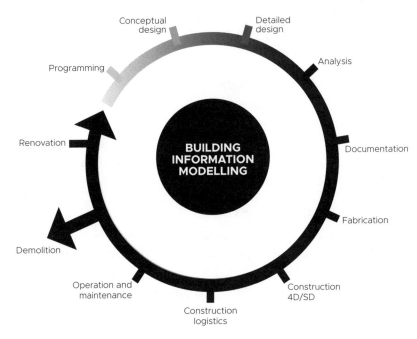

Figure 7.3: building information modelling

In simple terms, BIM is a way of working that accurately manages and models information in a team environment. The BIM software marketplace is saturated with similar features and functional tools, most of which can save time and money and increase productivity when leveraged correctly. Studies suggest that more than 65 per cent of businesses in the construction sector are using BIM processes and experiencing fewer construction errors as a result. The BIM model is most commonly used in large and small construction businesses, such as in the architectural, engineering and construction sectors.

What are the benefits of BIM?

The benefits of BIM tools and processes cannot be overstated. Above all, they enable the construction team to execute error-free projects. Although this list is far from comprehensive, a few of the most apparent advantages and rewards of the BIM process are described here.

PRECISE PLANNING

Compared with traditional computer spreadsheets, BIM collects and automates construction information. Automated data generation eliminates the problem of human error. Here are some common areas where BIM works in daily construction activities:

- BIM extracts or exports material information (types of material, quality, quantity and length needed) through a 3D model.

- BIM enables accurate cost estimates based on the list of materials and other information provided.

- BIM accurately determines expenses and payments during the construction process, reducing administration costs.

EARLY DETECTION

Even with this model there is a chance of inaccuracies passing undetected. While the construction model may look complete, variable site conditions may affect its accuracy and verification. It is here that BIM steps in to flush out any flaws in the modelling, such as a potential clash between electrical cables and air-conditioning ducts.

PROJECT VISUALISATION

Design concepts are often unclear, and changes may be made early in the design process. BIM enables the quick creation of 3D models for easy visualisation, facilitating the building presentation to clients who cannot grasp or understand building plans.

INFORMATION STORAGE SIMPLIFIED

Today most people and businesses store information and data on cloud servers. The BIM model is stored and accessed in any part of the world by authorised personnel. In addition, data is stored indefinitely.

REDUCTION IN ERRORS

BIM ensures a significant reduction in errors on the construction site. For example, errors can occur when the design office transfers construction drawings through manual processes, such as blueprints. BIM eliminates these problems by digitising the information and data transfer process in real time.

HIGHER-QUALITY WORK

A well-coordinated and reliable model is required to produce a high-quality construction project. This can be achieved if building contractors collaborate with the professional consultants such as the architect. By distributing the BIM tools to view the whole project in real time, the project can be better executed.

LOWER RISK AND COST

A recent study has shown that almost 75 per cent of construction companies using BIM have seen significant cost savings. In addition, by reviewing the project in the early design process, the building contractor can reduce the quantity of unused building materials, wastage and labour costs.

INCREASE IN PRODUCTIVITY

Since the introduction of BIM, productivity in construction projects has increased considerably. This has been made possible by automating tasks, the timely flow of materials on-site, and better coordination between suppliers and tradespeople through the expansion of BIM modelling.

■■■

This is only a small sample of BIM benefits. Others include more accurate pricing through a bill of quantities generated through the BIM model, and improved occupational safety and health (OSH) by identifying complex tasks before on-site construction starts. It is not surprise that more companies in the building sector are adopting the model, which is touted as a differentiator in the industry due to its benefits across a project's lifecycle, including, after construction, facility management.

The future of ConTech

The processes and technologies the construction industry is using today will look quite different five, 10 or 20 years from now, as ConTech, like

PropTech and FinTech, is constantly advancing and improving. It is now more popular than ever, and the construction industry and those who work in it will only benefit by keeping up with new ConTech trends. It will continue to benefit the construction industry, making the processes more efficient, the end products more professional and the workers happier, healthier and, most importantly, safer on the job than ever before.

ConTech represents enormous financial benefits for real estate developers. Construction costs have risen annually due to skilled labour shortages and more expensive building materials. It has therefore become increasingly challenging to build inexpensively. The best way to cut costs is to increase efficiency, which is precisely what ConTech applications do. Real estate developers who keep an eye out for new trends and innovations in ConTech will be best qualified to direct their team to take advantage of these innovations and incorporate them in their projects.

CONCLUSION

Developers who have been in the real estate industry for a good few years can find the prospect of adopting new technology overwhelming. Nevertheless, recognising and embracing changes and improvements in technology is fundamental to successful development. Ignore these shifts and you will be left behind, and so will your business. Finally, a few tips on improving your knowledge and experience of new technology.

Follow industry news

The more you keep up with the latest news and trends in technological innovation, the more informed you will be. It will also improve your ability to predict changes in the market and assist in your communications with other industry experts on the same level.

Talk to the younger generation

New technology is second nature to most young people. Talking with them will often alert you to new ideas and trends. They are also your future market, so it helps you to understand their real estate needs.

Invest in technology

It is wise to invest in and use new equipment and software related to real estate. Using hardware and software improves your technical skills and know-how.

Innovate

Becoming conversant with all aspects of the digital space will give you a platform from which to innovate. You will start to identify new ways to improve the performance of traditional real estate models. You may even come up with a new PropTech idea.

CHAPTER 8

BLOCKCHAIN TECHNOLOGY IN REAL ESTATE

One innovation that will have a significant impact on the real estate industry is blockchain technology. It has already disrupted the financial sector, with cryptocurrencies moving payments, remittances and foreign exchange. It is not surprising, therefore, that this technology is now being adopted in other commercial settings, including real estate. Real estate transactions are generally conducted offline and involve face-to-face meetings between the relevant parties. Smart contracts on blockchain platforms allow real estate assets to be tokenised and traded like cryptocurrencies such as bitcoin and ether.

When applied to real estate development, blockchain's transparent, cost-efficient and secure platform offers many social benefits. It provides a better system through which governments and businesses can improve operations and minimise opportunities for human interference while maximising access to professional services. It is a transparent system that can disrupt the norm to reduce fraud, speed up approvals and provide a more efficient way of completing a project.

With current transactions, most people use a bank as an intermediary. Blockchain allows the parties to a transaction to connect directly, which removes the need for intermediaries. In addition, blockchain uses cryptography and provides a secure decentralised database, or 'digital ledger', that allows all those on the network to see the transaction process. This network is essentially a chain of computers that must all approve before the transaction is verified and recorded.

What is blockchain?

Blockchain is a distributed database that shares data among several computers simultaneously. As a database, a blockchain stores information in a digital format. It is continually growing as new recordings, or 'blocks', are added. Each block contains a time-stamp and a link to the previous block, forming the chain. No specific person manages the database; everyone in the network receives a copy of the database. The older blocks are preserved, and new blocks are added to the ledger irreversibly, making it impossible to manipulate the documents, transactions or other information.

Furthermore, these blocks are encrypted and only a user who owns a unique cryptographic key can add a new record to a chain. In simple terms, blockchain can be explained as follows:

- Blockchain is a shared database that differs from a standard database in that it stores information in blocks that are then linked together via cryptography.

- When new data comes in, it is entered into a new block. Once the block is filled with data, it is chained to the previous block in chronological order.

- Various types of information are stored on a blockchain. The most common use so far has been as a ledger for transactions.

How does blockchain work?

Blockchain technology can work for almost any type of transaction involving value, including money, goods, contracts, services and real estate. Its potential in the commercial world is virtually limitless, including tracking the supply of goods, sending money overseas and payment of contract services on completion. Blockchain's technology can also help shut out fraudsters.

Each transaction is recorded and distributed on a digital ledger that can be seen by anyone on the network. The advantages of a distributed ledger include cost and risk reduction, data security and transaction transparency. As soon as a new transaction or new information is uploaded, the computers on that network validate it then store it as a block in the chain. This validation process ensures that no cheating occurs and everyone abides by the system's rules. Hacking such a network is next to impossible because of its decentralisation.

A typical blockchain transaction process (as illustrated in figure 8.1), may unfold in the following steps:

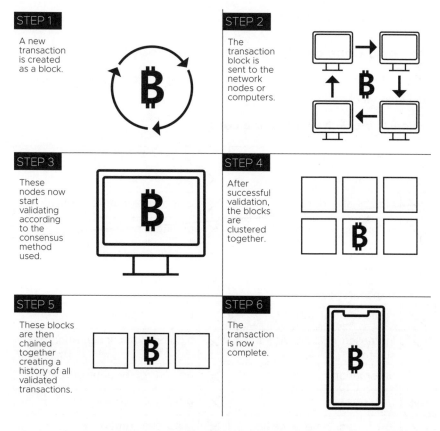

STEP 1

A new transaction is created as a block.

STEP 2

The transaction block is sent to the network nodes or computers.

STEP 3

These nodes now start validating according to the consensus method used.

STEP 4

After successful validation, the blocks are clustered together.

STEP 5

These blocks are then chained together creating a history of all validated transactions.

STEP 6

The transaction is now complete.

Figure 8.1: blockchain transaction process

1. A transaction is created as a block. This transaction can involve the transfer of information or an asset of monetary value.

2. The transaction block is then sent to the network nodes. If it is a public blockchain, it is sent to each node. Each block consists of the data, the previous block hash and the current block hash.

3. These nodes now start validating according to the consensus method used. In the case of bitcoin, proof-of-work (PoW) is used.

4. After successful validation, the blocks are chained together.

5. These blocks create a history of all validated transactions.

6. The transaction is now complete.

Pros and cons of blockchain technology

Table 8.1 lists some of the many advantages and disadvantages of blockchain technology.

Table 8.1: blockchain pros and cons

	Pros		Cons
✓	peer-to-peer	✗	repetitive process
✓	high-quality data	✗	complex signature verification
✓	enhanced security	✗	private keys
✓	high level of integrity	✗	lack of developers
✓	immutability and transparency	✗	integration concerns
✓	improved traceability	✗	unclear regulations
✓	increased efficiency and speed	✗	high energy consumption
✓	automation	✗	no control for enterprises
✓	faster transaction	✗	privacy concerns
✓	lower transactional costs	✗	cultural disruption
✓	longevity and reliability	✗	high cost
✓	empowered users		

Blockchain technology pros

First, we'll examine the many benefits of blockchain technology.

PEER-TO-PEER

As blockchain is a distributed system, it offers peer-to-peer transactions. It does not involve any third parties such as banks, which reduces transaction costs. It therefore helps a business to save more money that can be invested elsewhere. As a result, the business is more efficient.

HIGH-QUALITY DATA

Blockchain offers a high level of data quality. Every piece of information is verified before being added to the ledger, so there's no scope for human error.

ENHANCED SECURITY

Data is sensitive, and blockchain significantly changes how personal information is viewed. By creating a record that is encrypted end-to-end and cannot be altered, blockchain helps prevent fraud and unauthorised activity.

HIGH LEVEL OF INTEGRITY

Blockchain offers a higher level of integrity than other network systems. This means your data will always be correct, and no one can alter it once it's in the ledger. Storing the information and consensus processes is also robust.

IMMUTABILITY AND TRANSPARENCY

Because blockchain is a distributed ledger, transactions and data are recorded identically in multiple locations. In addition, all transactions are immutably recorded and time-stamped. This enables members to view the entire history and virtually eliminates any opportunity for fraud.

IMPROVED TRACEABILITY

Blockchain creates an audit trail that documents the provenance of an asset at every step on its journey. In addition, companies using blockchain can create a supply chain that works with both vendors and suppliers.

INCREASED EFFICIENCY AND SPEED

Traditional paper-heavy processes are time-consuming. Streamlining these processes with blockchain means transactions are completed faster and more efficiently. In addition, documentation can be stored on the blockchain, along with transaction details, eliminating the need to exchange paper documents.

AUTOMATION

Transactions are automated, with 'smart contracts' increasing efficiency and speed. When specified preconditions are met, the next step is automatically triggered. In addition, smart contracts reduce reliance on third parties to verify that the terms of a contract have been met.

FASTER TRANSACTIONS

Blockchain offers faster transactions. Centralised banks can take up to three days to process that transaction, and sometimes longer for overseas trade. With blockchain, transactions are completed within a few seconds!

LOWER TRANSACTIONAL COSTS

Other than offering faster transactions, it also offers a lower transaction cost. When using traditional methods, a transaction fee is applicable. Because of its efficiency, blockchain offers a lower transaction fee in exchange for a faster transaction process.

LONGEVITY AND RELIABILITY

Blockchain is immutable and transparent, which ensures integrity. These characteristics create reliability and longevity of the technology. Furthermore, as no one can change the blockchain's rules as they please, these rules remain intact.

EMPOWERED USERS

In a centralised system, users do not control their personal information. As a result, corrupt individuals can misuse the information for their own gain. Blockchain's peer-to-peer network gives users better control.

Blockchain technology cons

Having covered the main advantages of blockchain technology, we will now review the disadvantages.

REPETITIVE PROCESS

The computation of blockchain technology is more repetitive than that of a centralised system. Because of the distributed nature of the ledger system, every time the ledger is updated, all nodes need to be updated. This repetitive process costs time and burns electricity.

COMPLEX SIGNATURE VERIFICATION

Every transaction requires a private–public cryptographic signature verification. It uses the Elliptic Curve Digital Signature Algorithm (ECDSA) to ensure that the transaction happens between the correct nodes. This can be a tricky and complex process.

PRIVATE KEYS

A private key is needed to transact on a network. Other users can see your public key, but your private key remains hidden for security reasons and to ensure that others cannot access your personal assets. However, if you lose your private key, you lose your access to your funds on the network, with no way to recover them.

LACK OF DEVELOPERS

As blockchain is relatively new, there are as yet few capable blockchain developers who can work with it. So finding an experienced and talented development team to handle a blockchain project can be problematic.

INTEGRATION CONCERNS

The integration process of blockchain and legacy networks is not yet fully functional. As a result, many blockchain technologies cannot work with legacy networks, so companies must dispose of their legacy networks before they can use blockchain properly.

UNCLEAR REGULATIONS

Many blockchain platforms do not fall under a set of regulations, which creates mistrust in the industry. Many people have fallen victims to initial coin offering (ICO) scams, as there is no regulation related to cryptocurrencies. Government bodies also struggle to understand blockchain and regulate it.

HIGH ENERGY CONSUMPTION

Ensuring that every transaction is valid requires a consensus process. This process requires considerable computational power, increasing overall power consumption. (However, there are new consensus protocols that consume much less energy.)

NO CONTROL FOR ENTERPRISES

Enterprises require a specific authoritative process to use blockchain. Public blockchains do not offer these controlling aspects. (However, the rise of private and consortium blockchains seems to provide for both the technology's control and distributed nature.)

PRIVACY CONCERNS

Organisations requiring privacy to maintain their brand value cannot reveal their sensitive information either to the public or to their competitors. Many enterprises are therefore resistant to using blockchain for business purposes.

CULTURAL DISRUPTION

This is more a cultural disadvantage than a technical one. Businesses that have been running on a specific model for years feel the invention of blockchain threatens this model. Indeed, it has already started to change how the system works and has already disrupted many industries.

HIGH COST

Blockchain is much cheaper than other technology, but it can still be costly, depending on the features added. In addition, developing a solution from scratch requires significant capital, and replacing the legacy system adds further expense. You can reduce this burden by keeping your solutions to a minimum.

■■■

Blockchain is a relatively new technology and still has a long way to go before mass adoption. I have reviewed most of its pros and cons, but it is worth noting that blockchain companies are already addressing many of the disadvantages. For example, some blockchain enterprises now focus on using renewable energy such as solar, wind and hydrogen where high energy consumption is necessary. So give it a few more years to mature, and the benefits of blockchain will be irrefutable.

Blockchain in real estate

A real estate transaction involves many intermediaries such as mortgage brokers, lawyers and banks. Blockchain has the potential to streamline this complex process, making it faster, simpler and safer. In addition, the introduction of smart contracts on blockchain platforms allows assets such as real estate to be tokenised and traded like other cryptocurrencies such as bitcoin and ether. Here are some ways in which blockchain is likely to change the real estate industry.

Platforms and marketplaces

Real estate technology has mainly been concerned with connecting sellers with buyers. Blockchain introduces new ways to trade, allowing trading platforms and online markets to support real estate transactions comprehensively. By tokenising real estate, assets can be traded like shares and transactions can be completed online.

Security and trust

With decentralised technology, blockchain creates security and trust. Information stored in the blockchain is available to all parties on the network, making the data transparent and absolute. The decentralised exchange has trust and security built into the system, decreasing the possibility of fraud. As information is verified, buyers and sellers have more confidence in conducting transactions.

No intermediaries

Real estate agents, lawyers and banks have long been the main parties to real estate transactions. However, blockchain is likely to create a shift in their roles and participation. New platforms will eventually assume functions such as listings, payments and legal documentation, which will both save buyers and sellers commissions and fees, and speed up the process.

Liquidity

Real estate has always been considered an illiquid asset because of the sometimes lengthy process of matching a willing buyer and seller. Blockchain tokens are faster as they can be readily traded for fiat (government-issued) currencies through exchanges. In addition, a seller does not have to wait for a buyer who can afford the whole property.

Fractional ownership

With fractional ownership, blockchain lowers entry barriers to real estate ownership. For example, when buying a property, a large upfront deposit is needed to purchase the property, or buyers can pool their money to acquire a more substantial property. With blockchain, buyers can access a trading app to buy and sell fractional tokens.

Smart contracts

Blockchain's smart contracts provide a solution for managing real estate transactions through a universal distributed ledger open to the transacting parties. Altering any of the details of a transaction after it has been completed will not be possible. The smart contract operates with private keys that are used to digitally sign transactions and authenticate the transaction.

Lower costs

This transparency can lower all costs associated with real estate transactions. In addition to cutting out intermediaries' fees and commissions, other costs such as inspections, registration fees, loan fees, conveyancing fees and taxes associated with real estate can be reduced.

Peer-to-peer

The world's real estate industry is worth $217 trillion and is dominated by the wealthy and large corporations. With blockchain, more people can access the market when transactions are transparent, secure and equitable. Peer-to-peer activities with blockchain-powered platforms do most of the work. Buyers and sellers interact directly with each other in real time and in a cost-effective manner.

Blockchain in real estate development

The buying and selling of real estate involves one main contract between a buyer and a property seller, whereas in real estate development there are many contracts, agreements and payments from the start to the completion of a new building. As noted, on complicated real estate development projects, blockchain technology can significantly speed up the process transparently and efficiently. Of course, it will disrupt the current systems that have been in place for centuries and will force many players to change course or careers. Whether it is residential, commercial or just social infrastructure, areas where blockchain can add value and streamline development include the following.

Development site purchase

A smart contract can be in place to trigger payment or settlement of the land when due diligence and certain other conditions are met. Often settlement of land is a game of cat and mouse. Blockchain can ascertain milestones that will determine whether or not the transaction proceeds, therefore not wasting either the landowner's or the developer's time.

Approvals

Development approvals can be a long and drawn-out process. If local councils adopt blockchain technology, the approval process can run more efficiently and make those involved in the process more accountable for any delays.

Reduced risk

The blockchain environment creates a transparent platform and a lower risk process, and raises the question as to whether a developer is required in the delivery process. The alternative is to appoint a professional development manager and pay for the services provided. This reduces the excessive profit margins passed on to the purchasers.

Accountability

With so many people and contractors involved in the development process, from architects to engineers and contractors to subcontractors, every participant has a delivery role in the development process. Should there be any delay, everyone in the chain will know where it is occurring, and where the necessary action must be taken.

A broader range of investors

With entry for investors in real estate becoming increasingly expensive due to escalating values in growth locations, blockchain through a fractional investment structure allows smaller investors to invest in new developments. This creates a larger pool of investors.

Data history from initiation to operations

With the integration of blockchain, there is a robust and authentic system for recording the history of a development that can provide data on how the building was constructed. For example, the data captured includes the type, make and model of electrical systems or fittings that will need to be replaced from time to time during the building's operational period.

Blockchain's disruption

You may feel by now that blockchain conjures up a utopia for real estate development in which transparency will create a better world for all communities. Blockchain technology creates a 'socialist' platform that benefits the broader community. Unfortunately, though, we live in a capitalist society where the winner takes all. To implement blockchain concepts, a significant paradigm shift will have to occur. It may take several decades before there is anything like universal acceptance of this technology.

With the current real estate development structure, there are more winners than losers. Blockchain will work in areas of significant need, driven by our ever-increasing population and shortage of resources. The area that requires most attention is the delivery of social infrastructure, and the most critical is affordable housing.

The commercial adoption of blockchain will take time (consider the introduction of the internet some 25 years ago). The development and construction industries' culture and systems are well entrenched, and any change will take another decade. To prove blockchain technology's credibility, early adopters who take the first steps will set the benchmark for future developments. The technology will undoubtedly disrupt the current real estate development structure, including in the following areas.

Design and documentation

Architects and engineers have adopted building information modelling (BIM) in their design and documentation of new buildings over the past number of years. Blockchain technology can improve BIM in data security, liability and transferability. There is also the exciting possibility of linking digital components to their physical counterparts, enabling live data collection for BIM models. This creates an excellent opportunity to incorporate blockchain's decentralised ledger system to manage these various inputs. With blockchain, BIM model owners would have a 'common data environment' that is tamper-proof and time-stamped.

Development finance

Fractional ownership through digital tokens will allow a greater pool of investors and homebuyers to enter the real estate market. Developers will offer buyers and investors the opportunity to participate in their new projects early. These tokens can increase in value as the projects reach certain milestones. As various funding stages are reached, new tokens are offered to the public.

Role of developers

Blockchain's smart contracts and decentralised ledger help reduce several risks in a development project. So what will be the role of a real estate developer? Their current role will be filled by an experienced development manager who will provide the necessary development expertise for a fee. This will not apply to all projects, however. Some projects carry greater development risk, and developers must cost these risks in profit margins.

Role of builders

Similarly, builders will become construction managers as opposed to general building contractors. As construction managers, they will charge a fee for their services, including a performance fee for completing projects on time and within budget. Some builders are currently working on a similar model through a 'cost-plus' contract that can be improved using blockchain's technology.

■■■

More people in the real estate development industry will adopt blockchain as time passes. Whatever the disruption it brings, there can be no doubt that blockchain is here to stay and will continuously improve development systems and processes.

Blockchain and fractional ownership

The blending of fractional ownership and blockchain technology creates a blockchain-based marketplace. This marketplace is used for purchasing and exchanging real estate investment and development through crypto tokens, making transactions more accessible, efficient and transparent. In utilising this technology, a blockchain platform is created that lowers costs and provides affordable solutions for people to climb the real estate ladder.

What is fractional ownership?

Real estate has always been an attractive asset class for buyers and investors. Historically it has offered potentially high returns on a tangible asset. However, as real estate prices continue to rise, the ability to enter the real estate market moves further out of the average person's reach. Fractional ownership offers a solution for those looking to get a foot on the real estate ladder without a substantial initial investment.

With fractional real estate ownership, the cost of a property is divided into shares. These shares are then sold to investors who receive an income from rent charged together with capital returns on the property when sold or when they sell their shares. The cost of the shares will rise or fall in proportion to the change in the property's value. Generally, the ownership vehicle is under a company title and individual owners and investors have shares, as in a housing cooperative.

Blockchain for fractional property ownership

Combine blockchain technology with fractional property ownership, and we have a system open to anyone wanting to enter the real estate market. A blockchain-powered ledger can resolve complications by securely and reliably tracking the size and value of each person's stake in the property, in the same way as shares in companies are recorded on exchanges. The system also allows for incremental real estate ownership. For example, the UK Government offers a 'shared ownership' scheme to assist first-time buyers in purchasing part of a property and paying rent on the remaining value. The buyers can buy additional equity in the property when they can afford to. With blockchain, smart contracts make it possible to adopt this ownership model. Payments, automatically adjusted to the ownership level, are recorded in the blockchain ledger, and ongoing valuation of additional equity is also automated.

How does it work?

The combination of blockchain and fractions is based on smart contracts. You buy and sell real estate using digital tokens, and smart contracts control your real estate ownership rights and payouts. An exchange platform is created to 'tokenise' real estate assets like shares, which means a building such as an apartment block is broken into digital tokens. Investors can participate in the real estate economy by purchasing and selling these tokens without necessarily buying entire blocks of real estate. It allows investors to diversify their investment in real estate markets by location and asset class, all controlled and secured using smart contracts.

The investment model is based on a REIT (real estate investment trust) or PLT (property listed trust), in which the shares' value is based on the performance of the trusts. So the tokens can increase or decrease in value according to the real estate portfolio's performance. In addition, as these assets do not carry any debt, rental income minus expenses is distributed quarterly.

The investment process is as follows:

- An established property with a rental income is bought and placed on the blockchain.

- The shares are broken into tokens representing the common equity, transferrable and traceable on the blockchain.

- These tokens are sold to investors.

- The investors get access to cash flow generated by the asset quarterly.

- Investors can trade their tokens in the marketplace, making their investment liquid.

- Investors can see how each asset performs and can trade in and out of real estate faster than ever before.

The investor can buy and trade asset tokens on the blockchain platform. Real estate assets back up tokens that generally increase in value. Tokens are delivered to an investor's online wallet and dividends are paid quarterly.

A property seller can obtain faster liquidity through tokens than traditional property transactions.

They can hold their equity in tokens and sell their bank debt to investors. They can also benefit from the increased value spread over several other properties.

Blockchain in social infrastructure

In most democratic countries, elections have been fought over promises to deliver social infrastructure to communities.

Tight government budgets

With the tightening of budgets, governments are under increased pressure to find quick solutions to problems in maintaining public services and funding community infrastructure. The longer the process is delayed, the more pressure mounts to find answers. On top of this are the risks of forgetting the root causes of the problems, including greed, corruption, bureaucratic inefficiency and excessive faith in private corporations. Blockchain could radically change the situation by creating a new playing field accessible to all and not exclusive to government. Individuals in communities and the private sector need to take a leading role in delivering social infrastructure.

Changing demographics

The need for increased social infrastructure investment stems from various developments besides the increasing population. Changing demographics can affect the growing numbers of young and older people requiring different types of infrastructure. The unprecedented demand for social infrastructure worldwide presents both challenges and opportunities for governments and the private sector. They need to seek innovative ways to deliver essential health, education, housing and justice for our growing communities.

Blockchain's decentralised technology

To meet the community's demand for new social infrastructure, the aim should be to leverage blockchain's decentralised technology and initiate a people's protest where the community's needs are most felt. The focus would be on making a positive difference to the broader society, empowering ordinary people, and engaging the whole community. The blockchain alternative should be based on solidarity and putting people before profit, with a structure that can especially benefit communities in need. In addition, the technology can protect the public's interest to an unprecedented level by eliminating opportunities for bribery and corruption.

What is social infrastructure?

Social infrastructure is a subset of the infrastructure sector and typically includes assets that accommodate social services. However, social infrastructure does not typically provide social services themselves, such as teachers or protective services at a prison. Table 8.2 lists examples of social infrastructure assets, including schools, universities, hospitals, prisons and community housing.

Table 8.2: typical social infrastructure assets

Sector	Examples
Health	hospitals medical facilities aged care facilities medi-hotels
Education	childcare centres schools (primary and secondary) tertiary facilities student housing
Housing	affordable housing state or council housing defence force housing
Civic utilities	community and sports facilities local government facilities water and wastewater treatment
Transport	bus stations park-and-rides
Correctional and justice	prisons courthouses

The demand for new social infrastructure

Wherever you look around the world, infrastructure is in constant demand. In a recent report, PricewaterhouseCoopers (PwC) estimated that from 2020 to 2025 global spending on capital and infrastructure projects will total between $28 trillion and $30 trillion. Due to changing demographics in emerging and developed markets, social infrastructure will comprise a significant portion of this investment.

In developed markets, much infrastructure is aging and in need of renewal. Many emerging economies lack the infrastructure they need. Governments recognise that putting these buildings and systems in place will help support their economic growth. Besides the increasing population worldwide, the need for increased social infrastructure investment stems from various developments:

- **Aging population.** With the baby boomers reaching retirement and living longer due to better health, there is a growing need for aged care facilities and hospitals.

- **Working couples.** With both parents working full-time, there is an increased demand for childcare centres.

- **Tertiary education.** An increasing number of students are entering tertiary education, driving the demand for new education facilities and student housing.

- **New suburbs.** New housing developments and suburbs on the outskirts of cities are demanding new schools, community centres, police stations and other facilities.

- **Increased density.** Most cities are pushing for increased housing density close to the city centre, placing greater pressure on existing social infrastructure that needs upgrading.

How blockchain can meet the demand

Everywhere you go in the world, someone is talking about blockchain technology and its ability to reinvent the world of commerce and government and to challenge some of the most basic assumptions about society. While it is easy to get turned off by all the hype, the bottom line is that blockchain can be transformational and make a dramatic and positive social impact. Its potential to address some of the world's most pressing problems is exciting and inspiring. Still, blockchain strategies can only succeed if intentionality, a precise theory of change and quantitative metrics are assigned. Mechanisms by which blockchain technology can improve the delivery of social infrastructure include the following.

Universal access to financing

Blockchain-backed financial transfers do not require third-party intermediaries. Their resistance to fraud is another means to broaden global access to investments. For example, philanthropic donations can be tracked and delivered directly to the people in need, eliminating greedy intermediaries.

Smart contracts

The smart contracts system means the release of funding is pegged to achieving specific goals, for example in healthcare. Such applications can track the use of supplies, services delivery and disbursement of funds according to outcomes.

Transactions

The blockchain ledger is open and transparent. Anyone can look at it and easily track all trade flows, so any system based on an open public blockchain platform is transparent. The shutting down of any computer will not trigger the loss of information.

Security and ownership

Blockchain technology offers a way of representing almost any asset, whether tangible or intangible. As a result, the ownership of those assets can be readily identified, with no possibility of concealment or dishonesty, making it counterfeit-proof and very robust.

Why invest in social infrastructure?

Developers and investors are starting to turn their interest towards real estate social infrastructure sectors such as childcare, seniors housing, aged care, student accommodation, government premises, and medical and health facilities as viable investment alternatives. Following are the main drivers of this asset class and some insight into why it is preferred to traditional commercial investments such as retail, offices and industrial.

Demographic and social changes

The aging population is increasing the demand for senior housing and health services. In addition, the higher involvement of women in the workforce and the growing demographic of newborns to five-year-olds is escalating the demand for childcare. At the same time, the rise in international students is boosting the need for student accommodation.

Government budget constraints

Government's ability to fund the infrastructure required to meet community needs is under constant pressure. As a result, they are increasingly seeking private sector participation through private–public partnerships.

Increased urbanisation

Population growth and greater urbanisation of significant cities are increasing the need for social infrastructure to support communities in the inner city and on the urban fringes.

■■■

From a commercial investment perspective, social infrastructure projects have become attractive for most investors due to:

- **relatively high yields.** Social infrastructure assets commonly enjoy yields that are between 1 per cent and 1.5 per cent higher than significant office, retail and industrial assets.

- **attractive lease structure**. Longer-term lease rental increases are linked to CPI, and the tenant pays all outgoings, capital expenditure and refurbishments.

- **the strength of tenancies**. Tenants are inherently connected for the long term to their premises due to the specialised nature of the assets, particularly the internal fit-outs.

- **government support.** Many social infrastructure sectors receive some form of government subsidies or payments, and at times even the underwriting of a lease.

■ **attractive investment characteristics.** Social infrastructure assets typically exhibit low volatility and generate consistent cash flows due to less cyclical demand drivers.

Social infrastructure assets carry a lower risk level than other asset classes from a risk perspective. Two factors should still be considered, however. First, its specialised nature is often of critical importance to asset leasing. For example, a private hospital is a highly specialised asset and requires a well-capitalised and competent hospital operator. Then there is government regulation. Social infrastructure generally involves levels of government, high regulation and intervention, and these are susceptible to change. However, this can also be a positive, especially if the government is partially or fully underwriting the sector's cash flows.

Blockchain in affordable housing

Every major city in the world is experiencing a housing affordability crisis. It is not a new problem but a challenge that has faced governments for decades. Housing and shelter are basic human needs that fall under the social infrastructure banner. Whether for a first home buyer or a renter, housing has become very expensive. Taking that first step onto the real estate ladder raises many challenges for those on a relatively low income.

Why is housing unaffordable?

The most prominent element in the household budget is housing. House prices have skyrocketed relative to incomes in many cities, especially in countries with strict land-use regulations. The high cost of housing raises questions around why people are paying so much for housing and whether there are solutions to make it more affordable? Here is a look at just some of the reasons why real estate has become so expensive.

Government bureaucracy

Red tape, limited budgets, bribery and overpaid bureaucrats are primary causes of the non-delivery of affordable social housing. It has been found that when it comes to the provision of affordable housing, 50 per cent of an allocated budget is offered to the bureaucratic systems to monitor the process.

Government taxes

The costs of buying a property in most developed countries, such as taxes and transfer duty, have significantly impacted real estate prices. These taxes are levied against the percentage value of a property and not per transaction.

Transaction cost

In addition to taxes and transfer costs, there are also intermediary costs, such as fees and commissions charged by real estate agents, lawyers, conveyancers and banks.

Availability and affordability of land

A land shortage in densely populated city areas has also contributed to the rise in real estate prices. Limited land supply and more significant demand result in higher prices. Land has also become more expensive for developers to purchase, mainly due to the burden of government taxes passed on to buyers.

Labour and building costs

The cost of building has increased most significantly in the past two decades. Increasing labour and building material costs are major contributing factors to the rise in real estate prices. And GST or VAT adds to these costs.

■■■

Affordability comes down to cost. With layers of processes and entrenched housing delivery systems, it should be no surprise that housing has become unaffordable for many. So can blockchain streamline the process and cut out many of the layers of costs to ensure the delivery of a basic human need?

Can blockchain change the current status?

Blockchain's strategy is to create disruption, challenge the status quo and analyse each cost delivery element, including:

- **land cost.** It could be on a 60-year lease or government land sold at a peppercorn price. If the land is private, a development lease can be considered. In both cases, smart contracts can be used.

- **finance cost**. Finance can be raised through fractional tokens at each stage of the development process. However, as affordable housing is a government responsibility, they should underwrite the project.

- **soft cost**. Professional fees, rates and taxes, application fees and submission fees should be negotiated and tied to smart contracts.

- **developer's margin.** As a project's risk is minimised, there should be no developer's profit. Instead, a well-qualified and experienced development manager should oversee the project and be paid for their services.

- **builder's margin.** The builder should act as a construction manager, with a fixed fee for services rendered plus a performance bonus for completing the project on time and within budget.

- **accurate construction pricing.** Using the BIM model's Bill of Quantities, tradespeople and suppliers can bid on projects more accurately, which will help reduce costs.

The material supply source can be verified and the materials procured on an open platform on an ethical and sustainable basis.

Other blockchain opportunities

Blockchain technology can be utilised in other projects, especially where several people are involved. Whenever there is a group of decision-makers in any project, situations or conflicts may arise as one party does not trust another. Blockchain's transparency can eliminate any potential misunderstanding between parties. Here are three areas in the real estate development space where blockchain can be adopted.

Real estate syndicates

There will always be a manager or initiator who starts a real estate syndicate and invites other investors to participate. Most invitees are excited in the initial stages, when they think only of the benefits and financial rewards. As the project progresses, however, conflicts may develop or decisions are postponed, delaying the completion of the project. Syndicate members then start turning against the manager, holding them responsible for the project's problems without fully understanding the issues.

Through blockchain, each syndicate member is part of that chain and can see the project's delay and its probable causes. This eliminates suspicion that might otherwise generate further conflict among syndicate members. The blockchain system will also keep the manager in check and ensure they are performing in the syndicate members' best interest.

Cooperatives and co-housing

Blockchain is the ideal platform to operate in a structure where people of similar interests develop a project to share amenities and provide communal support. Whether it is a cooperative network or a co-housing project, a smart contract will assist in the initial stage of setting up members, as will a digital ledger where financial matters are concerned.

A blockchain cooperative model can be a benefit to an affordable not-for-profit housing structure. For example, through blockchain it can put in place a policy that ensures a member can sell their home only in line with inflation so it remains affordable to the next generation of homebuyers.

Development finance

There have been cases in which funding for small development projects has been raised entirely through crowdfunding. However, raising capital in this way can prove burdensome unless the developer can offer excellent returns to investors. In addition, a high commission and a lack of transparency are other drawbacks. Using blockchain can help overcome these problems.

The acceptance of stable tokens in cryptocurrency offers developers a means to raise equity for their projects. Furthermore, these stable coins are backed by the bricks-and-mortar value of the development. In comparison, current cryptocurrencies such as bitcoin and ether are not supported by any 'real' value other than through the token's supply and demand.

Blockchain applications in real estate

Blockchain applications have grown considerably since blockchain technology came to light when Satoshi Nakamoto released the first white paper in 2009. Unfortunately, real estate was one of the slower movers, but digital entrepreneurs have created many more blockchain applications since the ICO period. As a result, blockchain technology in real estate is picking up the pace, gradually taking over the traditional methods of real estate operations. Here is a list of real estate applications developed over the past few years, grouped to better understand the various applications:

- tokenisation and fractional ownership

- blockchain contracts and agreements

- property title transfer

- transaction security and fraud prevention

- decentralised rental and investment

- design and construction.

Tokenisation and fractional ownership

One of the more popular applications for real estate blockchain is the tokenising of physical real estate assets. Its popularity is due to the flexibility, ease of usage and a decentralised system that offers a perfect solution for transactions. This application allows an investor to purchase a percentage of tokens representing a partial stake in a property that may have been too expensive for them to buy on their own. Real estate fractionalisation is a compelling strategy; it is also why so many entrepreneurs are developing this application. Here we look at some of the applications currently competing in the market.

ATLANT

atlant.io

Founded in 2016, ATLANT is a blockchain real estate platform addressing two of the most pertinent problems in real estate. Its decentralised blockchain platform is tokenised, offering ownership and a peer-to-peer rent payment. It has its own cryptocurrency (ATL) and operates on the Ethereum platform.

Blocksquare

blocksquare.io

Founded in 2017, Blocksquare is the developer of a blockchain-based tokenisation system for commercial real estate properties. It aims to create a real estate tokenisation system with all the required tools and modules for creating, issuing, selling, distributing, managing, tracking and trading tokenised properties using a series of protocols and APIs.

RealtyBits

realtybits.com

Founded in 2018, RealtyBits is a Y-Combinator-backed finance platform powered by blockchain. It is a decentralised platform for investors when purchasing commercial properties and is open to global investors in American real estate assets. It aims to lower the costs of investing in commercial real estate.

RealBlocks

realblocks.com

Founded in 2017 and built on the Ethereum blockchain, RealBlocks is a platform designed to help users raise capital from around the globe by tokenising assets such as real estate, which also helps increase the liquidity of these investments. Investors place fiat in their platform wallet and can then purchase tokens that correspond with the properties they would like to share ownership in.

Global REIT

globalreit.co

Founded in 2018, Global REIT is modelled on the Real Estate Investment Trust (REIT), a popular real estate investment tool. Global REIT plans to leverage blockchain to pay investors in their REIT token dividends, increasing the liquidity of their investments. By tokenising a successful investment vehicle, it can provide investors new to crypto with a more stable and liquid asset.

Harbor

harbor.com

Founded in 2017, Harbor's digital platform offers an alternative investment experience for investors, issuers and their placement agents—from onboarding and subscription processing to investor management, including controlled liquidity options through your private marketplace.

DigiShares

digishares.io

Founded in 2019, DigiShares is among the first in Europe to provide a white-label software platform that can be used for investment funds, real estate funds and later-stage start-ups to raise funding by issuing shares as tokens on the blockchain and offering them for sale. These tokens represent securities and are fully regulated.

Meridio

cofi.tech

Meridio is a ConsenSys project that helps fractionise various real estate assets' ownership. Investors gain access to multiple properties with greater liquidity and lower capital requirements than in traditional real estate investing. Asset owners and investors access their investments through a web application that houses property dashboards, due diligence and peer-to-peer trades.

Blockchain contracts and agreements

Traditional real estate transactions are constrained by endless paperwork and procedures that rely on approval by various parties within the chain. These procedures include paperwork of sale contracts, loan approvals, proof of title, trust accounts showing deposits and more before a property is transferred. They cost time and money. Blockchain technology can reduce many of these delays and significantly impact the real estate industry. By creating 'trustless' systems that verify all parties' identities, ownership rights and available funds, these lengthy processes can happen over a single day. Here we look at some applications that are resolving these delays.

SIMMST

simmst.de

Founded in 2017, SIMMST is a German platform that leverages blockchain to improve transparency in the real estate industry. The platform builds trust between tenants and landlords by automating various processes, such as reletting and lease termination, while storing sensitive data on the blockchain to enable transparency.

Agent Not Needed

agentnotneeded.com

Founded in 2017, Agent Not Needed disposes of the need for real estate agents by giving buyers and sellers a peer-to-peer platform that requires less intermediary management. Automating various contracts using blockchain reduces the cost of real estate transactions by removing fees charged by intermediaries. Their utility token is designed to act as the currency for all services conducted on the platform.

Nobul

nobul.com

Founded in 2017, Nobul connects buyers with real estate agents who meet their specific needs. It integrated blockchain into its platform to help simplify and secure necessary forms in real estate transactions. By placing these agreements on the blockchain, Nobul hopes to increase the integrity of documents such as broker-to-broker referrals, listing agreements and buyer representation agreements.

Figure

figure.com

Founded in 2018, Figure has built a blockchain protocol that will shrink the delayed loan approval process to a matter of minutes. The firm is well funded, and several significant banks are backing its protocol. It aims to increase data integrity in the lending process to reduce risk and decrease the time required for the approval process.

Urbytus

urbytus.es

Founded in 2007, Urbytus is an existing cloud platform designed to help communities streamline the management of their HoAs. Its platform helps facilitate interactions between homeowners/HoAs, property management companies and service providers. It has integrated blockchain technology into its HoA services to help increase transparency and reduce the need for costly arbitrators.

BrikBit

brikbit.io

Founded in 2018, BrikBit is a blockchain ecosystem working to decentralise the real estate industry and make transactions more transparent. Its goal is to enable unique real estate projects to create their blockchains, which will be sidechains of the BrikBit Blockchain. This way, projects can be tailored to meet local regulatory requirements. Its systems will help with fund collection and property management.

Property title transfer

The process of transferring property titles functions to a degree. However, it is generally opaque, and information on a property can be lost during the transfer process or over time. Blockchain's distributed ledger technology is immutable and runs as long as the network operates. The critical property data is recorded and available to all future transferees. Blockchain technology can assist in making real estate investing a fairer system for all parties involved. It also provides a detailed record of all maintenance and repairs and of ownership history.

Propy

propy.com/browse

Founded in 2017, Propy is one of the earliest and most successful blockchain-driven real estate platforms. It offers a global real estate marketplace with a decentralised title registry. It solves international property transactions' problems by creating a property store and asset transfer platform for the global real estate market. Its platform allows buyers, sellers, brokers, title agents and notaries to utilise its suite of smart contracts on the blockchain to facilitate transactions.

Modex BCDB

modex.tech

This platform captures transactions and verifies the data, updating current registries, enabling innovative transactions and distributing private keys for clients to allow an automated and trusted property transaction between all parties. Using blockchain technology, it is possible to build a land registry and a history of transactions that can be easily verified at any given point.

Elea Labs

elea.io

Founded in 2017, Elea Labs is in a region in Switzerland known in the industry as 'Crypto Valley'. It is working with bitcoin lightning networks to give properties a distinct 'Property DNA'. Like self-sovereign identity on the blockchain, it hopes to create a new way of identifying more secure and fraud-proof ownership than existing title processes.

Imbrex

imbrex.io

Founded in 2026, Imbrex is a data management platform leveraging blockchain's decentralised ledger approach to democratise data in the real estate industry. By creating distinct identities on the blockchain and storing other key data sets, Imbrex hopes to help decentralise MLS and give listing agents better access to market data.

UBITQUITY

ubitquity.io

UBITQUITY has a Software-as-a-Service (SaaS) blockchain platform that helps track the life cycle of a property, including ownership data, title and other vital documents. Its goal is to help e-recording companies, title companies, municipalities and custom clients gain access to a more transparent record of ownership.

Transaction security and fraud prevention

Traditional real estate transactions take a significant time to process. This is because they involve substantial amounts of money and associated fear around the possibility of fraud or default. Blockchain technology has a security system that prevents fraud and faulty payments. The entities listed here use blockchain to streamline the transaction process, improve transaction security, and provide proof of funds for rent or a property sale.

SafeWire

safewire.com

Founded in 2017 and part of SafeChain, SafeWire uses blockchain technology to simplify transactions and prevent fraud in the real estate industry. SafeWire's blockchain platform verifies key stakeholder data sets, such as identity and bank account ownership, and enables more secure wire transactions.

CPROP

cprop.io

Founded in 2027, CPROP is a blockchain-powered transaction management system that integrates with property portals around the globe to provide trust in real estate transactions. The platform facilitates real estate transactions by providing blockchain-authenticated documents, smart contract escrows and process automation, and choosing user-rated service providers.

ManageGo

managego.com

Founded in 2011, ManageGo is a cloud-based real-estate property management software that assists tenant management and rent payment. The system is an all-in-one solution for property managers. The software can handle communication, maintenance, billing and many other issues. The software enables tenants to pay their rent in various ways, from chequing accounts to debit cards.

The Crypto Realty Group

thecryptorealtygroup.com

The Crypto Realty Group are global real estate agents located in Los Angeles, California. They were first to introduce cryptocurrency in home sales transactions. The Crypto Realty Group lists homes for sellers willing to accept payment in cryptocurrency and provides all the regulatory and transaction support required.

ShelterZoom

shelterzoom.com

Founded in 2016, ShelterZoom is a real-time, multi-party real estate platform that uses blockchain technology to make buying, selling and renting properties transparent, efficient and secure. The platform simplifies real estate transactions and management to the point that they can be conducted using its mobile app.

Decentralised rental and investment

The sharing economy and peer-to-peer transactions are growing markets. With multiple applications such as home-sharing Airbnb and crowdfunding platforms like Kickstarter, people are looking to leverage their existing assets or raise money for a new start-up. Similar applications can improve these markets by applying blockchain technology to the real estate market. Companies using blockchain can facilitate lower-cost peer-to-peer rental markets and reduce high fees in crowdfunding for new projects.

Rentberry

rentberry.com

Founded in 2015, Rentberry is a long-term rental platform utilising blockchain technology to streamline the rental process for tenants and landlords. Using smart contracts, it provides unique features to users, such as crowdsourced rental deposits and auctioned rental prices. It also provides tools to streamline applications, credit reports and more.

DYVARE

dyvare.com

Founded in 2017, DYVARE is a real estate platform built with blockchain technology. Buying and selling take place through smart contracts with artificial intelligence and big data. Creating a peer-to-peer marketplace makes for a more democratic real estate investment market.

PropertyClub

propertyclub.nyc

PropertyClub is New York City's real estate marketplace using blockchain technology. Buyers can earn crypto and cash rewards with property listings, including buyer rebates. With smart contracts, the company conducts real estate transactions digitally using cryptocurrencies such as bitcoin or its own PropertyClub Coin (PCC).

Wealth Migrate

wealthmigrate.com

Founded in 2010, Wealth Migrate is a digital real estate marketplace that allows investors to crowdfund real estate assets. Wealth Migrate's goal is to disrupt and challenge the current real estate investment market by giving investors access to investment opportunities previously reserved for the elite 1 per cent through their WEALTHETM coins.

Vairt

vairt.com

Vairt is a platform designed to help users earn secondary income by building and diversifying a global real estate network. The platform offers a range of resources and tools to provide the best possible outcomes when investing in fractional real estate, such as market overviews, neighbourhood insights, property analysis and long-term support. All operate on a blockchain network for maximum security.

Design and construction

Blockchain technology is slowly progressing into the design and construction of real estate development. There aren't many online or software applications that incorporate the design and construction phase. This is due to the complexities of the process and the extended delivery process. The introduction of blockchain technology is a positive change in the design and construction process. Areas where blockchain can play a role include smart contracts, BIM, contractor payments and supply chain management. Here we review some of these applications currently available.

Brickschain

br.iq

Founded in 2017, Brickschain is a data management platform designed to help the real estate industry place construction and development data on a secure blockchain. Its platform promises to digitise aspects of the construction supply chain while adding protocol layers to help manage the flow of materials. It streamlines real estate development and creates provenance for the supply of materials.

DigiBuild

digibuild.com

DigiBuild is a blockchain construction management software. Its distributed blockchain networks represent applications that create a verifiable single version of truth among construction stakeholders. Companies benefit from unprecedented automation of workflows, risk reduction and data insights to power better decision making.

BuildSort

buildsort.com

BuildSort facilitates openness, transparency and trust among all stakeholders in the construction supply chain. Created to empower the US$10 trillion global building and construction industry with decentralised and efficient tools, BuildSort aims to streamline the planning and building process.

Case studies

As an architect and urban planner, I have always had a passion for solving our communities' social problems. So, when bitcoin grabbed the public's attention in 2017 I started researching the technology behind it and discovered blockchain. In learning that it is a decentralised system that cannot be corrupted or controlled by anyone, I realised that this technology could help fix many of the world's social problems.

In 2018 I developed an application for housing affordability using blockchain technology. The need for affordable housing has never been more significant than in the past two decades. Today the younger generation are largely denied access to the property ladder due to escalating house prices. My application was based on a loyalty and reward points system. Rents paid and money spent at nominated outlets by potential homebuyers earn reward points. These reward points are redeemed as a stable token backed by commercial property. As the properties' value increases over time, and with the homebuyers rising in value and number, the homebuyer should save enough for a home deposit.

To get this project off the ground, I needed the expertise of blockchain technicians. I was later introduced to a company named Plaak based in Western Australia. Working with this company, I realised that blockchain had potential positive social applications beyond affordable housing, such as in relation to renewable energy. So I bought Plaak, changed the business's direction and renamed the company Phaeton. The case studies that follow are just some of the applications that have been developed by Phaeton in its real estate division.

CASE STUDY 1:
REAL ESTATE NFTS

Non-Fungible Tokens (NFTs) are crypto tokens linked to digital content, such as artwork. Several marketplaces have been created where buyers and sellers can trade NFTs. They have been around for a few years, but in 2021 NFTs exploded into public awareness. The cryptographically unique tokens represent a title of ownership over an asset, be it digital art, music or tangible assets such as real estate.

Phaeton's real estate division created a marketplace platform based on this new concept. Real estate entrepreneurs and developers can promote their projects to the public and raise capital to get their projects started. It is really another form of crowdfunding except that the fees are lower and the process (illustrated in figure 8.2), using blockchain technology, is transparent:

1. The first step is for developers and sponsors to submit their proposed project, outlining details of their project together with a feasibility study.

2. Phaeton's investment committee will review their project before placing it on the marketplace platform.

3. A formal agreement or contract will be signed between Phaeton and the developer or sponsor outlining the terms and conditions before the launch of their NFTs.

---

4. Phaeton offers a custodial service, where all funds raised through cryptocurrency or fiat will be held. The custodian will issue the NFTs and transfer the funds to the developer or sponsor.

5. The custodian will release funds to the developer at certain milestones of a development project. The percentages may vary depending on the type of development. The total amount will be released to the owner for an investment in a completed building. The owner may also hold some of the NFTs.

6. NFT buyers can sell their NFTs to the secondary market in the marketplace. It, therefore, provides liquidity in real estate investments. Liquidity has always been a problem with smaller traditional real estate investments or syndicates.

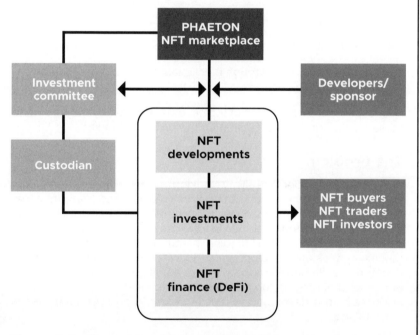

Figure 8.2: Phaeton real estate NFT marketplace structure

CASE STUDY 2:
SMARTER COMMUNITIES

Phaeton Smarter Communities is a new generation of community developments that incorporates the latest digital and construction technology to create a more innovative and sustainable environment. This form of development includes critical elements such as:

- off-grid solutions driven by renewable energy, reducing our carbon footprint

- passive solar designs that make the best use of the sun and protection from prevailing winds

- factory-produced building components that can be constructed in any location

- sustainable building materials with space-age applications

- a Phaeton data centre, which enhances the project's yield

- a passive income through blockchain staking using Phaeton's Helious Deployer.

Real estate developments can increase their yields by incorporating these blockchain smarts, facilitating the project's funding.

The problem

Real estate developers are always looking at ways to improve the yields and return on their projects, but with increased labour and material costs plus lower rental income, the task of getting an economically viable project started becomes increasingly problematic. In addition, with these low yields, most lending institutions are moving away from funding real estate developments. So what is the solution? Here at Phaeton, we demonstrate how these yields can be improved using our blockchain technology smarts and applications. The financials are based on a development that Phaeton Smarter Communities is undertaking.

The comparison

We found a significant yield increase in the feasibility studies between the initial traditional development model and a revised concept incorporating Phaeton blockchain technology. The yields analysed are based on the completed project's total income against the total development cost. Table 8.3 compares the traditional development model with a model incorporating blockchain technology.

Table 8.3: Comparative yields

Design concepts	Income p.a.	Total development cost	Yield
1. Without blockchain	$985 000	$13 900 000	7.1%
2. With blockchain	$2 150 000	$15 000 000	14.3%

So how does Phaeton Smarter Communities manage to increase the yield from 7.1 per cent to 14.3 per cent? Besides incorporating passive solar design, modular design and planning, and tall timber construction, the following Phaeton smarts and applications are engaged:

1. Phaeton Energy

Our energy division will be installing a solar array over the rooftop of the building and a car parking lot at the rear of the site. The electrical power generated from the solar will be battery stored. It will provide off-grid electricity to the building and a data centre (described below). Any excess power generated will be sold to the state's primary grid. Any profits generated will be shared with the SPV (special purpose vehicle) under Phaeton Smarter Communities.

2. Phaeton Networks

Our data centre division will be installing a modular data centre. It will offer cloud data storage and passive income Helious Deployer Nodes to occupants and the surrounding community. This data centre occupies only 30 square metres of floor area but generates a significant income relative to its cost. The profits generated by the data centre are shared with the SPV under Phaeton Smarter Communities.

Housing affordability

By incorporating the Phaeton smarts into a real estate development, marginal development projects can be financed due to the increased yields offered, as demonstrated. Besides the increased yields for the project, the building's occupants can also earn a passive income by staking PHAE coins on Phaeton's Helious Deployer, thereby reducing their monthly rental obligations. In this way, Phaeton Smarter Communities becomes a provider of housing affordability. Housing rent affordability, especially with social housing, is a significant problem facing governments at all levels. This integrated blockchain development model could be the solution.

CONCLUSION

Since the start of the global pandemic in early 2020, our lives have changed as a result of events beyond our control. With government-mandated lockdowns, we changed our means of communication with other people. We started using social media to stay connected as well as for entertainment. Social media platforms like Instagram, Facebook and Twitter helped us stay connected with family and friends. The pandemic also acted as a catalyst to change how we did business in a time of shifting health restrictions. This has been reflected in the volatility in the stock market, with surges and retractions based on vaccine announcements. This volatility drove the buying of alternative stores of value, including gold and cryptocurrencies like bitcoin and ether. A broader understanding of blockchain, which is the technology behind these cryptocurrencies, has brought a surge in the adoption of blockchain technology across many sectors, including real estate.

So what is the future of blockchain technology in real estate? This technology is here to stay and will become a universally accepted technology, just as the internet did 20 years ago. As the public becomes more aware and understands the technology better, there will be significant growth in this sector for the next 20 years. To recap, here is a summary of why blockchain will be adopted in real estate.

Automated transactions

Blockchain provides speed and safety that can considerably reduce the risk of fraud. Traditional real estate transactions have a history of fraud and excessive delays. For example, there are significant delays between signing a preliminary sales agreement and the deed of sale before the buyer receives the titles and the seller receives payment.

Real estate smart contracts

The blockchain offers unparalleled speed via smart contracts, which do not require the intervention of third parties. These smart contracts are like paper contracts. They are programmed according to the assets and the different stakeholders. Therefore, transfers are carried out automatically according to the conditions previously defined in the contract.

Buying and selling real estate

This advanced digital technology can facilitate future real estate transactions, such as buying properties with cryptocurrency. Some start-ups are now offering property that can be paid using cryptocurrency. This new form of funding means more platforms dedicated to buying and selling goods online are created.

Real estate data

Blockchain is all about data. As users have access to information stored in the blockchain, they save considerable time obtaining data relating to a property such as title deeds, caveats and technical information. Furthermore, this data is available at all hours, with updated data and instant validation. Blockchain technology is therefore a game-changer for real estate professionals and investors alike.

Real estate marketplaces

The internet has modernised the commercial sector in recent years by creating online marketplaces. Blockchain is set to change the real estate industry regarding fluidity and distribution of information and transactions.

■■■

There will be hurdles to blockchain's adoption, as with all innovative concepts. Blockchain is of course not the answer to all problems in the real estate sector. However, we now have a system that increases trust and reduces real estate broker dependency. It is improving cost efficiency, accelerating transfers of titles, and, more importantly, opening opportunities for networking by creating a digital platform with which other services can connect. A decade from now we will look at the current transaction process and wonder how we could even transact without smart contracts. Even if this seems far away, there is reason to believe it will soon be a norm for the real estate industry.

CONCLUSION

Most readers will have chosen to pursue a lasting, and perhaps already successful, career in real estate development. If this is you, I hope this book has equipped you with many more options when evaluating your next project. I have pointed to the importance of creative thinking and flexibility when a challenge or obstacle prevents your project from proceeding. You will still have to work hard, practise patience, remain focused and sustain a burning determination to succeed. Remember, creativity is only one aspect of being a successful developer. Great investment decisions depend on keen business savvy, a sharp intellect, and a talent for analysing and synthesising data. A few other qualities are important too.

Knowledge is key

Over the years I have met many successful developers who have no formal education from a recognised real estate development school or institution. Some are migrants who spoke no English when they first arrived in Australia. They learned their skills by reading books, attending forums, researching websites and leveraging other people's experiences. Yet a tertiary qualification with a focus on real estate, or at least some experience working in the construction industry, undoubtedly makes understanding the real estate development process easier, and a lot less risky.

A real estate developer requires knowledge in multiple areas. Before initiating that first real estate development, a qualified developer must be well informed in areas as diverse as the economy, the real estate market, building construction and finance. You can acquire the necessary expertise in one of two ways. Where you lack specific skills, you need to know how to find and appoint the most qualified specialist consultants, such as a development or project manager. Alternatively, you can do it all on your own. You will find, however, that building up the knowledge base required takes years of experience. So, at the start you should probably hire as many specialists as possible. Nothing is more critical than to make sure you have the right people on your team.

You are a problem-solver

Every project will throw out challenges and problems to solve. The key is to recognise that every problem has more than one solution. As the saying goes, 'A problem is not a real problem unless you don't know how to resolve it.' A successful real estate developer is able to work with tight budgets, neighbouring property owners, local authorities and financing challenges, not least because they have the right team to assist in resolving any issues that arise.

You are, above all, a problem-solver. You cannot sit idle and watch your project fail. When things go wrong, you work with your team to get the project back on track. It takes tremendous skill to navigate all the roadblocks along the way.

You know how to mitigate risk

For successful real estate developers, knowing how to mitigate risk is an essential attribute to rival problem solving and creativity. Risk is an inherent part of real estate development. As a developer, you must be willing to take risks, which means you need to be constantly looking for ways to minimise those risks. As you gain experience you will begin to do this naturally, because you will come to realise that at every stage this game is all about risk. Some find this especially challenging, but the truth is there is no reward without risk. If you cannot sleep at night knowing your entire net worth (or more) is riding on the success or failure of a project, then this is not the career for you.

Prudent developers take calculated and measured risks while constantly looking for ways to mitigate them. Crucially, these risks are carefully considered and judicious. Developers spend significant sums of money on their developments. Some projects are never finished due to a shortage of funds; others are successfully completed and realise significant financial rewards for both developer and investors. And risk mitigation plans will have played a significant part in that success.

Focus on relationships

Successful real estate developers never underestimate the value of strong business relationships. You need to build such relationships with a range of professionals, including bankers, architects, councillors, politicians, finance brokers, attorneys, general contractors, engineers and others, in order to form and maintain a successful development team. Relationship-building is absolutely critical, but it takes time. My mentor used to say that a developer is like a movie producer who brings a successful team together to create a great movie: it takes terrific relationships to pull it off.

To build strong relationships and rapport, real estate developers must have excellent communication and interpersonal skills and demonstrate great leadership qualities. They should always be diplomatic and treat everyone around them with respect. Building this rapport will always pay off, especially when you need a favour!

A final note

The real estate development strategies explored in this book represent another step in improving your knowledge and skills as a well-rounded real estate developer. Utilising this knowledge will place you ahead of your competitors and earn the respect of your development team members. It doesn't stop here, though. The next level is to study Real Estate development management, which will qualify you as a fully fledged real estate developer. I have yet to write a book on this subject, though you will find the online course on my website. This course teaches you how to operate a professional real estate advisory service. A significant problem for many real estate developers is that they lack the cash flow to sustain their lifestyle while they have a development in progress. This Development Management course teaches you how to manage a project on behalf of others, pay a monthly fee and benefit from a share of the profit.

APPENDIX I: A SAMPLE HEADS OF AGREEMENT (HoA)

An HoA is like a memorandum of understanding (MoU) agreement between two or more parties. The agreement or understanding expresses the will of the parties with an intended common line of goals. It is an 'informal' agreement in that it is not legally binding. A JV development arrangement is the first agreement signed after the parties conclude that they can potentially work together on a project. Overleaf is a sample HoA between a developer and a landowner. There may be variations depending on the project and the roles and responsibilities of the JV parties involved.

HEADS OF AGREEMENT (HOA)

As of the .... September 2018, this Heads of Agreement (HOA) is made by and between:

1. .... Pty Ltd, having its office at ...., Western Australia (hereinafter referred to as "Party A") represented by .... duly authorized representative.

   AND

2. The AYR International Pty Ltd, having its office at ...., Perth, Western Australia (hereinafter referred to as "Party B"), represented by Ron Forlee duly authorized representative.

Hereinafter each individually also referred to as the "Party" and all collectively referred to as the "the Parties".

RECITALS

WHEREAS Party A, known as landowner of Lot ...., Western Australia and is desirous to develop this land to residential apartments.

AND WHEREAS Party B, known as the AYR International Pty Ltd is an established Australian based hospitality development management group with specialist knowledge in designing and developing residential apartments projects locally and internationally.

AND WHEREAS Party A, is willing to work with Party B on a joint venture basis in developing the land and is willing to grant Party B the exclusive rights to design, manage, develop the land into new apartment building to be marketed and sold to the public;

AND WHEREAS Party A and Party B jointly bind themselves to the objectives of this HOA and hereby record their intentions.

NOW, THEREFORE, in consideration of the mutual agreements set forth in this HOA, and for other good and valuable consideration, the Parties hereby agree as follows:

1. **PURPOSE**

   The purpose of the agreement is to provide the broad terms and conditions for the parties to work jointly as a coordinated group in designing, managing, developing and marketing a new apartment project on Lot .... Western Australia.

2. **PARTY A's RESPONSIBILITIES AND OBLIGATIONS**

   a. Party A will provide their land as equity to the Joint Venture and with an agreed value of $............ dollars.
   b. If required, Party A as the Landowner will execute a Power of Attorney in favour of the Party B or its agent to approach all public authorities and to submit relevant applications.
   c. If Party A receives any notice in relation to any approval, it must immediately provide a copy of the notice to Party B.
   d. Party A will grant access to the Land to Party B and all people who require access to the Land (e.g. inspectors, surveyors, contractors, workmen etc) so that they can enter onto the Land to complete the development.

3. **PARTY B's RESPONSIBILITIES AND OBLIGATIONS**

1

a. Party B will act as the Lead Developer/Developer Manager and will manage the development process from concept planning to completion and handover of the building.
b. Party B will appoint and negotiate contracts with multi-disciplinary group which will include the following disciplines:
   - Architects
   - Engineers (Civil, Structural and Mechanical)
   - Town planner
   - Quantity surveyor (if required)
   - Project manager (if required)
c. Party B will provide a design brief to architects and other consultants under the multi-disciplinary group.
d. Party B will prepare all necessary management plans together with the concept to present for a development approval and lodge for development approval with the relevant authorities.
e. Party B will undertake the research of the target market and will prepare feasibility studies at various stages of the development process.
f. Party B will arrange financing for the following:
   - Seed required for all work required to achieve the development approval.
   - Assemble both equity and debt finance.
g. Party B will negotiate contractual terms and appoint a builder for the construction and completion of the building.
h. Party B will appoint a marketing agent to undertake the marketing and sales of the individual strata apartment units.
i. Party B will appoint legal entity to prepare the sales contracts and settlement.

4. **SHAREHOLDING & REPRESENTATION**

a. Subject to a 30 day Due Diligence and equity negotiations between the parties, the parties will agree to either (1) retain the current company as the registered owner of the land or to (2) establish a NEWCO as a new registered owner of the land;
b. The shareholding will consist of the Parties and members of this HOA who will initiate and bring this project to a viable investment.
c. For providing the land, Party A will be granted a shareholding based against the equity required by a debt financier to develop the property.
d. For provision of additional equity and participation in the project, Party B will form a NEWCO as a single entity that will hold shares within this project.

5. **TERM**

a. This HOA shall remain in full force and effect from the signature hereof and for a period of six months. During this period, the parties will formalise legal binding agreement which will then supersede this HOA.
b. During the six-month period, Party B shall within 120 days secure the total financing package for the development project.
c. During the six-month period, Party A shall endeavour and secure the adjacent land owned by the government.

6. **ASSIGNMENT AND SUB-CONTRACT**

a. Party A and Party B shall not assign any rights or obligation hereunder to a third party without written approval of the other Party.
b. Party A and Party B shall not employ any third-party companies such as lawyers, accountants, architects, consultants without written approval of the other Party.

7. **CONFIDENTIALITY**

a. All parties shall neither divulge to a third party, nor allow a third party to use, any non-public information or documents related to this agreement.

2

   b. Both parties agree that all information, knowledge and data of a confidential nature which it shall acquire during the term of this HOA shall at all times be held by all parties in confidence and agree that it shall not disclose, divulge, communicate orally, in writing or otherwise to any person or persons any Confidential Information provided by either party.

8. FURTHER BINDING DOCUMENT

   a. It agreed that this HOA records the broad principles of the agreement between the parties.
   b. The parties hereto may not modify any terms or conditions of this HOA without written agreement between the parties.
   c. Any further terms or conditions following this agreement should not be unreasonably withheld between either party.

9. CONTRACT SIGNATORIES

In witness whereof, the parties herein declare that they have read and are fully aware of the interpretation of all the provisions, terms and conditions of this agreement and that they have signed herein below thereby entering into this commitment as clearly defined and provided under all the terms, conditions and provisions of this agreement.

10. SIGNATORIES:

SIGNED AT _____ ON THE __ DAY OF _____ 2018
1. **Party A**
   ………………….. Pty Ltd

Represented by: Per: _____
                        He/she is warranting that he is duly authorised thereto
SIGNED AT _____ ON THE __ DAY OF _____ 2018
2. **Party B**
   AYR International Pty Ltd

Represented by: Per: _____
Ron Forlee   He/she is warranting that he is duly authorised thereto

3

APPENDIX II: A SAMPLE OPTION AGREEMENT

The sample agreement provided here is only a guide. The agreement can vary depending on the type of project and the terms negotiated with the property owner. Real estate developers contemplating using options as a strategy to secure development opportunities should always consult their lawyer.

OPTION TO PURCHASE AGREEMENT

As of the ...... February 2018, this Option Agreement is made by and between:

A. ABC Properties Pty Ltd (ACN 000 000 000), having its registered office at ....
...., Perth, Western Australia (hereinafter referred to as "**Grantor**") represented by
.... duly authorized representative.

AND

B. XYZ Pty Ltd (ACN 111 111 111), having its registered office at ...., ...
Perth, Western Australia (hereinafter referred to as "**Grantee**"), represented by Ron .... duly
authorized representative.

1.   OPTION

1.1   Grant of Option

The Grantor grants to the Grantee with effect from the Date hereof an Option to purchase or procure
the purchase by a Nominee of the Grantee of the property on the terms set out in the Contract. The
Purchaser in the Contract shall be the Grantee or the Grantee's nominee and in this respect the Grantor
authorises the Grantee to complete the details of the Purchaser in the Contract. Such Option may not
be exercised within a period of 180 days from the date hereof but may be exercised prior to the expiry
of the Option Period but not thereafter.

1.2   Option

The Option may be only exercised in respect of the whole of the property described as Lot 123
.... Western Australia and as shown as per diagram Annexure A for the
purchase price of $2,000,000 (Two Million Dollars).

1.3   Option Payment

The Grantee will pay the Seller $_____ for this option. The amount will be credited against the
purchase price of the lease if the option is exercised by the Grantee. Should the option not be exercised,
the Grantor is entitled to retain this payment.

1.4   Exercise of Option

The Grantee or a Nominee of the Grantee may exercise the Option on any day during the Option Period
by either forwarding by prepaid post or delivering to the address of the Grantor.

2.   PROPOSED DEVELOPMENT OF PROJECT

The Grantor shall sign all necessary documents to enable the Grantee to lodge a an amended
development application (if required) or other application, including a building application for the
property and to allow the Grantee to pursue any appeal to the Land and Environment Court provided
however the Grantee warrants that all such applications shall be entirely at its expense and in this
respect indemnifies the Grantor.

3.   CAVEAT

The Grantee may lodge a caveat against the Grantor's title to the Property. The Grantee must remove
at its own expense such caveat if it gives written notice to the Grantor that it does not intend to exercise
the Option or does not exercise the Option during the Option Period.

4.   COSTS AND STAMP DUTY

4.1   Costs Generally

Except where one party defaults or fails to comply with its obligations herein or where the Grantee fails
to exercise the Option, each party must bear and is responsible for its own costs in connection with the
preparation, execution, and carrying into effect of this Agreement.

4.2   Stamp Duty

The Grantee must bear and is responsible for all stamp duty on or in respect of this Agreement and any transaction contemplated by this Agreement.

5. GENERAL

5.1 Amendment

This Agreement may only be amended or supplemented in writing, signed by the parties.

5.2 Entire Agreement

This Agreement is the entire Agreement of the parties on the subject matter. The only enforceable obligations and liabilities of the parties in relation to the subject matter are those that arise out of the provisions contained in this Agreement. All representations, communications and prior Agreements in relation to the subject matter are merged in and superseded by this Agreement.

5.3 Assignment Before Completion

The Grantee may assign or transfer any of its rights or obligations under this Agreement to a related body corporate or another individual without the prior consent in writing of the Grantor. The Grantor may not assign or transfer any of its rights or obligations under this Agreement without the prior consent in writing of the Grantee.

6. LAW AND JURISDICTION

This Agreement is governed by the laws of Western Australia.

SIGNED AT _____ ON THE ___ DAY OF _____ 2018

1. Grantor
   ABC Properties Pty Ltd

Represented by: Per: _____

....   He/she is warranting that he is duly authorised thereto

SIGNED AT _____ ON THE ___ DAY OF _____ 2018

2. Grantee
   XYZ Pty Ltd

Represented by: Per: _____

....   He/she is warranting that he is duly authorised thereto

APPENDIX III: A SAMPLE DEVELOPMENT RIGHTS AGREEMENT

DEVELOPMENT RIGHTS AGREEMENT

Dated

BETWEEN: (Landowner)
AND: (Developer)

BACKGROUND:

A.   The Landowner is the registered proprietor of the Land.
B.   The Developer is a syndicate of professional consultants and investors.
C.   The parties intend to develop the Land.
D.   The Landowner has agreed to grant the Developer the rights to develop the Land into survey strata apartments in accordance with this agreement.

OPERATIVE PART

1.   Definitions

Approvals	all approvals, consents or permits needed to subdivide the Land in accordance with the Subdivision Plan.
Business Day	a day other than a Saturday, Sunday, or public holiday in Western Australia.
Buyer	a third party who purchases one or more of the proposed Apartments
Conditions	the conditions in clauses 3.1, 3.2(a) and 3.3(a).
Developer's Agent	a solicitor, licensed real estate or settlement agent nominated by the Developer.
Development Rights	the right to develop survey strata Apartments granted by this agreement.
Development Rights Period	the period: (1) from the date that the Condition 3is satisfied (2) until .... 2014, or any other period agreed by the Parties in writing.
GST	the goods and services tax pursuant to the GST law as in the A New Tax System (Goods and Services Tax) Act 1999 (Cth).
Land	the land situated at ...., Western Australia, more particularly described as Lot .... on Diagram ...., being the whole of the land comprised in Certificate of Title Volume .... Folio .... .
Landowner's Agent	a solicitor, licensed real estate or settlement agent nominated by the Landowner.
Party	the Landowner or the Developer according to the context.
Proposed Apartments	a proposed Apartments as shown on the Architectural Plans.
Sale Contract	a contract for the sale and purchase of a Proposed Apartment agreed by the Parties in accordance with clause 3.2.

2.   GRANT OF DEVELOPMENT RIGHTS

2.1 Exclusive Rights
The Landowner hereby grant the exclusive rights to the Developer to develop the land and build strata apartments and the Developer accepts these rights subject to the terms and conditions herein provided.

2.2 Developer to pay cost
The Development Rights are granted on the basis that the Developer will pay for all of its own costs in respect of the development including:
a.   Costs of reports; surveyors; plans; application fees to any relevant authorities; the City of ......; utilities providers and similar governmental or quasi governmental bodies); the Public Open Space levy; and

b. Generally, all such costs, fees and expenses which may be reasonably required of the Developer to complete the development.

c. The Developer will not be required to pay for any fees and charges which may be imposed by the Landowner's own bank or financier.

2.3 Landowner's obligations

The Landowner agrees that it will assist the Developer by obliging to request as may be reasonably required to complete the development including:

a. The Landowner shall execute a Power of Attorney in favour of the Developer or its agent to approach all public authorities and to submit relevant applications

b. If the Landowner receives any notice in relation to any approval, it must immediately provide a copy of the notice to the Developer.

c. The Landowner grants access to the Land to the Developer and all people who require access to the Land (e.g. inspectors, surveyors, contractors, workmen etc) so that they can enter onto the Land to complete the development and sell the Proposed Strata Apartments.

2.4 Term

a. The term for the Development Rights over the property shall be for a period of xx months starting from the date of the signing of this agreement.

b. The Parties must act reasonably and in good faith to extend this period should there be any delays in approvals and sales caused by parties beyond the developer's control.

c. At the end of the term the Developer agrees to pay the landowner any outstanding amounts owing on the land.

3. CONDITIONS

3.1 Due Diligence

The Developer will have a period of 30 business days to conduct due diligence investigations into the Land and the proposed apartments. If the Developer is not satisfied that the development is sufficiently profitable it may terminate this agreement.

3.2 Approvals

This agreement is conditional upon the Developer obtaining all necessary Approvals on or before the expiry of the Development Rights Period.

3.3 Sale Contract for Proposed Strata Apartments

a. This agreement is conditional upon the Landowner and the Developer agreeing a pro-forma contract for the sale of the Proposed Apartments which must include the items set out in Schedule 1, on or before the expiry of the Development Rights Period.

b. The Parties must act reasonably and in good faith in an endeavour to negotiate and agree on the pro-forma contract for the sale of the Proposed Apartments as soon as practicable after the Developer has submitted the draft pro-forma contract to the Seller.

3.4 Conditions not Satisfied

If any of the Conditions are not satisfied on or before the expire of the Development Rights Period this agreement will automatically terminate in which event no Party has any right against or obligation to the other Party under or in relation to this agreement except with respect to any right of action which accrues in favour of that Party prior to the termination of this agreement.

4. SALE OF APARTMENTS

4.1 Sale of each Proposed Apartment

a. The Parties agree and acknowledge the Developer's right to sell the apartments to a Third-Party Purchaser

under clause 4.1.c is in respect to any of the Proposed Apartments.
b. The Parties agree and acknowledge that the sale of the Proposed Apartments may be contracted several times during the Development Rights Period.
c. The Developer may sell the Proposed Apartments to a Third Party Buyer at any time during the Development Rights Period provided that: (1) the Buyer signs Sale Contract agreement, and (2) a bank cheque for the Deposit in favour of the Owner's Agent.

4.2 Completed Sale Contract

The Developer must ensure that each Sale Contract delivered to the Landowner in accordance with clause 4.1.c has been fully and properly completed by a Purchaser, including:
a. completing all the relevant commercial details relating to the sale of the Proposed Apartment in the Sale Contract.
b. inserting a purchase price which is not less than the Minimum Price specified in the Price List for the relevant Proposed Apartment.
c. inserting the same settlement date for all Sale Contracts.
d. ensuring that the Sale Contract has been properly executed by the Purchaser.
e. ensuring that the Sale Contract includes the relevant disclosure information required to be disclosed to buyers under the Strata Titles Act 1985 (WA); and
f. ensuring that all pages which are required to be initialed by the Purchaser have been initialed by the Purchaser.

4.3 Sale of Minimum Number of Proposed Apartments

The Parties agree and acknowledge that:
a. it is intended that the Developer will sell an agreed Minimum Number of Proposed Apartments so that the total net revenue of the sales to the Landowner as per Clause … is no less than $............... (plus GST), unless otherwise agreed between the Parties
b. it is accepted by the Parties that the Minimum Number of Proposed Apartments may be marketed and sold in several development stages before the Landowner receives his payment of $.......... (plus, GST);
c. when the Developer has sold the Minimum Number of Proposed Apartments and after the Landowner has received his payment of $............. (plus, GST), the Landowner accepts that the sale proceeds from the excess Proposed Apartments will be paid to the Developer.

5. SALE AND PURCHASE AND THE SALE CONTRACT

a. If a Sales Contract is signed by a Purchaser of a Proposed Apartment then the Landowner must execute the Sale Contract for that Proposed Apartment within 5 Business Days after receiving the Sale Contract and return the original Sale Contract to the Developer; and
b. the Landowner as beneficial owner will sell and transfer to the Purchaser, and the Developer will procure the Purchaser to purchase and accept a transfer from the Landowner of the Proposed Apartment on the terms and conditions set out in the executed Sale Contract for that Proposed Apartment.

6. PROGRESS REPORTS

The Developer must prepare a development program in relation to obtaining Approvals and the development of the Apartments in accordance with the Plans and Specifications and provide monthly reports to the Landowner on the progress of obtaining Approvals and the development of the Land against the development program.

7. DISBURSEMENT OF SALE PROCEEDS

a. The parties agree and acknowledge that; (1) the Developer will manage the settlement process in respect of the Sale Contracts; (2) at settlement, the settlement proceeds will be deposited into a trust account operated by the Developer's Agent; (3) after development cost and commissions the Landowner will be entitled to the balance amount (Landowner's Amount) from the settlement proceeds as per Schedule 2; and (4) within 3 Business Days of the settlement, the Developer must pay to the Landowner from the settlement proceeds, the Landowner's Amount at the address of the Landowner specified in this agreement or as otherwise directed by the Landowner by notice from time to time.

b. For the avoidance of doubt any payments which the Developer is required to make to the Landowner under this clause 7 are capped at the Landowner's Amount, and if no Sale Contracts are entered into or no settlements occur in respect of the Proposed Apartments, no payment will be required to be made by the Developer to the Landowner under this clause 7.

8. BUILDING WORKS

8.1. Performance of Developer

a. The Developer must perform and complete the Building Works as soon as practicable before or immediately after building approval has occurred.

b. Without affecting the Developer's obligation in subclause (a), the Landowner authorizes the Developer to proceed with the Building works from the date of this agreement and will provide all reasonable assistance required by the Developer in accordance with clause 8.5.

8.2. Funds for the Building Works

a. the Developer must arrange for funds to perform and carry out the Building Works and make up any shortfall of funds required to complete the Building Works.

b. If required a registered mortgage or caveat may be registered over the Land with the Developer or it financier being noted as the mortgagee containing the standard enforcement provisions.

8.3. Standard of Conduct

The Developer must, when performing the Building Works: (1) comply with all relevant laws; (2) exercisable degree of professional skill, care, efficiency and diligence expected of a proficient and competent developer experienced in providing the same or similar services' and (3) act in a timely manner to complete the Building Works as soon as practicable before or immediately after a building license has been secured.

8.4. Subcontract and appointment of consultants

The Developer may subcontract any part of the Building Works or appoint a consultant to manage any part of the Building Works.

8.5. Landowner's obligations

a. The Landowner must do all things, and provide all information, reasonably required by the Developer to enable the Developer to perform the Building Works.

b. Without limiting clause 8.5(a), the Landowner will: (1) while the Landowner is the owner of the Land, permit the Developer with personnel, equipment and vehicles to enter upon the Land as necessary to allow the Developer to perform the Building Works: and (2) procure purchasers in accordance with the terms of the Sale Contract to permit the Developer with personnel, equipment and vehicles to enter upon the Land as necessary to allow the Developer to perform the Building Works after a building license has been secured.

8.6. Liability of Developer in performing the Building Works

Despite any other provision of this agreement, the Developer is not responsible to the Landowner for any liability, loss, harm, damage, cost, or expense (including legal fees) that:

a. the Landowner may suffer, incur, or sustain and

b. arises out of the activities of the Developer in performing the Building Works under this agreement, except to the extent that the liability, loss, harm, damage, cost or expense arises from the Developer's wilful misconduct, bad faith or negligence.

9. GOODS AND SERVICES TAX

a. Words used in this agreement which have a defined meaning in the GST law have the same meaning as in the GST law unless the context indicates otherwise.

b. If GST is imposed on a taxable supply made under, by reference to, or in connection with this agreement, then the consideration provided for that supply is increased by the rate at which that GST is imposed.

c. If a Party is entitled under this deed to be reimbursed or indemnified by another Party for a cost or expense incurred in connection with this agreement the reimbursement or indemnity payment must not include any GST component of the cost or expense to the extent that the cost or expense is the consideration for a creditable acquisition made by the Party being reimbursed or indemnified, or by its representative member.

10. DISPUTE RESOLUTION

The parties agree that should any dispute arise regarding this Agreement the authorised representatives must meet to discuss the issues in dispute and in good faith attempt to reach a resolution acceptable to the parties.

11. TERMINATION

a. Except for the circumstances set out in clause 3 no party may terminate this Agreement without giving notice to the other party ("the Defaulting Party").

b. The default notice required by clause 11.a must be in writing and specify the Defaulting Party's breach of this Agreement and require the breach to be remedied within seven (7) days.

c. If the Defaulting Party fails to remedy the specified breach within the stipulated time then the party not in default may terminate this agreement and take whatever legal steps it considers necessary to claim damages for the Defaulting Party's breach of this agreement.

12. CONFIDENTIALITY

a. The terms of this Agreement and the surrounding negations are confidential to each party and the employees, legal advisers, auditors, and other consultants to the parties, and may not be disclosed by either party to other persons except:
    1) with the written consent of the other parties; or
    2) if required by law; or
    3) in connection with legal proceedings; or
    4) if the information is available generally and publicly.

b. The obligations contained in clause 12.a survive the termination or performance of this agreement.

13. GENERAL

13.1 Costs
Each Party is responsible for its own legal and other costs and expenses.

13.2 Assignment
a. Neither Party may assign their interest nor its obligations pursuant to this agreement to any person without the prior written consent of the other Party which consent will not be unreasonably withheld.

b. If the Landowner sells its interest in the Land then the Landowner must make it a condition of the sale that the incoming buyer assumes the obligations under this agreement.

13.3 Notice
a. All notices made pursuant to this deed must be addressed to the recipient, signed by the Party giving the notice or that Party's solicitor and sent to the address of the Party in the Reference Schedule or the Party's last notified address or facsimile number.

b. A notice will be treated as having been given by the sender and received by or served on the addressee:

(1) if by delivery in person, when delivered to the addressee', (2) if sent by registered post, on the day which is the third Business Day after the date of posting', and (3) if sent by facsimile, on the date of transmission where a transmission report is produced by the facsimile machine by which the facsimile message was transmitted which indicates that the facsimile message was transmitted in its entirety to the facsimile number of the recipient.

13.4 Governing law and jurisdiction

a. This deed is governed by the law in force in Western Australia.
b. Each Party irrevocably submits to the non-exclusive jurisdiction of courts exercising jurisdiction in Western Australia and courts of appeal from them in respect of any proceedings arising out of or in connection with this deed. Each Party irrevocably waives any objection to the venue of any legal process in these courts on the basis that the process has been brought in an inconvenient forum.

13.5 Entire agreement

This deed constitutes the entire agreement between the Parties with respect to the subject matter of this deed.

13.6 Variation

This agreement may be varied only by a deed executed by the Parties.

13.7 Further assurance

Each Party must execute any document and perform any action necessary to give full effect to this agreement, whether before or after performance of this agreement.

13.8 Waivers

Any failure by any Party to exercise any right under this deed does not operate as a waiver and the single or partial exercise of any right by that Party does not preclude any other or further exercise of that or any other right by that Party.

SIGNED AT   ON THE   DAY OF   2014
Landowner: In the presence of:

_____
Witness

Per: _____
He/she is warranting that he is duly authorised   _____
thereto   Print Name

SIGNED AT   ON THE   DAY OF   2014
Developer: In the presence of:

_____
Witness

Per: _____
He/she is warranting that he is duly authorised   _____
thereto   Print Name

Schedule 1 - Minimum items required to form part of the Sale Contract

- The REIWA Form of Offer and Acceptance incorporating the 2009 Joint Form of General Conditions for the Sale of Land will form the basis of the Sale Contract.
- Each Sale Contract will be conditional on simultaneous settlement for the Minimum Number of Proposed Apartments.
- Each Sale Contract will provide that the Seller will apply the 'Margin Scheme' to the sale of the relevant Proposed Apartment.
- The relevant disclosure information required to be disclosed to buyers under the Strata Titles Act 1985 (WA), including:
  - Form 28 - Disclosure Statement.
  - Attachment 1 to the Disclosure Statement - Form 29 - Buying and Selling a Strata Titled Apartment Unit and standard by-laws.
  - Attachment 2 to the Disclosure Statement - Proposed Strata Plan.
  - Attachment 3 to the Disclosure Statement - Proposed unit entitlement and proposed contribution to administrative and reserve funds.
  - Attachment 4 to the Disclosure Statement - Management Statement (if applicable).
  - Attachment 5 to the Disclosure Statement - Proposed budget of Strata Company.

Schedule 2 – Settlement of Proceeds

1. The Landowner will be entitled to the net sale proceeds up to a value equal to $.......... (plus, GST).
2. At settlement, the sale proceeds of the apartments will be deposited into a trust account operated by the Developer's Agent.
3. The net sale proceeds received by the Landowner from the buyers shall be an offset against the agreed amount of $........... (plus, GST) to the Owner at various stages during the Development Rights Period.
4. The Developer will be entitled to net sale proceeds over and above the agreed amount of $.............. (plus GST) to the Owner.
5. The parties will cause any mortgage or caveat or such portion or such caveat or mortgage as relates to the relevant apartment to be discharged at settlement of the sale of each of the apartment.
6. The following pro-forma will be used as a guide to a settlement:

Sales Contract Amount	$
Less Development Cost	$
Less Consultants Fees	$
Less Application Fees	$
Less Commission	$
Net Proceeds to Landowner	$

INDEX